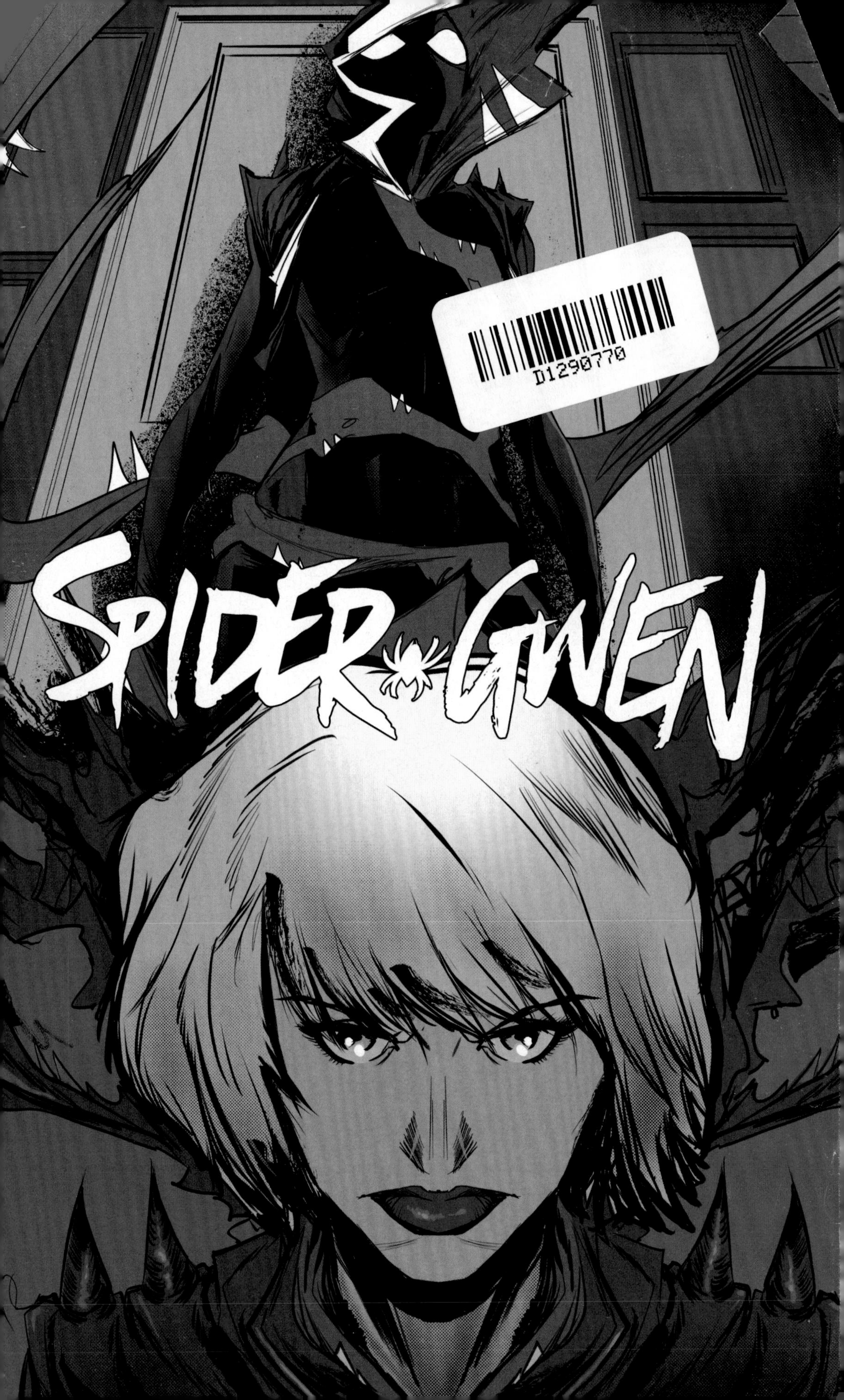
SPIDER-GWEN

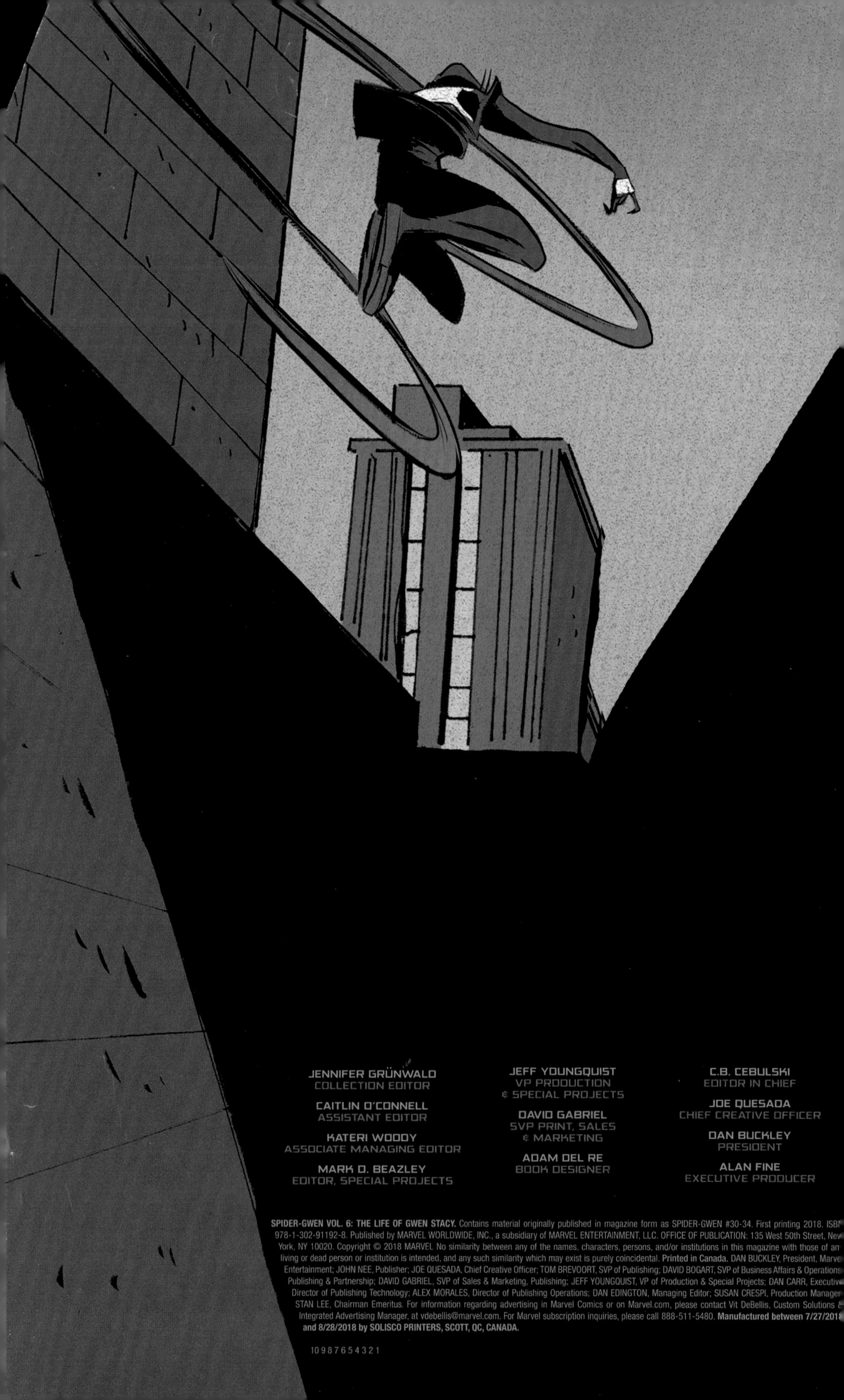

JENNIFER GRÜNWALD
COLLECTION EDITOR

CAITLIN O'CONNELL
ASSISTANT EDITOR

KATERI WOODY
ASSOCIATE MANAGING EDITOR

MARK D. BEAZLEY
EDITOR, SPECIAL PROJECTS

JEFF YOUNGQUIST
VP PRODUCTION & SPECIAL PROJECTS

DAVID GABRIEL
SVP PRINT, SALES & MARKETING

ADAM DEL RE
BOOK DESIGNER

C.B. CEBULSKI
EDITOR IN CHIEF

JOE QUESADA
CHIEF CREATIVE OFFICER

DAN BUCKLEY
PRESIDENT

ALAN FINE
EXECUTIVE PRODUCER

SPIDER-GWEN VOL. 6: THE LIFE OF GWEN STACY. Contains material originally published in magazine form as SPIDER-GWEN #30-34. First printing 2018. ISBN 978-1-302-91192-8. Published by MARVEL WORLDWIDE, INC., a subsidiary of MARVEL ENTERTAINMENT, LLC. OFFICE OF PUBLICATION: 135 West 50th Street, New York, NY 10020.

Printed in Canada. DAN BUCKLEY, President, Marvel Entertainment; JOHN NEE, Publisher; JOE QUESADA, Chief Creative Officer; TOM BREVOORT, SVP of Publishing; DAVID BOGART, SVP of Business Affairs & Operations, Publishing & Partnership; DAVID GABRIEL, SVP of Sales & Marketing, Publishing; JEFF YOUNGQUIST, VP of Production & Special Projects; DAN CARR, Executive Director of Publishing Technology; ALEX MORALES, Director of Publishing Operations; DAN EDINGTON, Managing Editor; SUSAN CRESPI, Production Manager; STAN LEE, Chairman Emeritus. For information regarding advertising in Marvel Comics or on Marvel.com, please contact Vit DeBellis, Custom Solutions & Integrated Advertising Manager, at vdebellis@marvel.com. For Marvel subscription inquiries, please call 888-511-5480. **Manufactured between 7/27/2018 and 8/28/2018 by SOLISCO PRINTERS, SCOTT, QC, CANADA.**

10 9 8 7 6 5 4 3 2 1

SPIDER ✱ GWEN

THE LIFE OF GWEN STACY

JASON LATOUR
WRITER

ROBBI RODRIGUEZ
WITH **CHRIS VISIONS** (#33)
ARTISTS

RICO RENZI
WITH **LAUREN AFFE** (#34)
COLOR ARTISTS

VC'S CLAYTON COWLES
LETTERER

ROBBI RODRIGUEZ
COVER ART

KATHLEEN WISNESKI
ASSISTANT EDITOR

DEVIN LEWIS
EDITOR

NICK LOWE
EXECUTIVE EDITOR

GWEN STACY CREATED BY
STAN LEE & **STEVE DITKO**

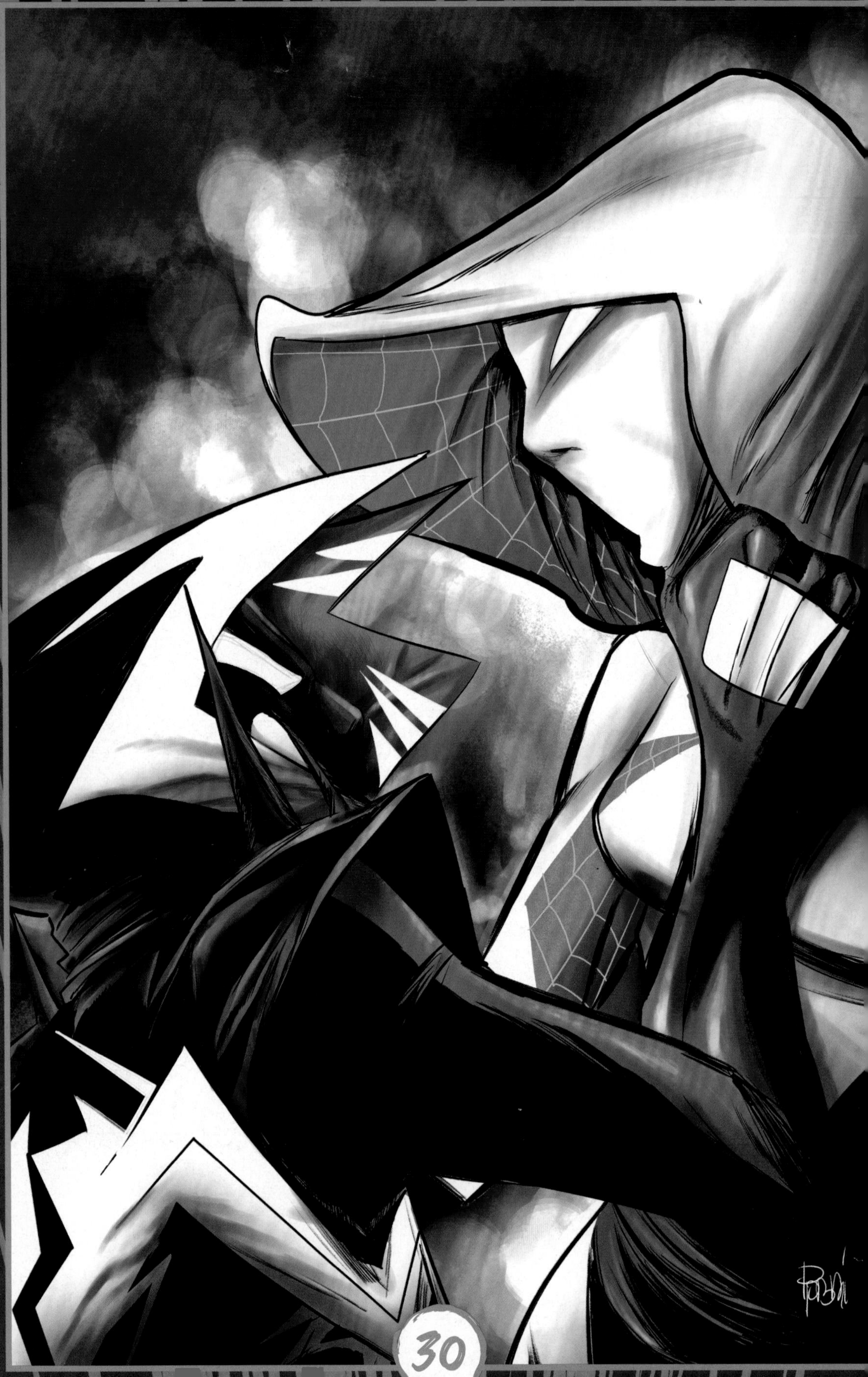

AS A TEENAGER, GWEN STACY WAS BITTEN BY A MUTATED SPIDER. THE BITE TRANSFORMED HER, GRANTING HER AMAZING POWERS: A PRECOGNITIVE AWARENESS OF DANGER, ADHESIVE FINGERTIPS AND TOES, AND THE PROPORTIONAL SPEED AND STRENGTH OF A SPIDER. BUT THOSE GIFTS WERE TAKEN AWAY WHEN A SUPER VILLAIN FURTHER TAMPERED WITH HER GENETICS, AND GWEN HAD NO CHOICE BUT TO EMBRACE A SYMBIOTIC PARASITE CALLED VENOM TO RESTORE THEM. TO THE RESIDENTS OF NEW YORK, SHE IS THE DANGEROUS OUTLAW CALLED SPIDER-WOMAN, BUT YOU KNOW HER AS…

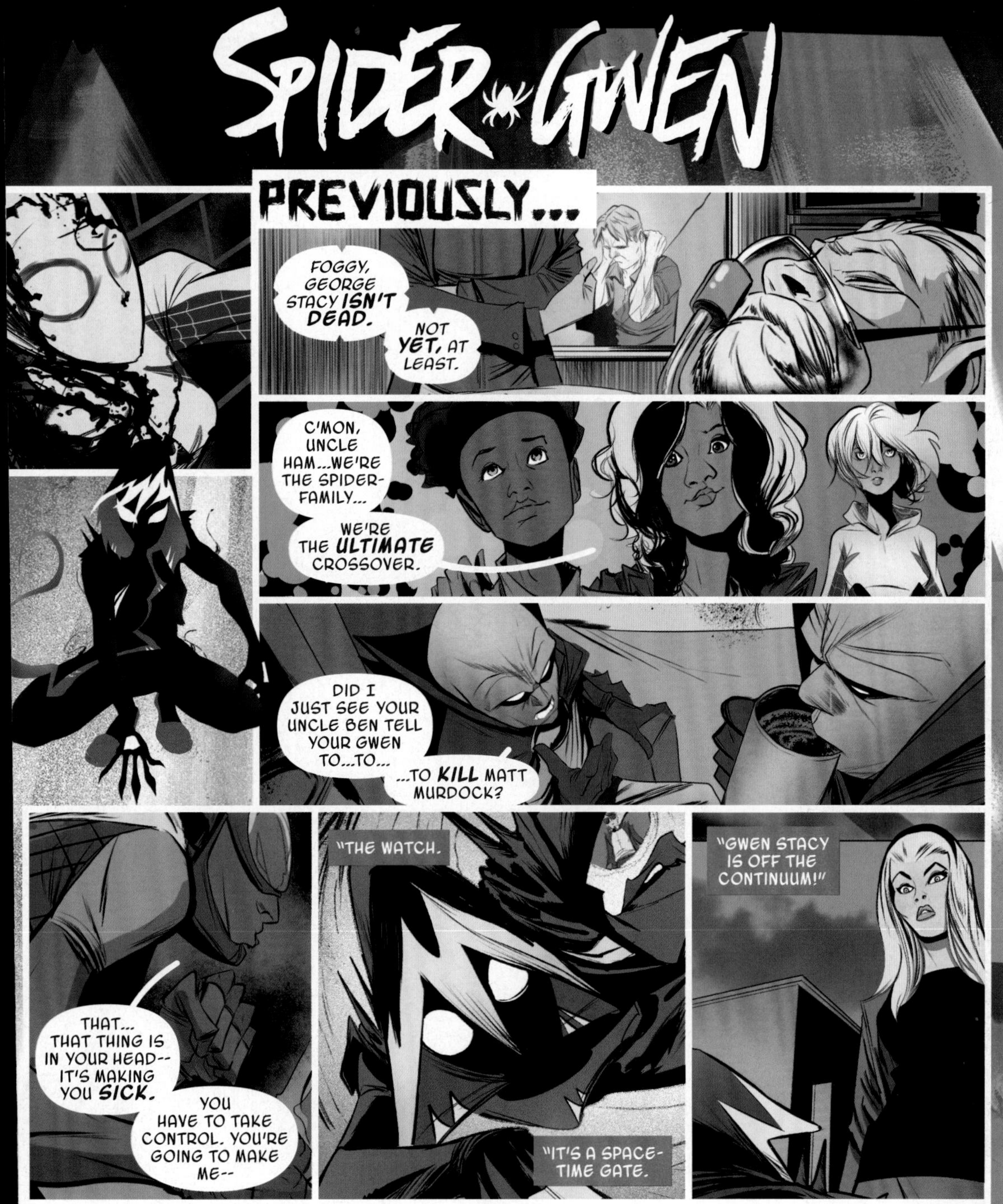
SPIDER-GWEN
PREVIOUSLY...
FOGGY, GEORGE STACY ISN'T DEAD.
NOT YET, AT LEAST.
C'MON, UNCLE HAM...WE'RE THE SPIDER-FAMILY...
WE'RE THE ULTIMATE CROSSOVER.
DID I JUST SEE YOUR UNCLE BEN TELL YOUR GWEN TO...TO...
...TO KILL MATT MURDOCK?
THAT... THAT THING IS IN YOUR HEAD-- IT'S MAKING YOU SICK.
YOU HAVE TO TAKE CONTROL. YOU'RE GOING TO MAKE ME--
"THE WATCH.
"IT'S A SPACE-TIME GATE.
"GWEN STACY IS OFF THE CONTINUUM!"

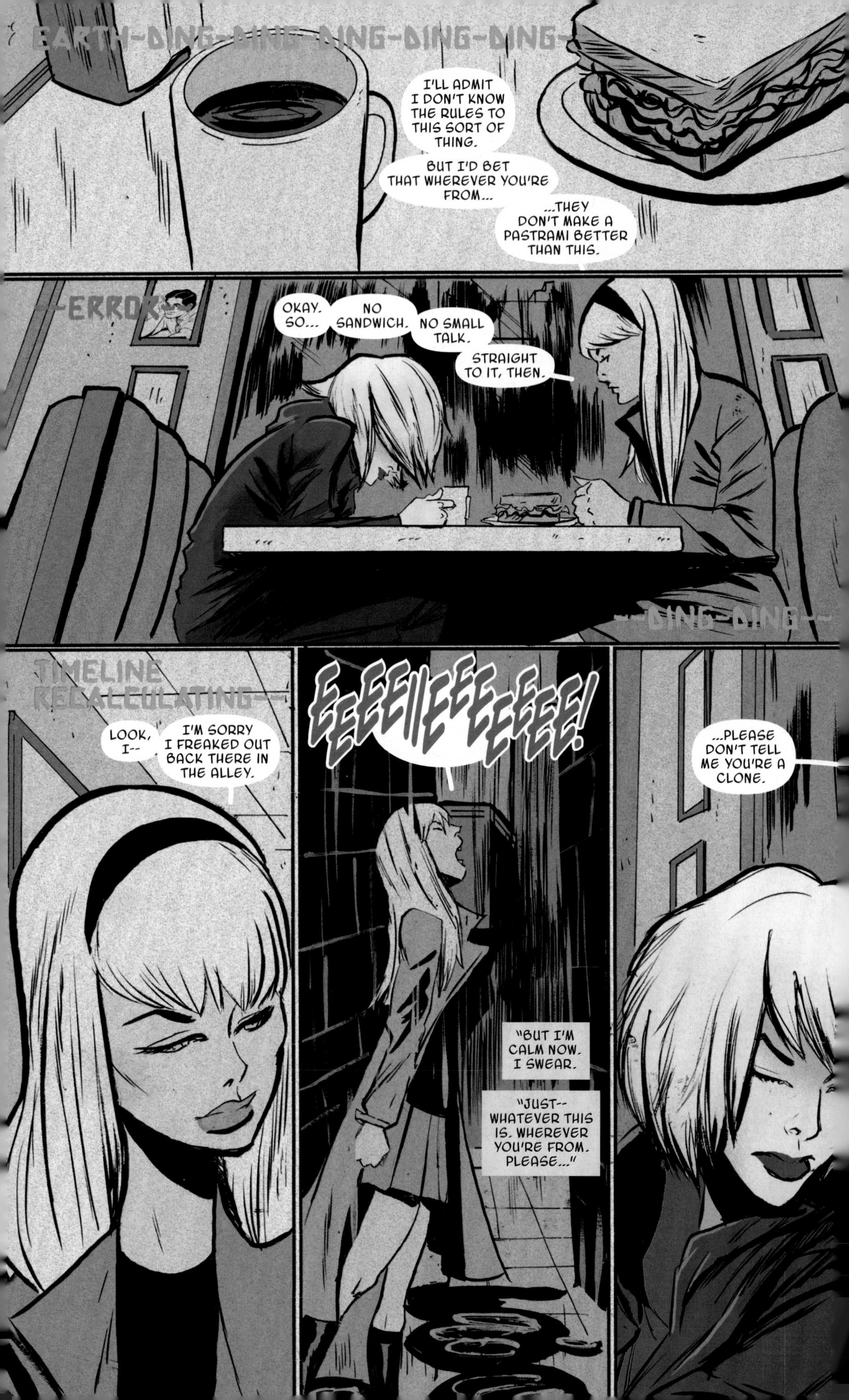
EARTH-DING-DING-DING-DING-DING--
I'LL ADMIT I DON'T KNOW THE RULES TO THIS SORT OF THING.
BUT I'D BET THAT WHEREVER YOU'RE FROM...
...THEY DON'T MAKE A PASTRAMI BETTER THAN THIS.
--ERROR--
OKAY. SO...
NO SANDWICH.
NO SMALL TALK.
STRAIGHT TO IT, THEN.
--DING-DING--
TIMELINE RECALCULATING--
LOOK, I--
I'M SORRY I FREAKED OUT BACK THERE IN THE ALLEY.
EEEEIIEEEEEEEE!
"BUT I'M CALM NOW. I SWEAR.
"JUST-- WHATEVER THIS IS. WHEREVER YOU'RE FROM. PLEASE..."
...PLEASE DON'T TELL ME YOU'RE A CLONE.

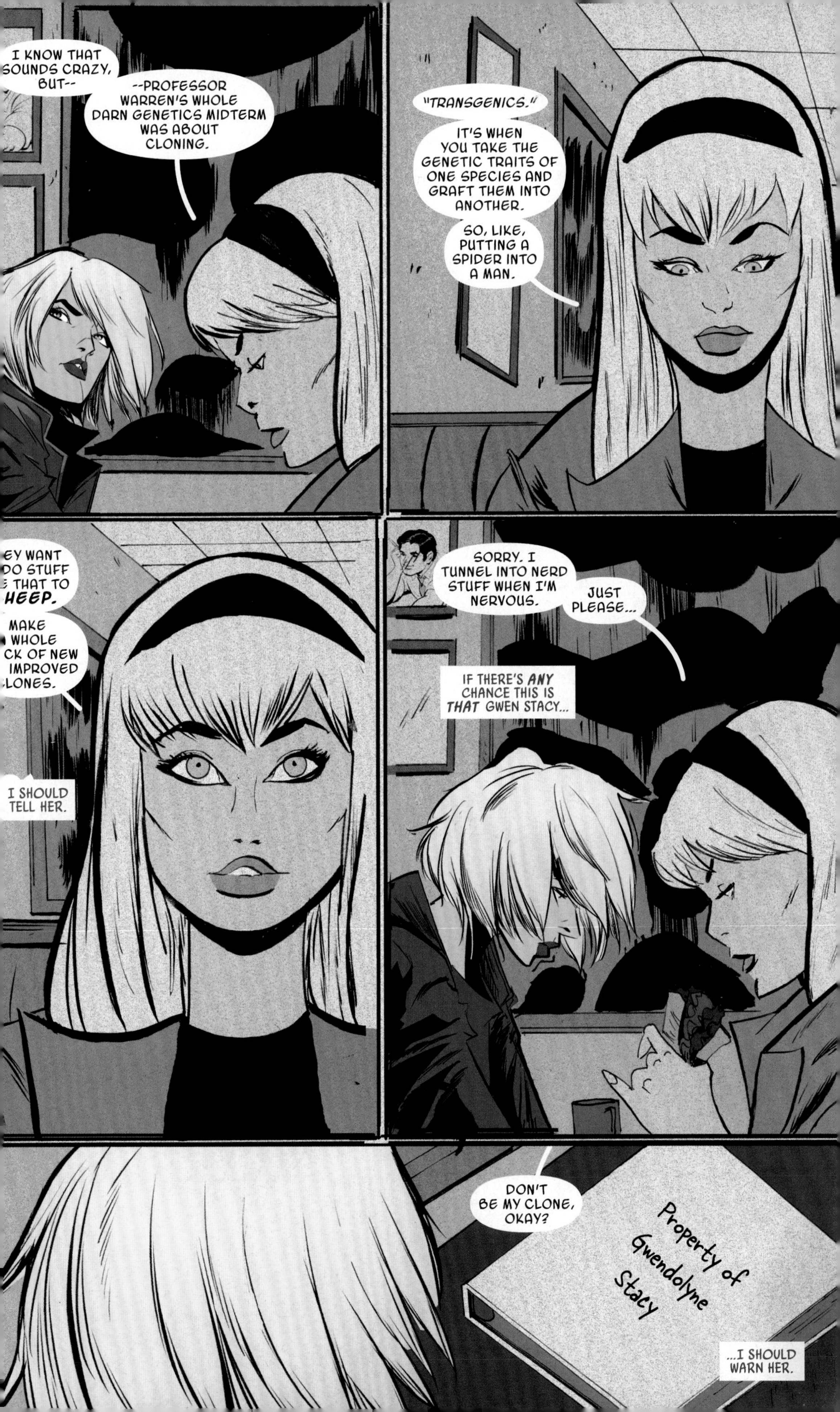
I KNOW THAT SOUNDS CRAZY, BUT--
--PROFESSOR WARREN'S WHOLE DARN GENETICS MIDTERM WAS ABOUT CLONING.
"TRANSGENICS."
IT'S WHEN YOU TAKE THE GENETIC TRAITS OF ONE SPECIES AND GRAFT THEM INTO ANOTHER.
SO, LIKE, PUTTING A SPIDER INTO A MAN.
EY WANT DO STUFF THAT TO HEEP.
MAKE WHOLE CK OF NEW IMPROVED LONES.
I SHOULD TELL HER.
SORRY. I TUNNEL INTO NERD STUFF WHEN I'M NERVOUS.
JUST PLEASE...
IF THERE'S ANY CHANCE THIS IS THAT GWEN STACY...
DON'T BE MY CLONE, OKAY?
Property of Gwendolyne Stacy
...I SHOULD WARN HER.

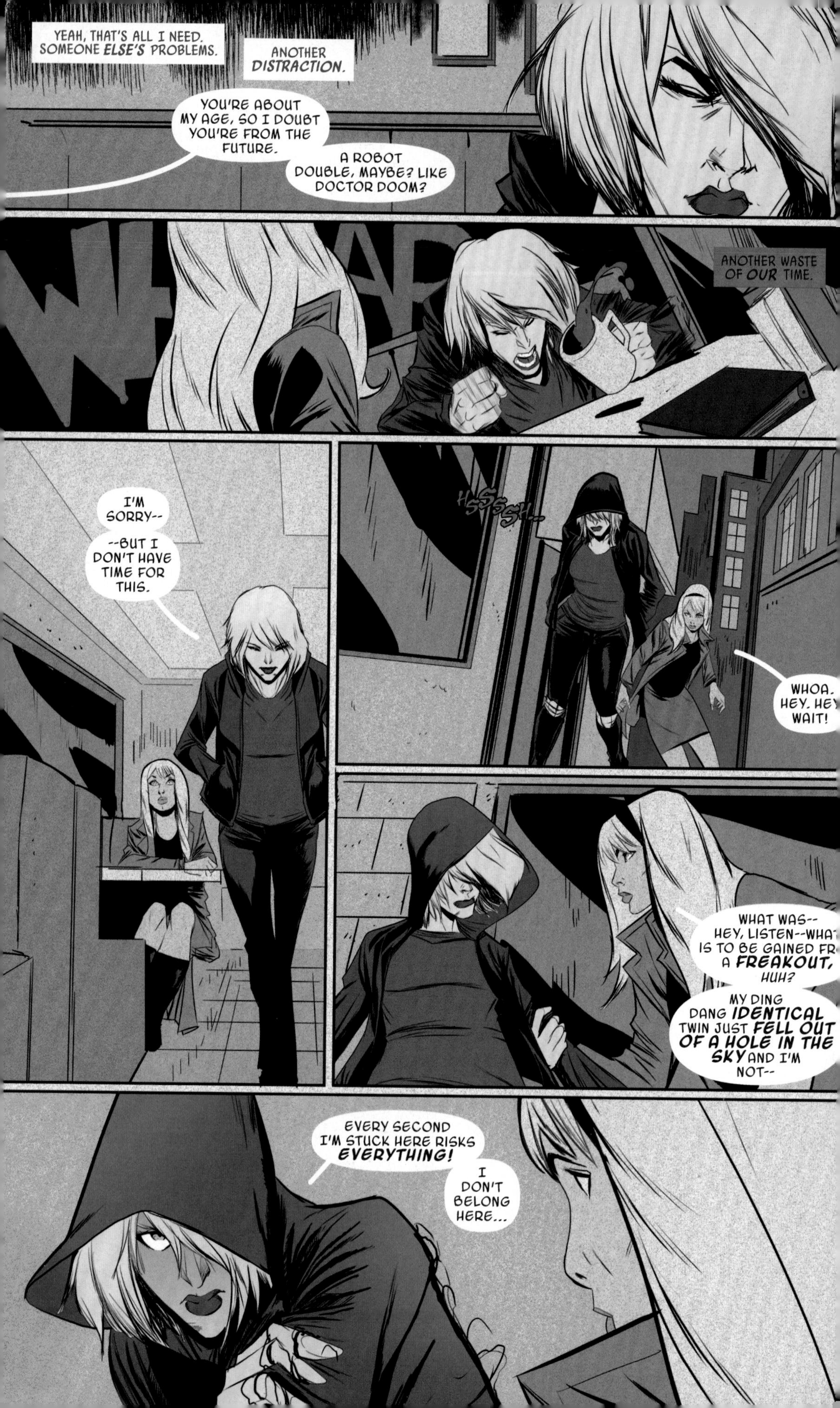

YEAH, THAT'S ALL I NEED. SOMEONE ELSE'S PROBLEMS.
ANOTHER DISTRACTION.
YOU'RE ABOUT MY AGE, SO I DOUBT YOU'RE FROM THE FUTURE.
A ROBOT DOUBLE, MAYBE? LIKE DOCTOR DOOM?
ANOTHER WASTE OF OUR TIME.
I'M SORRY--
--BUT I DON'T HAVE TIME FOR THIS.
HSSSSH...
WHOA. HEY. HEY WAIT!
WHAT WAS-- HEY, LISTEN--WHAT IS TO BE GAINED FR A FREAKOUT, HUH?
MY DING DANG IDENTICAL TWIN JUST FELL OUT OF A HOLE IN THE SKY AND I'M NOT--
EVERY SECOND I'M STUCK HERE RISKS EVERYTHING!
I DON'T BELONG HERE...

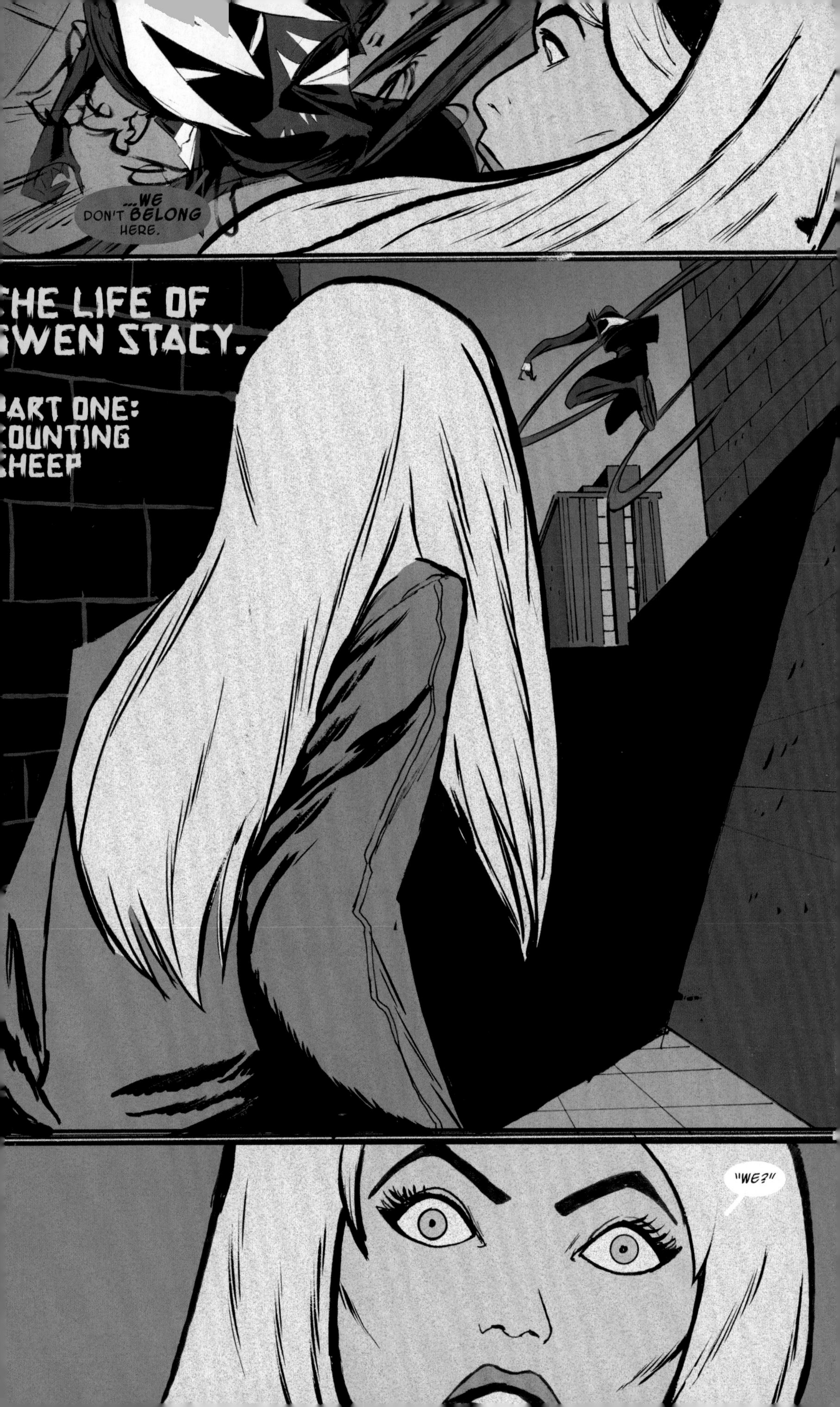
...WE DON'T BELONG HERE.
THE LIFE OF GWEN STACY.
PART ONE: COUNTING SHEEP
"WE?"

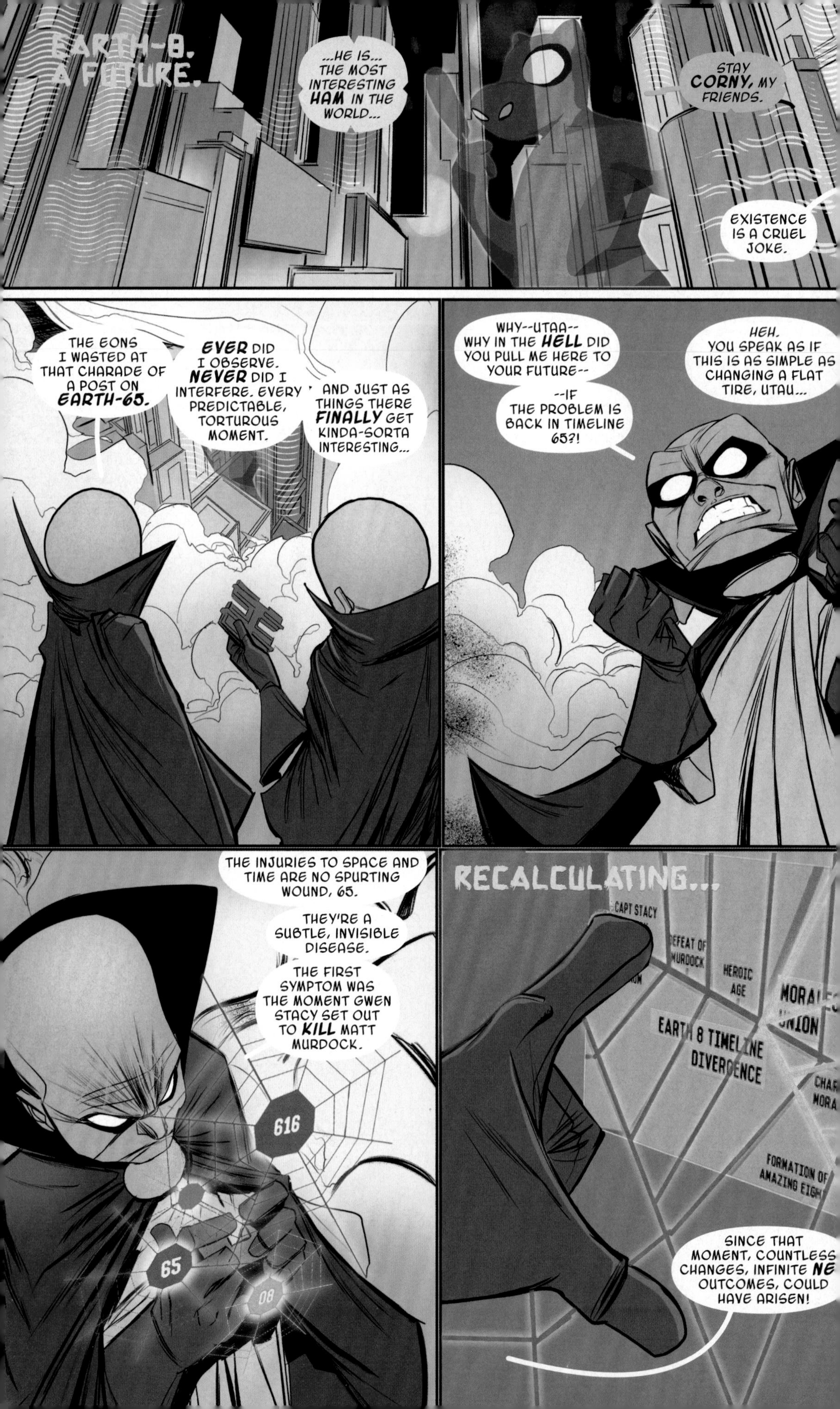
EARTH-8. A FUTURE.
...HE IS... THE MOST INTERESTING HAM IN THE WORLD...
STAY CORNY, MY FRIENDS.
EXISTENCE IS A CRUEL JOKE.
THE EONS I WASTED AT THAT CHARADE OF A POST ON EARTH-65.
EVER DID I OBSERVE. NEVER DID I INTERFERE. EVERY PREDICTABLE, TORTUROUS MOMENT.
AND JUST AS THINGS THERE FINALLY GET KINDA-SORTA INTERESTING...
WHY--UTAA-- WHY IN THE HELL DID YOU PULL ME HERE TO YOUR FUTURE--
--IF THE PROBLEM IS BACK IN TIMELINE 65?!
HEH. YOU SPEAK AS IF THIS IS AS SIMPLE AS CHANGING A FLAT TIRE, UTAU...
THE INJURIES TO SPACE AND TIME ARE NO SPURTING WOUND, 65.
THEY'RE A SUBTLE, INVISIBLE DISEASE.
THE FIRST SYMPTOM WAS THE MOMENT GWEN STACY SET OUT TO KILL MATT MURDOCK.
616
65
08
RECALCULATING...
CAPT STACY
DEFEAT OF MURDOCK
HEROIC AGE
EARTH 8 TIMELINE DIVERGENCE
FORMATION OF AMAZING EIGH
SINCE THAT MOMENT, COUNTLESS CHANGES, INFINITE NE OUTCOMES, COULD HAVE ARISEN!

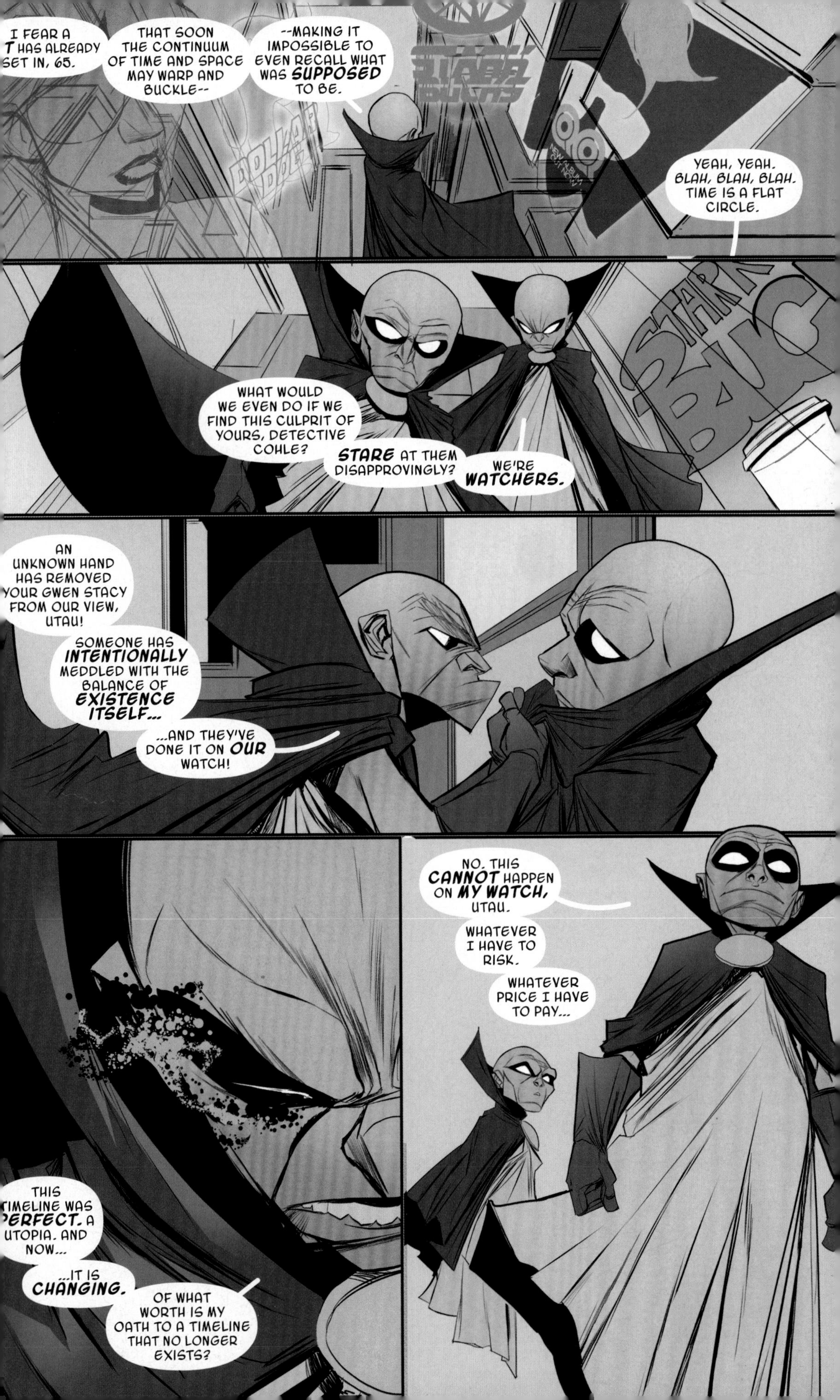

I FEAR A
T HAS ALREADY
SET IN, 65.
THAT SOON THE CONTINUUM OF TIME AND SPACE MAY WARP AND BUCKLE--
--MAKING IT IMPOSSIBLE TO EVEN RECALL WHAT WAS SUPPOSED TO BE.
YEAH, YEAH. BLAH, BLAH, BLAH. TIME IS A FLAT CIRCLE.
WHAT WOULD WE EVEN DO IF WE FIND THIS CULPRIT OF YOURS, DETECTIVE COHLE?
STARE AT THEM DISAPPROVINGLY?
WE'RE WATCHERS.
AN UNKNOWN HAND HAS REMOVED YOUR GWEN STACY FROM OUR VIEW, UTAU!
SOMEONE HAS INTENTIONALLY MEDDLED WITH THE BALANCE OF EXISTENCE ITSELF...
...AND THEY'VE DONE IT ON OUR WATCH!
THIS TIMELINE WAS PERFECT. A UTOPIA. AND NOW...
...IT IS CHANGING.
OF WHAT WORTH IS MY OATH TO A TIMELINE THAT NO LONGER EXISTS?
NO. THIS CANNOT HAPPEN ON MY WATCH, UTAU.
WHATEVER I HAVE TO RISK.
WHATEVER PRICE I HAVE TO PAY...

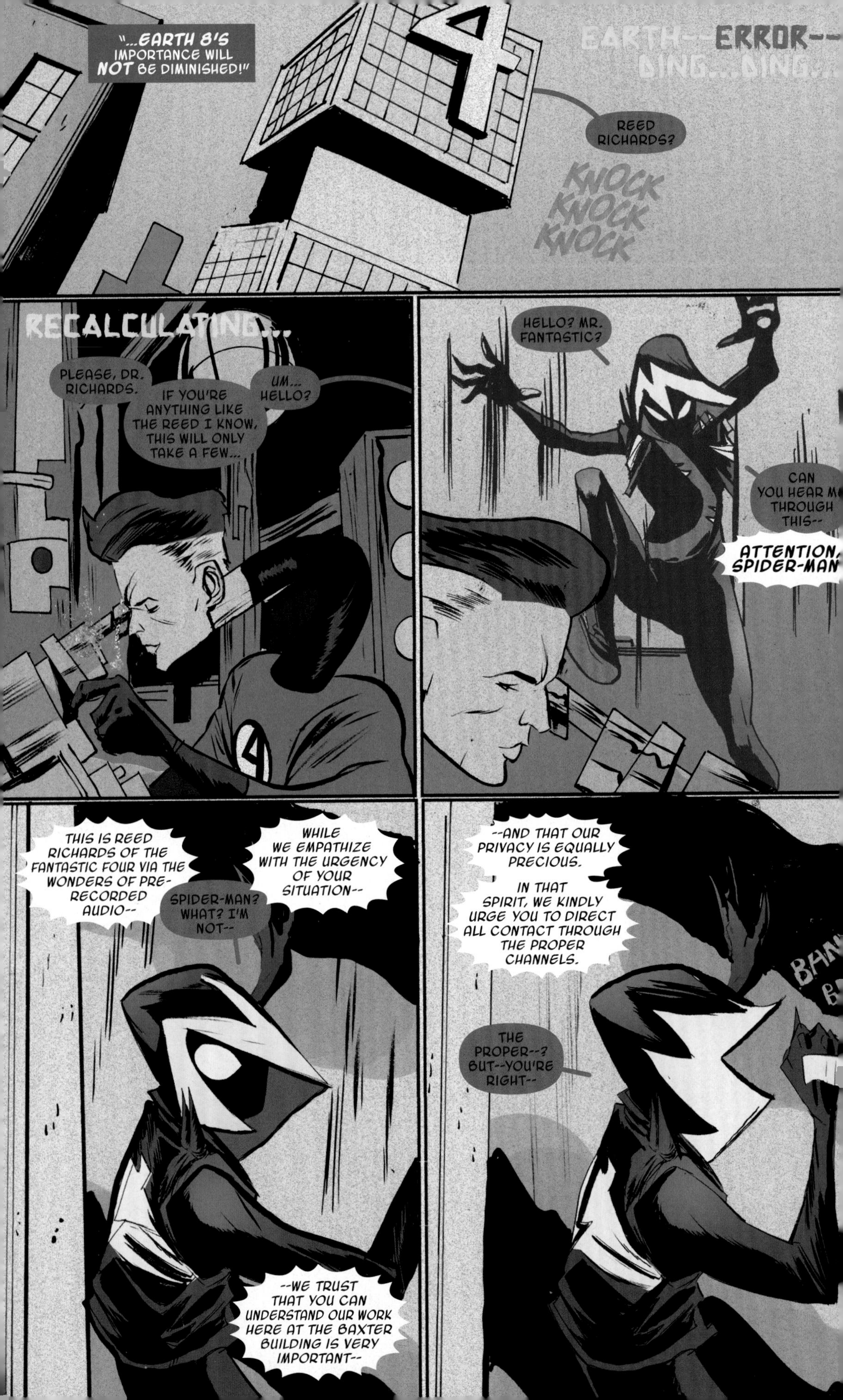
"...EARTH 8'S IMPORTANCE WILL NOT BE DIMINISHED!"
EARTH--ERROR--
DING...DING...
REED RICHARDS?
KNOCK KNOCK KNOCK
RECALCULATING...
PLEASE, DR. RICHARDS.
IF YOU'RE ANYTHING LIKE THE REED I KNOW, THIS WILL ONLY TAKE A FEW...
UM... HELLO?
HELLO? MR. FANTASTIC?
CAN YOU HEAR M THROUGH THIS--
ATTENTION, SPIDER-MAN
THIS IS REED RICHARDS OF THE FANTASTIC FOUR VIA THE WONDERS OF PRE-RECORDED AUDIO--
SPIDER-MAN? WHAT? I'M NOT--
WHILE WE EMPATHIZE WITH THE URGENCY OF YOUR SITUATION--
--WE TRUST THAT YOU CAN UNDERSTAND OUR WORK HERE AT THE BAXTER BUILDING IS VERY IMPORTANT--
--AND THAT OUR PRIVACY IS EQUALLY PRECIOUS.
IN THAT SPIRIT, WE KINDLY URGE YOU TO DIRECT ALL CONTACT THROUGH THE PROPER CHANNELS.
THE PROPER--? BUT--YOU'RE RIGHT--

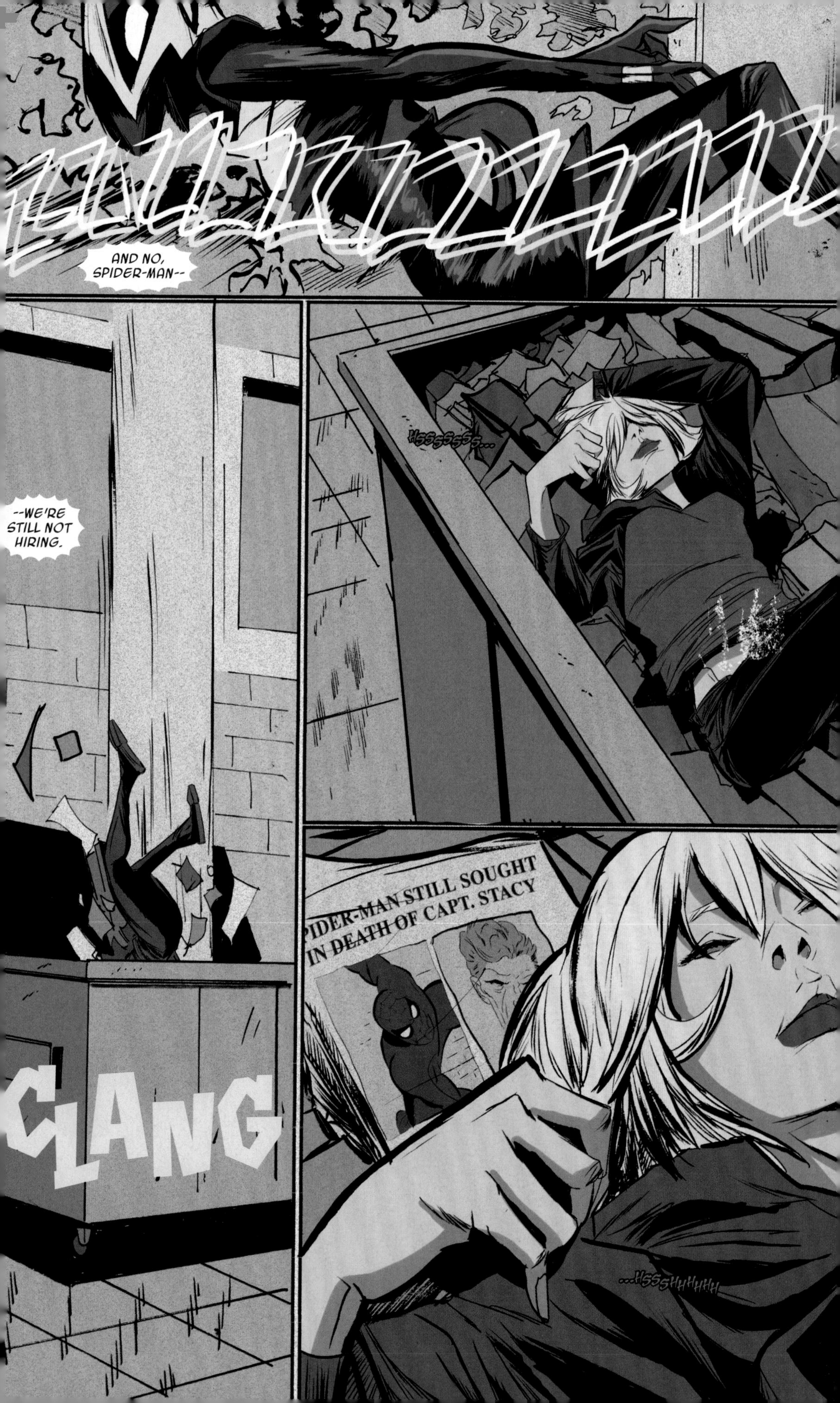
AND NO, SPIDER-MAN--
--WE'RE STILL NOT HIRING.
CLANG
HSSSSSSS...
PIDER-MAN STILL SOUGHT IN DEATH OF CAPT. STACY
...HSSSHHHHHH

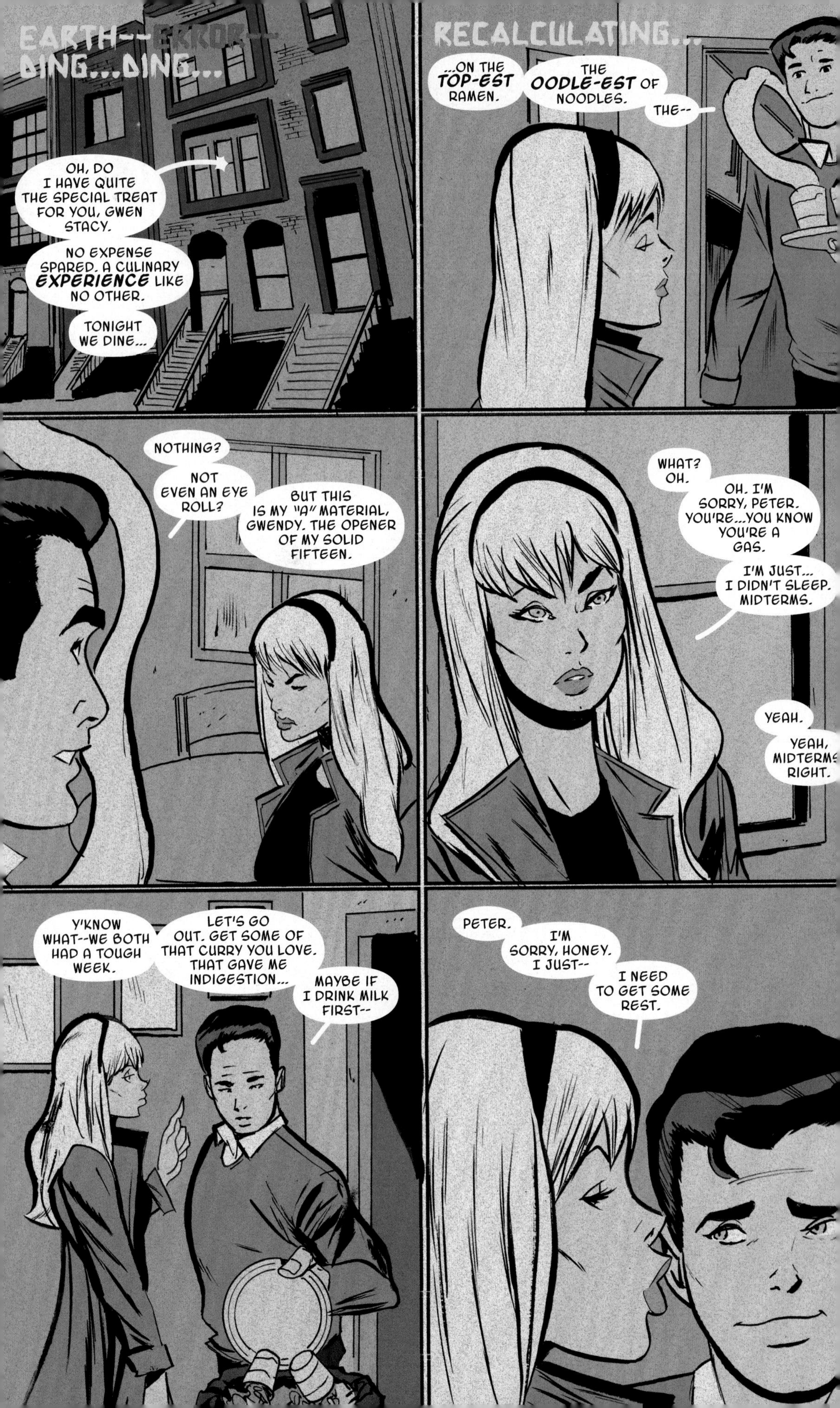
EARTH--ERROR--
DING...DING...
OH, DO I HAVE QUITE THE SPECIAL TREAT FOR YOU, GWEN STACY.
NO EXPENSE SPARED. A CULINARY EXPERIENCE LIKE NO OTHER.
TONIGHT WE DINE...
RECALCULATING...
...ON THE TOP-EST RAMEN.
THE OODLE-EST OF NOODLES.
THE--
NOTHING?
NOT EVEN AN EYE ROLL?
BUT THIS IS MY "A" MATERIAL, GWENDY. THE OPENER OF MY SOLID FIFTEEN.
WHAT? OH.
OH. I'M SORRY, PETER. YOU'RE...YOU KNOW YOU'RE A GAS.
I'M JUST... I DIDN'T SLEEP. MIDTERMS.
YEAH.
YEAH, MIDTERMS RIGHT.
Y'KNOW WHAT--WE BOTH HAD A TOUGH WEEK.
LET'S GO OUT. GET SOME OF THAT CURRY YOU LOVE. THAT GAVE ME INDIGESTION...
MAYBE IF I DRINK MILK FIRST--
PETER.
I'M SORRY, HONEY. I JUST--
I NEED TO GET SOME REST.

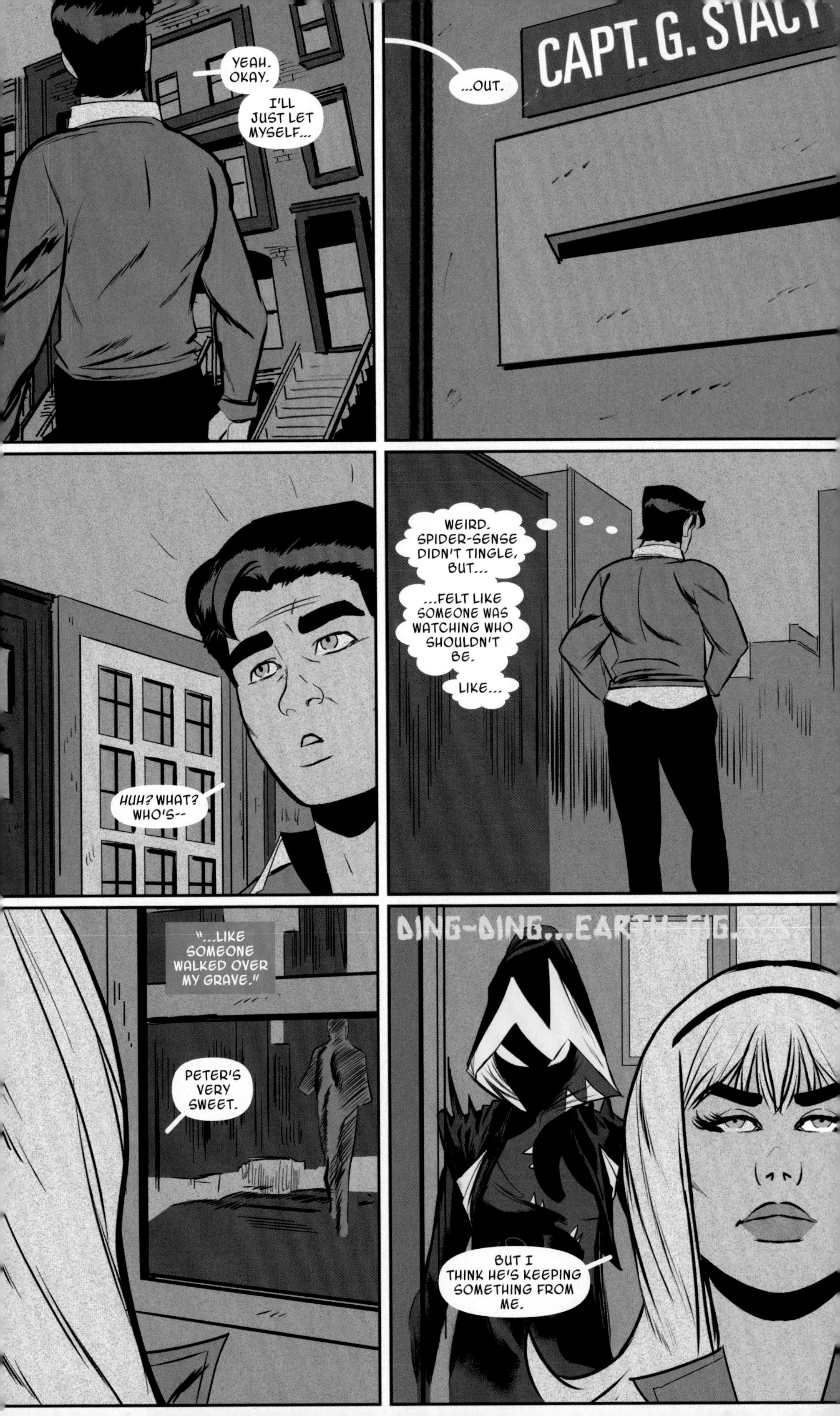

YEAH. OKAY.
I'LL JUST LET MYSELF...
...OUT.
CAPT. G. STACY
HUH? WHAT? WHO'S--
WEIRD. SPIDER-SENSE DIDN'T TINGLE, BUT...
...FELT LIKE SOMEONE WAS WATCHING WHO SHOULDN'T BE.
LIKE...
"...LIKE SOMEONE WALKED OVER MY GRAVE."
PETER'S VERY SWEET.
DING-DING...EARTH-
BUT I THINK HE'S KEEPING SOMETHING FROM ME.

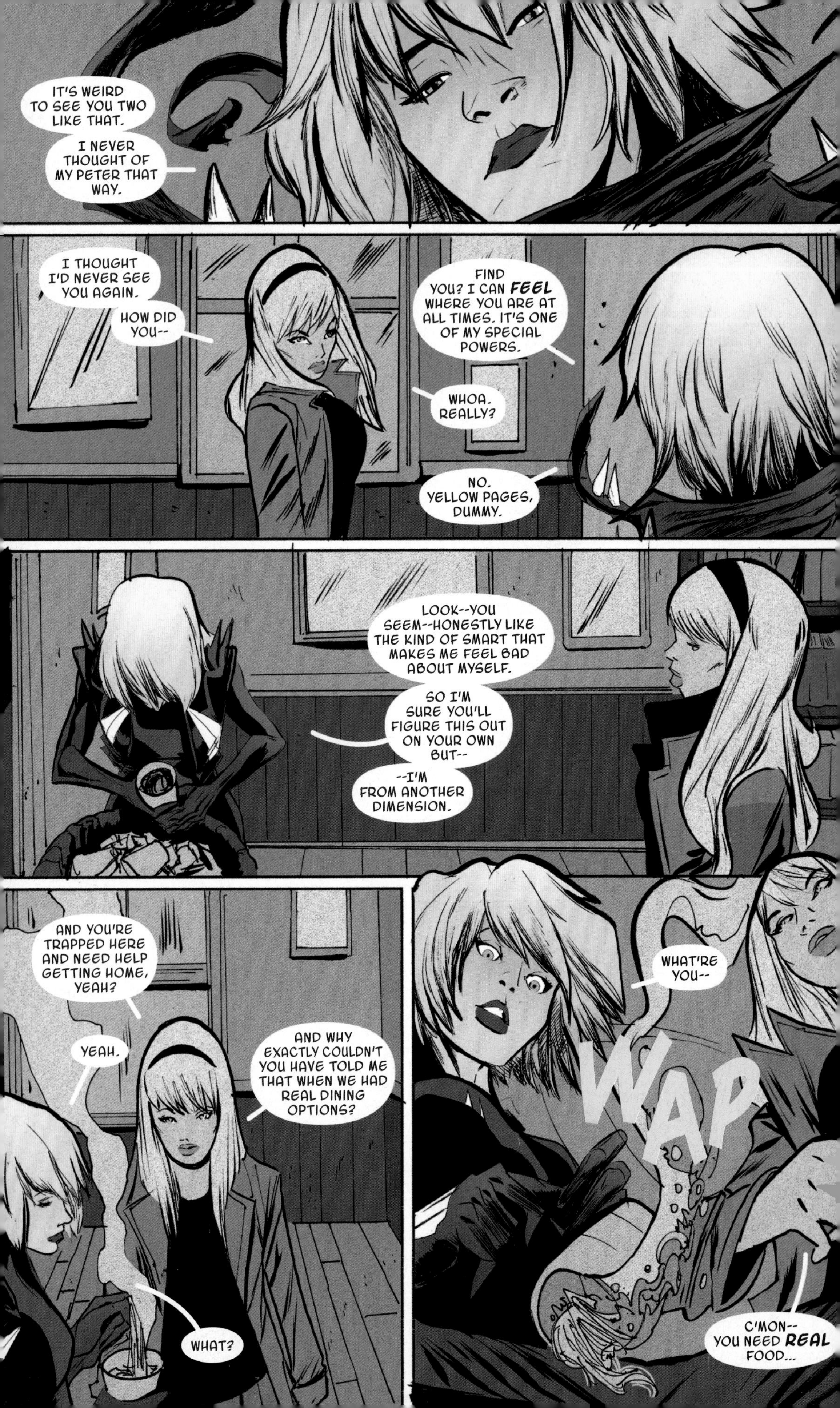
IT'S WEIRD TO SEE YOU TWO LIKE THAT.
I NEVER THOUGHT OF MY PETER THAT WAY.
I THOUGHT I'D NEVER SEE YOU AGAIN.
HOW DID YOU--
FIND YOU? I CAN FEEL WHERE YOU ARE AT ALL TIMES. IT'S ONE OF MY SPECIAL POWERS.
WHOA. REALLY?
NO. YELLOW PAGES, DUMMY.
LOOK--YOU SEEM--HONESTLY LIKE THE KIND OF SMART THAT MAKES ME FEEL BAD ABOUT MYSELF.
SO I'M SURE YOU'LL FIGURE THIS OUT ON YOUR OWN BUT--
--I'M FROM ANOTHER DIMENSION.
AND YOU'RE TRAPPED HERE AND NEED HELP GETTING HOME, YEAH?
YEAH.
AND WHY EXACTLY COULDN'T YOU HAVE TOLD ME THAT WHEN WE HAD REAL DINING OPTIONS?
WHAT?
WHAT'RE YOU--
WAP
C'MON-- YOU NEED REAL FOOD...

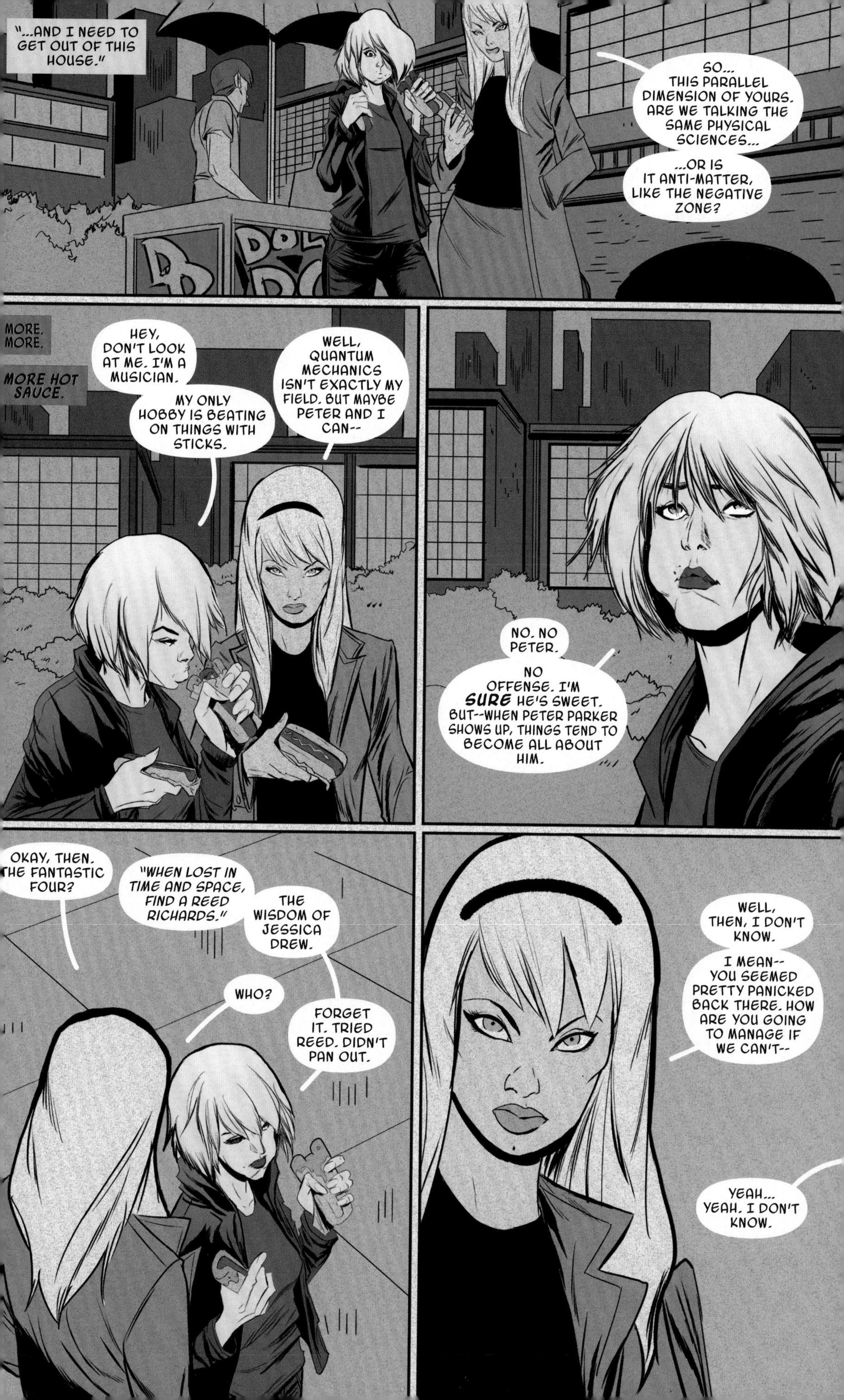
"...AND I NEED TO GET OUT OF THIS HOUSE."
SO... THIS PARALLEL DIMENSION OF YOURS. ARE WE TALKING THE SAME PHYSICAL SCIENCES...
...OR IS IT ANTI-MATTER, LIKE THE NEGATIVE ZONE?
MORE. MORE.
MORE HOT SAUCE.
HEY, DON'T LOOK AT ME. I'M A MUSICIAN.
MY ONLY HOBBY IS BEATING ON THINGS WITH STICKS.
WELL, QUANTUM MECHANICS ISN'T EXACTLY MY FIELD. BUT MAYBE PETER AND I CAN--
NO. NO PETER.
NO OFFENSE. I'M SURE HE'S SWEET. BUT--WHEN PETER PARKER SHOWS UP, THINGS TEND TO BECOME ALL ABOUT HIM.
OKAY, THEN. THE FANTASTIC FOUR?
"WHEN LOST IN TIME AND SPACE, FIND A REED RICHARDS."
THE WISDOM OF JESSICA DREW.
WHO?
FORGET IT. TRIED REED. DIDN'T PAN OUT.
WELL, THEN, I DON'T KNOW.
I MEAN-- YOU SEEMED PRETTY PANICKED BACK THERE. HOW ARE YOU GOING TO MANAGE IF WE CAN'T--
YEAH... YEAH. I DON'T KNOW.

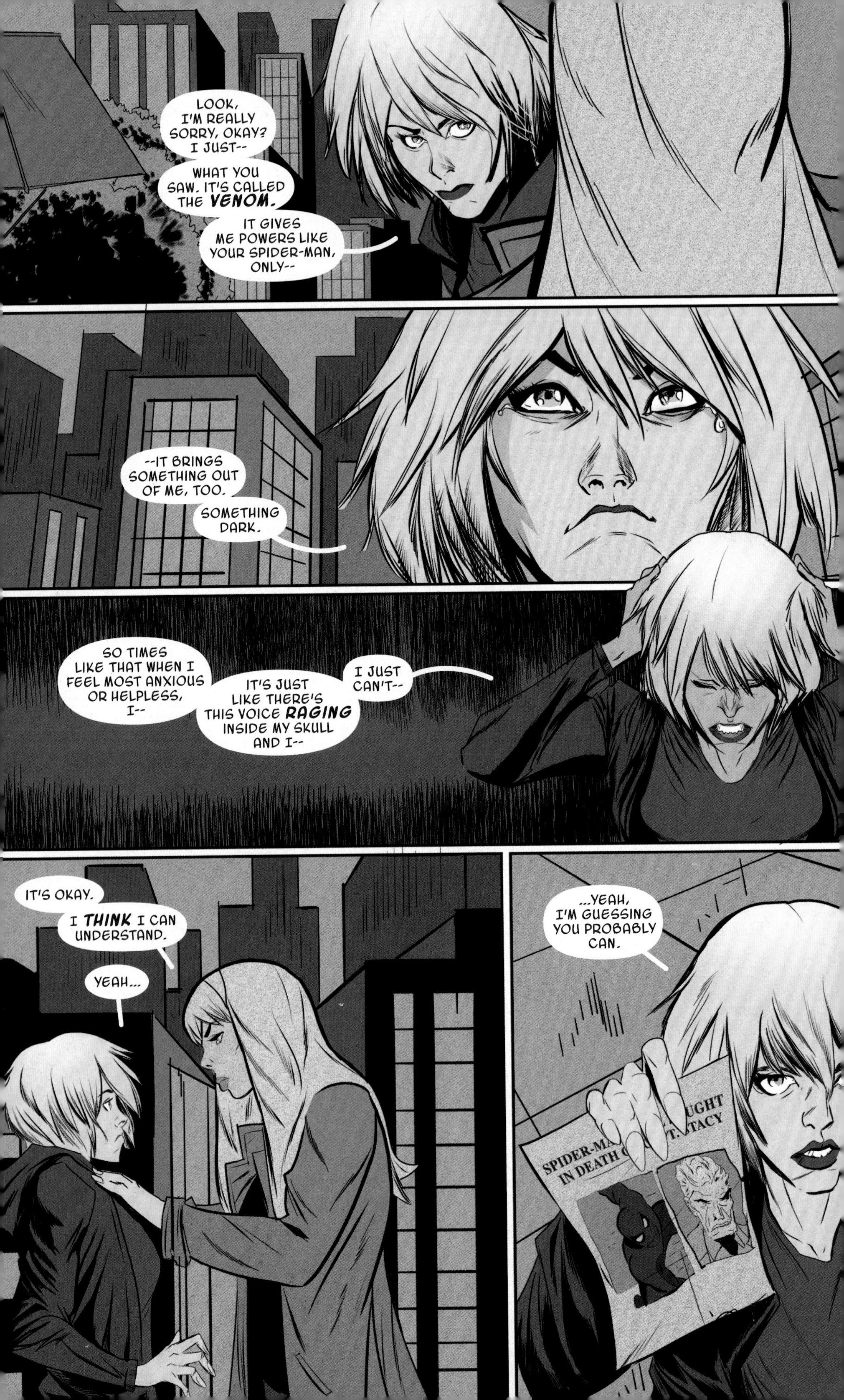
LOOK, I'M REALLY SORRY, OKAY? I JUST--
WHAT YOU SAW. IT'S CALLED THE VENOM.
IT GIVES ME POWERS LIKE YOUR SPIDER-MAN, ONLY--
--IT BRINGS SOMETHING OUT OF ME, TOO.
SOMETHING DARK.
SO TIMES LIKE THAT WHEN I FEEL MOST ANXIOUS OR HELPLESS, I--
IT'S JUST LIKE THERE'S THIS VOICE RAGING INSIDE MY SKULL AND I--
I JUST CAN'T--
IT'S OKAY.
I THINK I CAN UNDERSTAND.
YEAH...
...YEAH, I'M GUESSING YOU PROBABLY CAN.

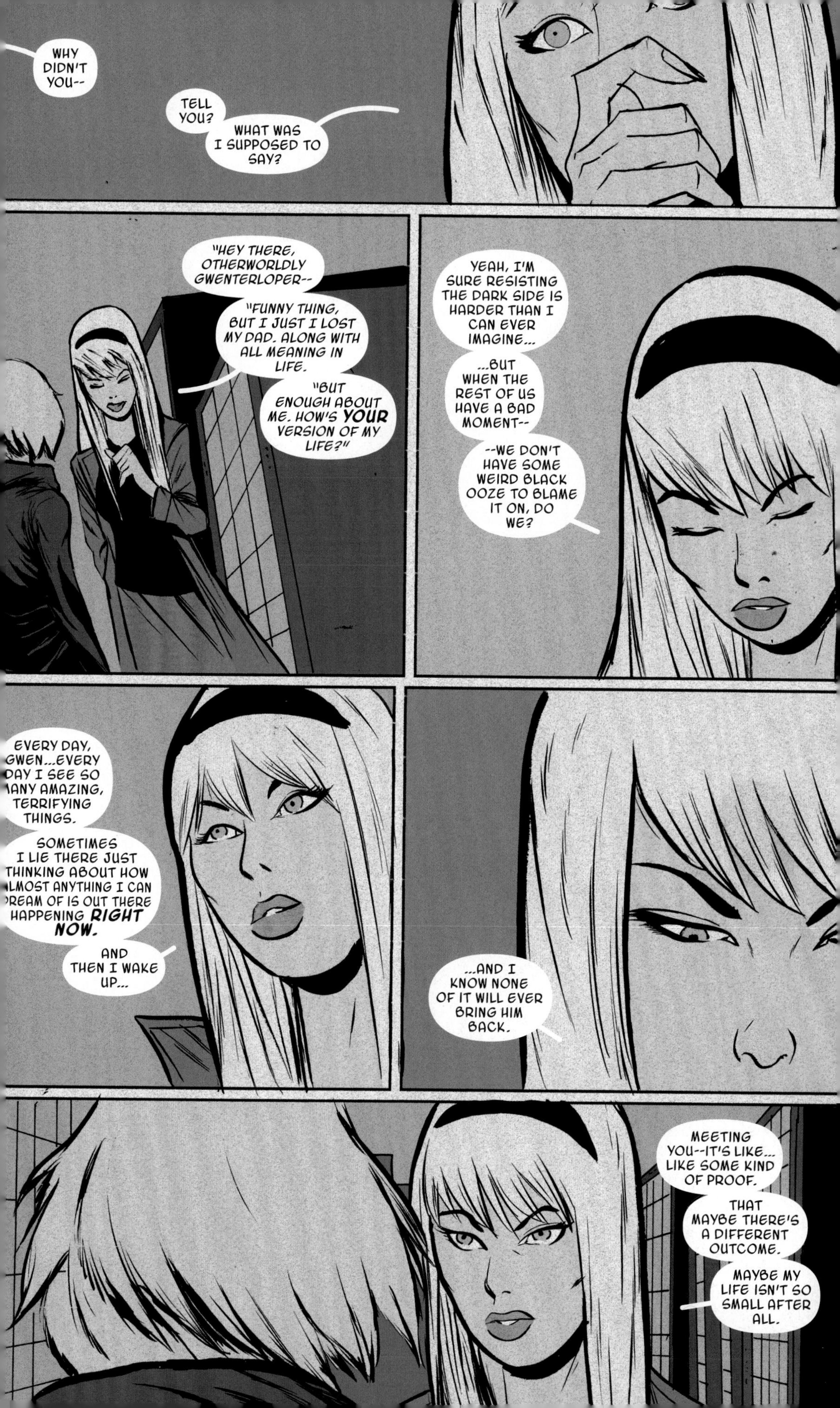
WHY DIDN'T YOU--
TELL YOU?
WHAT WAS I SUPPOSED TO SAY?
"HEY THERE, OTHERWORLDLY GWENTERLOPER--
"FUNNY THING, BUT I JUST I LOST MY DAD. ALONG WITH ALL MEANING IN LIFE.
"BUT ENOUGH ABOUT ME. HOW'S YOUR VERSION OF MY LIFE?"
YEAH, I'M SURE RESISTING THE DARK SIDE IS HARDER THAN I CAN EVER IMAGINE...
...BUT WHEN THE REST OF US HAVE A BAD MOMENT--
--WE DON'T HAVE SOME WEIRD BLACK OOZE TO BLAME IT ON, DO WE?
EVERY DAY, GWEN...EVERY DAY I SEE SO MANY AMAZING, TERRIFYING THINGS.
SOMETIMES I LIE THERE JUST THINKING ABOUT HOW ALMOST ANYTHING I CAN DREAM OF IS OUT THERE HAPPENING RIGHT NOW.
AND THEN I WAKE UP...
...AND I KNOW NONE OF IT WILL EVER BRING HIM BACK.
MEETING YOU--IT'S LIKE... LIKE SOME KIND OF PROOF.
THAT MAYBE THERE'S A DIFFERENT OUTCOME.
MAYBE MY LIFE ISN'T SO SMALL AFTER ALL.

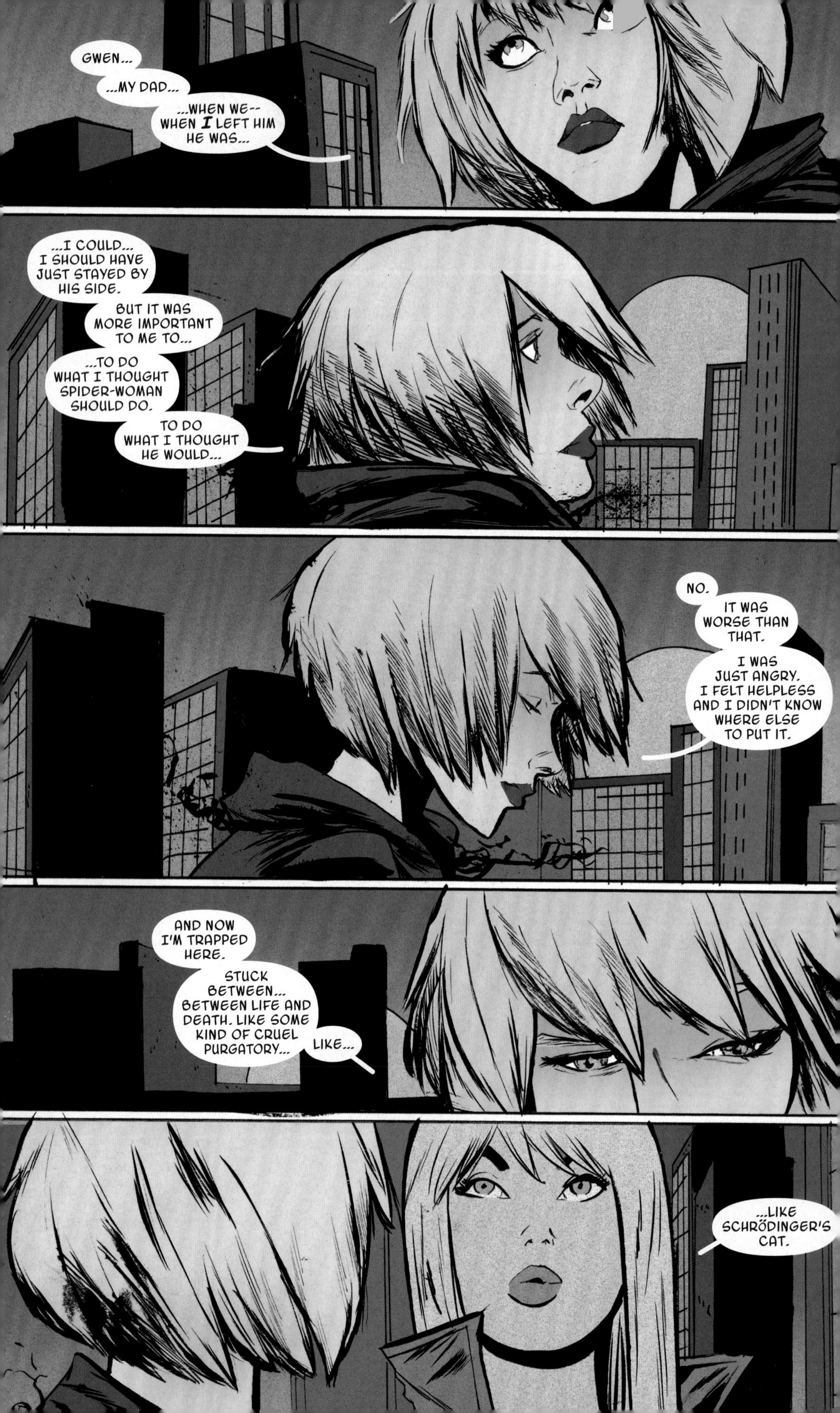
GWEN...
...MY DAD...
...WHEN WE-- WHEN I LEFT HIM HE WAS...
...I COULD... I SHOULD HAVE JUST STAYED BY HIS SIDE.
BUT IT WAS MORE IMPORTANT TO ME TO...
...TO DO WHAT I THOUGHT SPIDER-WOMAN SHOULD DO.
TO DO WHAT I THOUGHT HE WOULD...
NO.
IT WAS WORSE THAN THAT.
I WAS JUST ANGRY. I FELT HELPLESS AND I DIDN'T KNOW WHERE ELSE TO PUT IT.
AND NOW I'M TRAPPED HERE.
STUCK BETWEEN... BETWEEN LIFE AND DEATH. LIKE SOME KIND OF CRUEL PURGATORY...
LIKE...
...LIKE SCHRÖDINGER'S CAT.

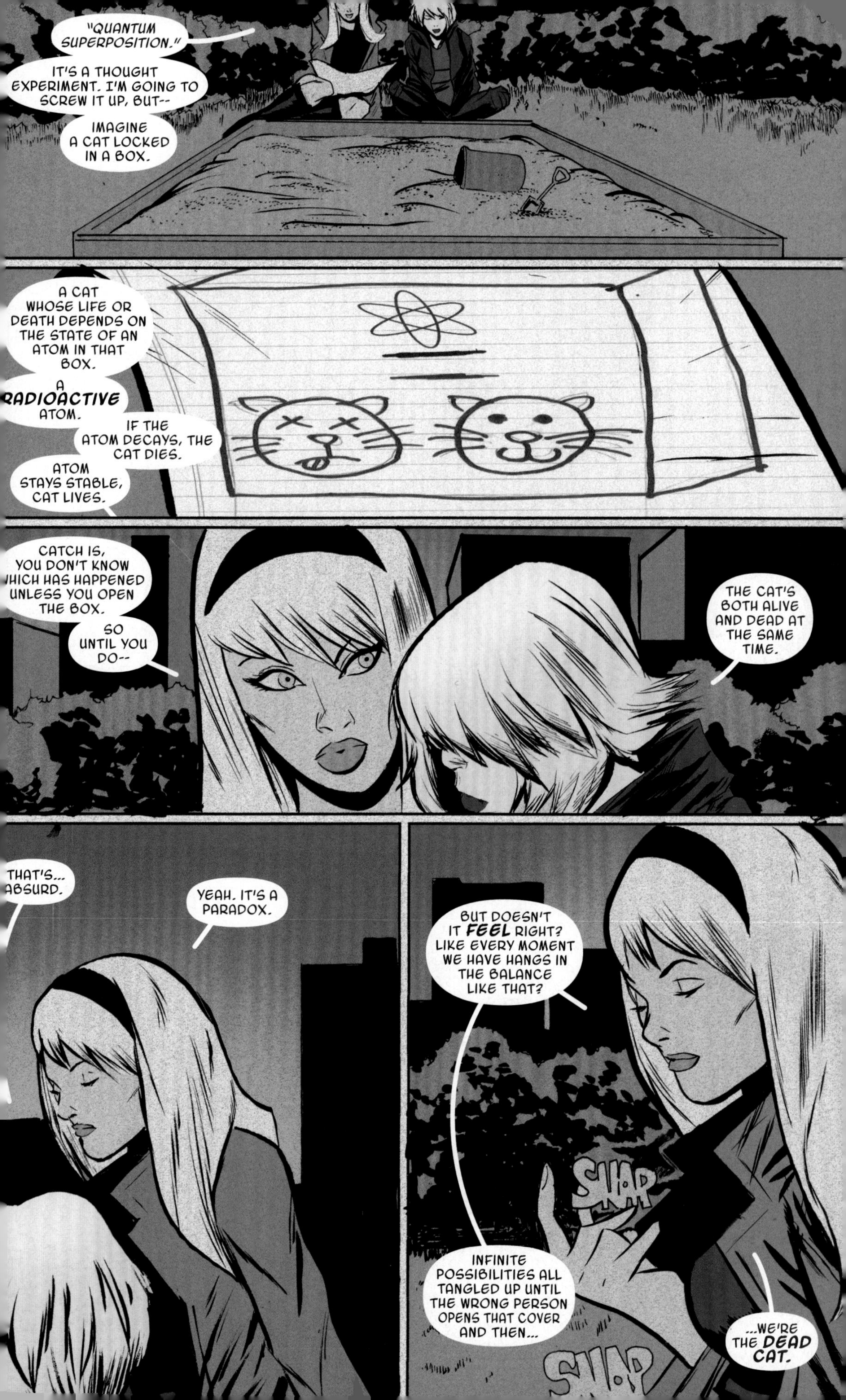
"QUANTUM SUPERPOSITION."
IT'S A THOUGHT EXPERIMENT. I'M GOING TO SCREW IT UP, BUT--
IMAGINE A CAT LOCKED IN A BOX.
A CAT WHOSE LIFE OR DEATH DEPENDS ON THE STATE OF AN ATOM IN THAT BOX.
A RADIOACTIVE ATOM.
IF THE ATOM DECAYS, THE CAT DIES.
ATOM STAYS STABLE, CAT LIVES.
CATCH IS, YOU DON'T KNOW WHICH HAS HAPPENED UNLESS YOU OPEN THE BOX.
SO UNTIL YOU DO--
THE CAT'S BOTH ALIVE AND DEAD AT THE SAME TIME.
THAT'S... ABSURD.
YEAH. IT'S A PARADOX.
BUT DOESN'T IT FEEL RIGHT? LIKE EVERY MOMENT WE HAVE HANGS IN THE BALANCE LIKE THAT?
SNAP
INFINITE POSSIBILITIES ALL TANGLED UP UNTIL THE WRONG PERSON OPENS THAT COVER AND THEN...
...WE'RE THE DEAD CAT.
SNAP

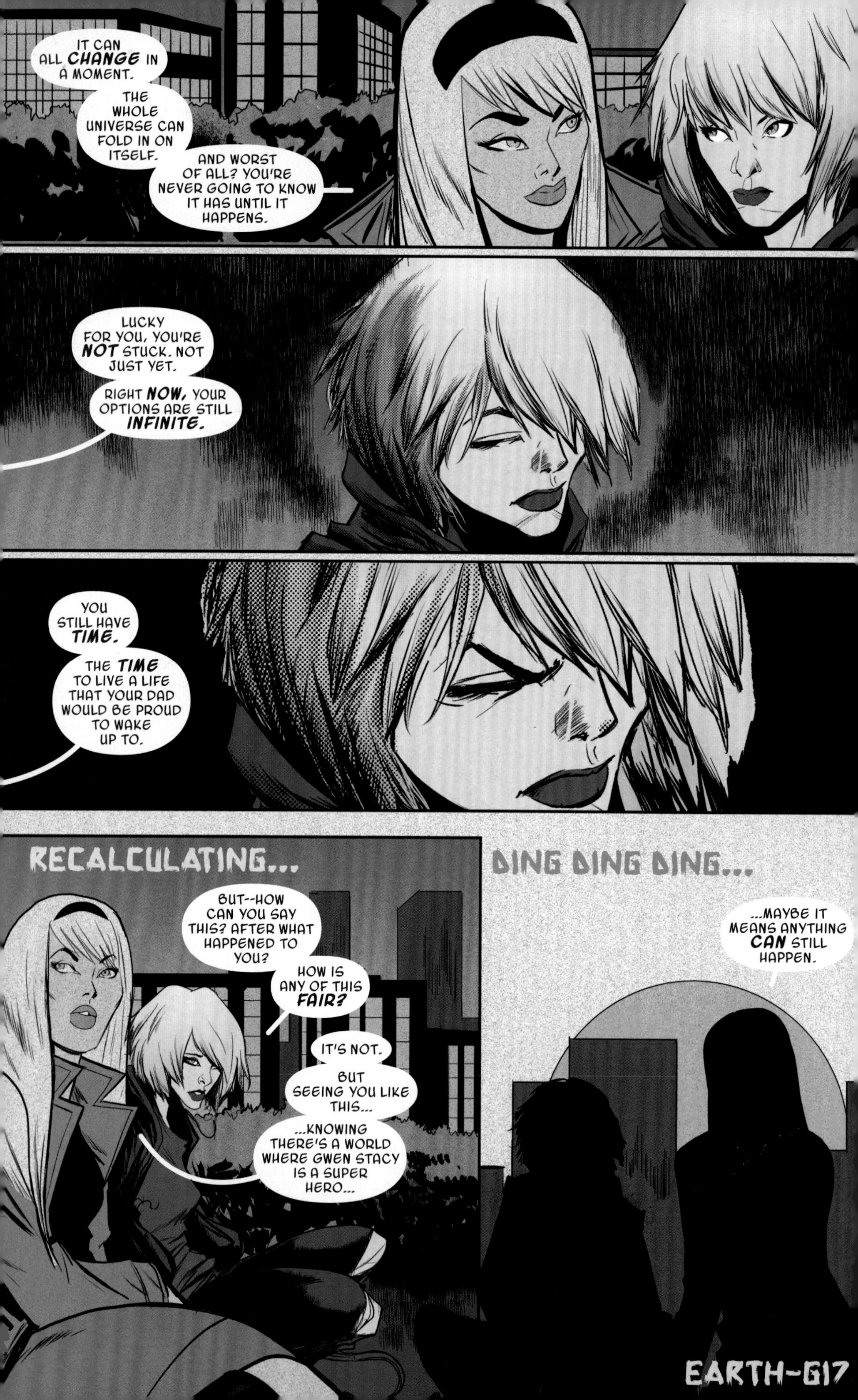
IT CAN ALL CHANGE IN A MOMENT.
THE WHOLE UNIVERSE CAN FOLD IN ON ITSELF.
AND WORST OF ALL? YOU'RE NEVER GOING TO KNOW IT HAS UNTIL IT HAPPENS.
LUCKY FOR YOU, YOU'RE NOT STUCK. NOT JUST YET.
RIGHT NOW, YOUR OPTIONS ARE STILL INFINITE.
YOU STILL HAVE TIME.
THE TIME TO LIVE A LIFE THAT YOUR DAD WOULD BE PROUD TO WAKE UP TO.
RECALCULATING...
BUT--HOW CAN YOU SAY THIS? AFTER WHAT HAPPENED TO YOU?
HOW IS ANY OF THIS FAIR?
IT'S NOT.
BUT SEEING YOU LIKE THIS...
...KNOWING THERE'S A WORLD WHERE GWEN STACY IS A SUPER HERO...
DING DING DING...
...MAYBE IT MEANS ANYTHING CAN STILL HAPPEN.
EARTH-617

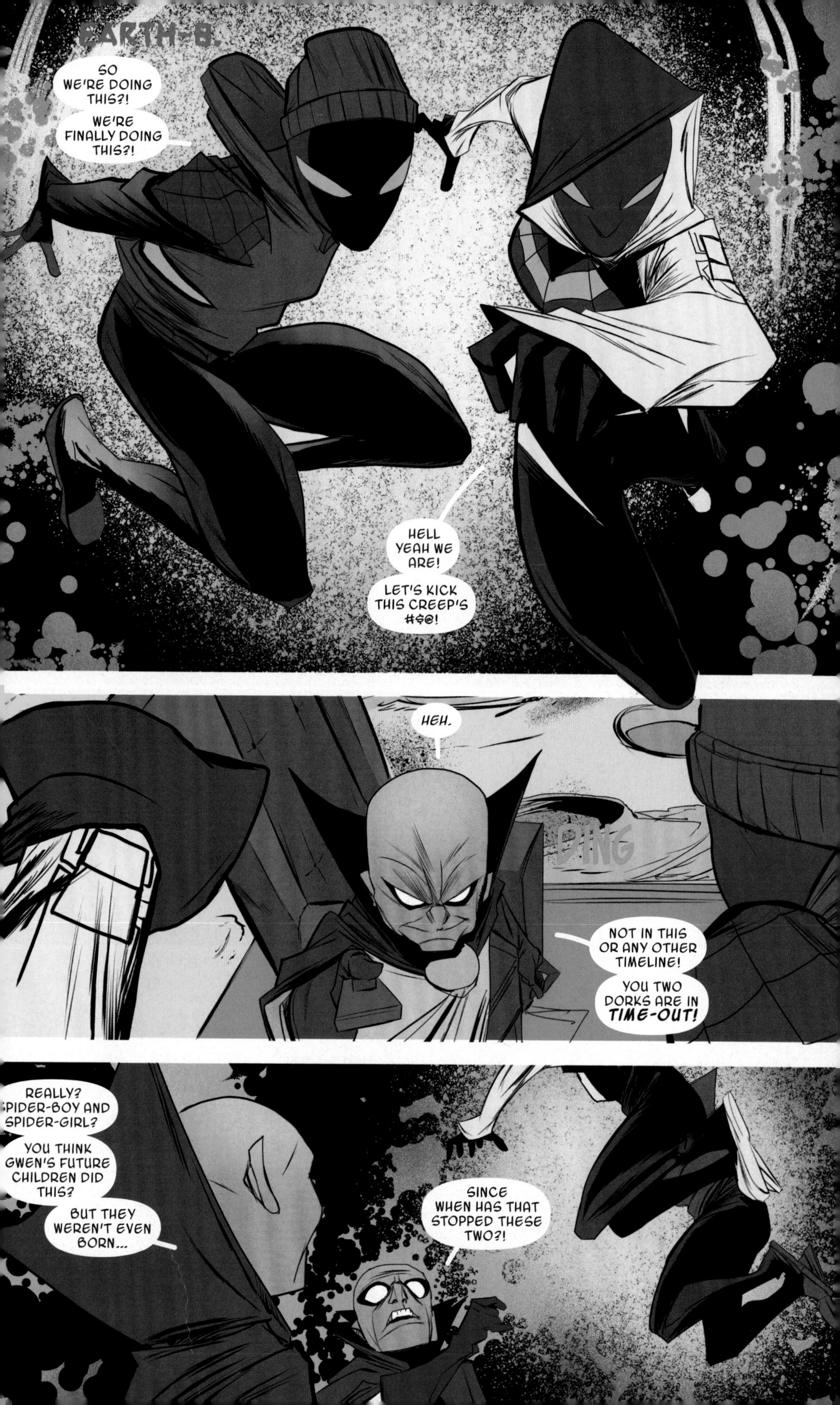
EARTH-8.
SO WE'RE DOING THIS?!
WE'RE FINALLY DOING THIS?!
HELL YEAH WE ARE!
LET'S KICK THIS CREEP'S #$@!
HEH.
DING
NOT IN THIS OR ANY OTHER TIMELINE!
YOU TWO DORKS ARE IN TIME-OUT!
REALLY? SPIDER-BOY AND SPIDER-GIRL?
YOU THINK GWEN'S FUTURE CHILDREN DID THIS?
BUT THEY WEREN'T EVEN BORN...
SINCE WHEN HAS THAT STOPPED THESE TWO?!

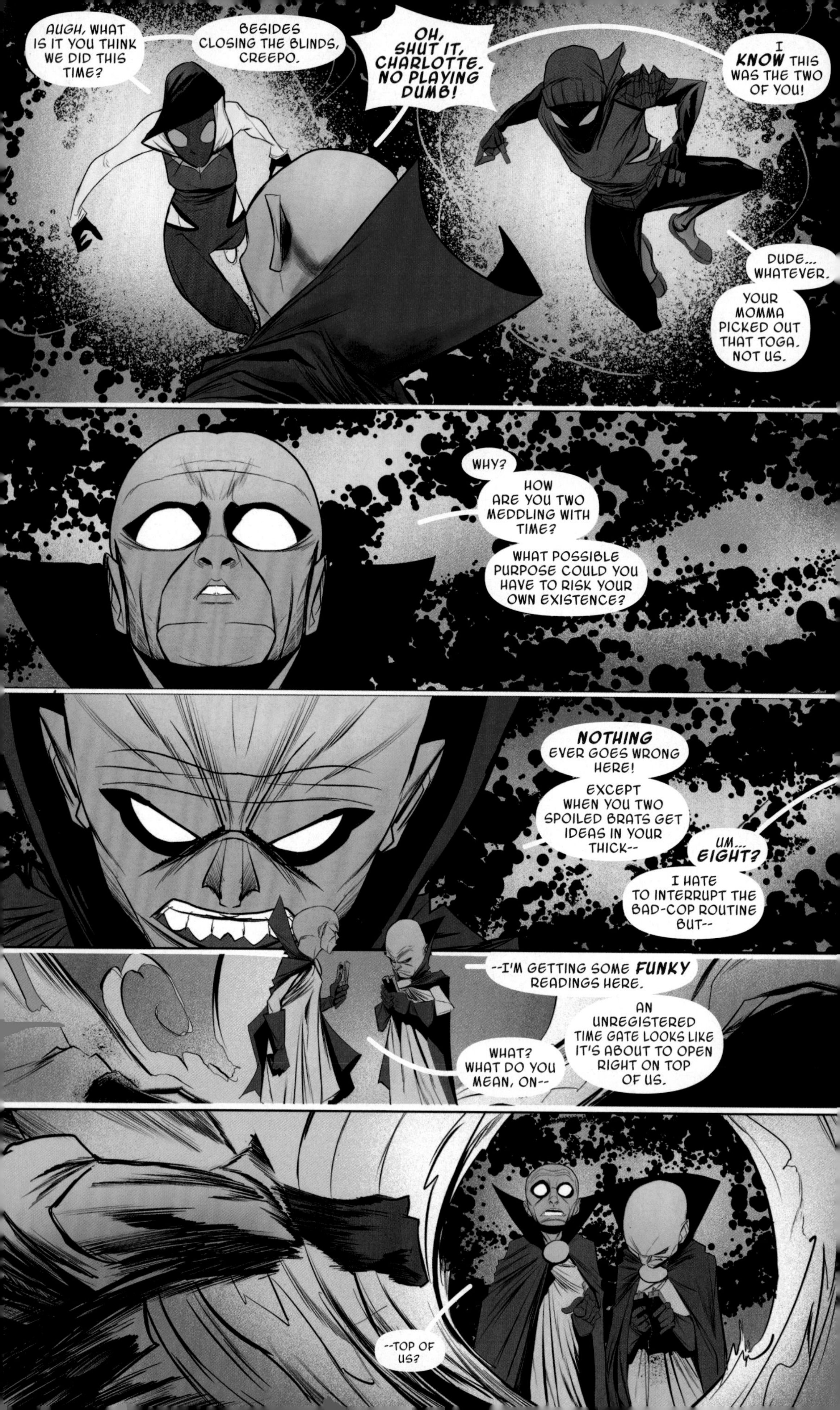

AUGH, WHAT IS IT YOU THINK WE DID THIS TIME?
BESIDES CLOSING THE BLINDS, CREEPO.
OH, SHUT IT, CHARLOTTE. NO PLAYING DUMB!
I KNOW THIS WAS THE TWO OF YOU!
DUDE... WHATEVER.
YOUR MOMMA PICKED OUT THAT TOGA. NOT US.
WHY?
HOW ARE YOU TWO MEDDLING WITH TIME?
WHAT POSSIBLE PURPOSE COULD YOU HAVE TO RISK YOUR OWN EXISTENCE?
NOTHING EVER GOES WRONG HERE!
EXCEPT WHEN YOU TWO SPOILED BRATS GET IDEAS IN YOUR THICK--
UM... EIGHT?
I HATE TO INTERRUPT THE BAD-COP ROUTINE BUT--
--I'M GETTING SOME FUNKY READINGS HERE.
AN UNREGISTERED TIME GATE LOOKS LIKE IT'S ABOUT TO OPEN RIGHT ON TOP OF US.
WHAT? WHAT DO YOU MEAN, ON--
--TOP OF US?

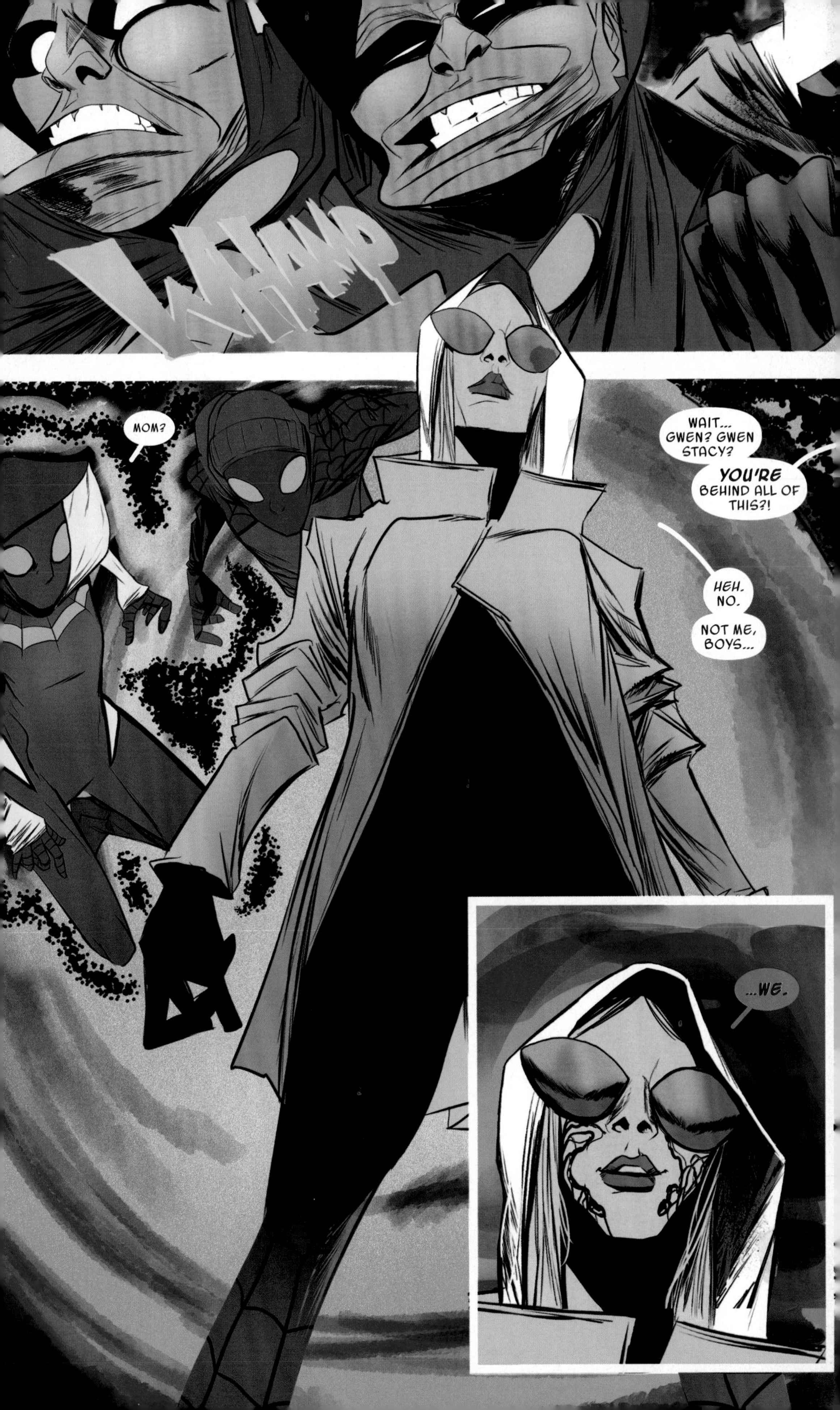
WHAMP
MOM?
WAIT... GWEN? GWEN STACY?
YOU'RE BEHIND ALL OF THIS?!
HEH. NO.
NOT ME, BOYS...
...WE.

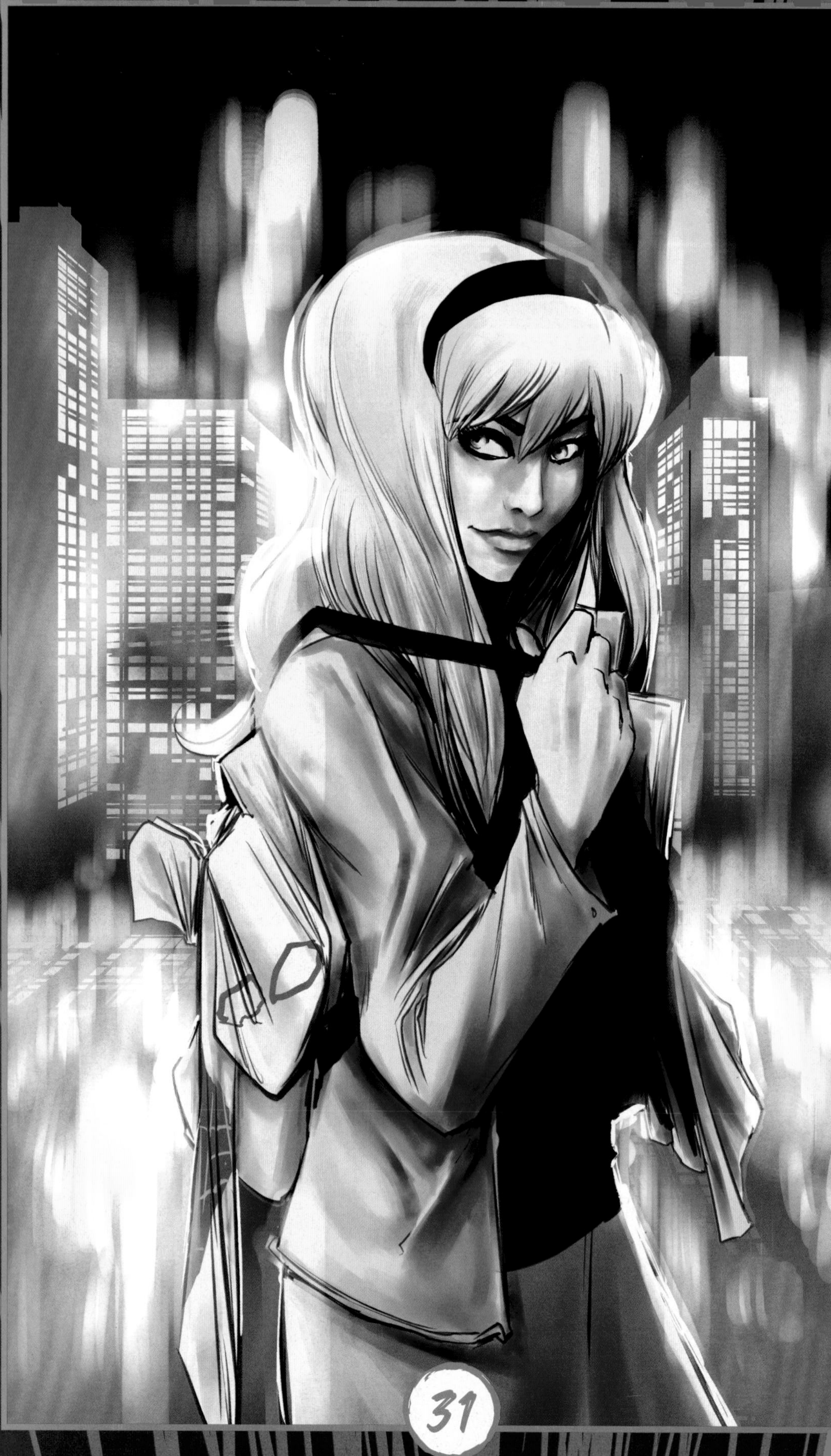

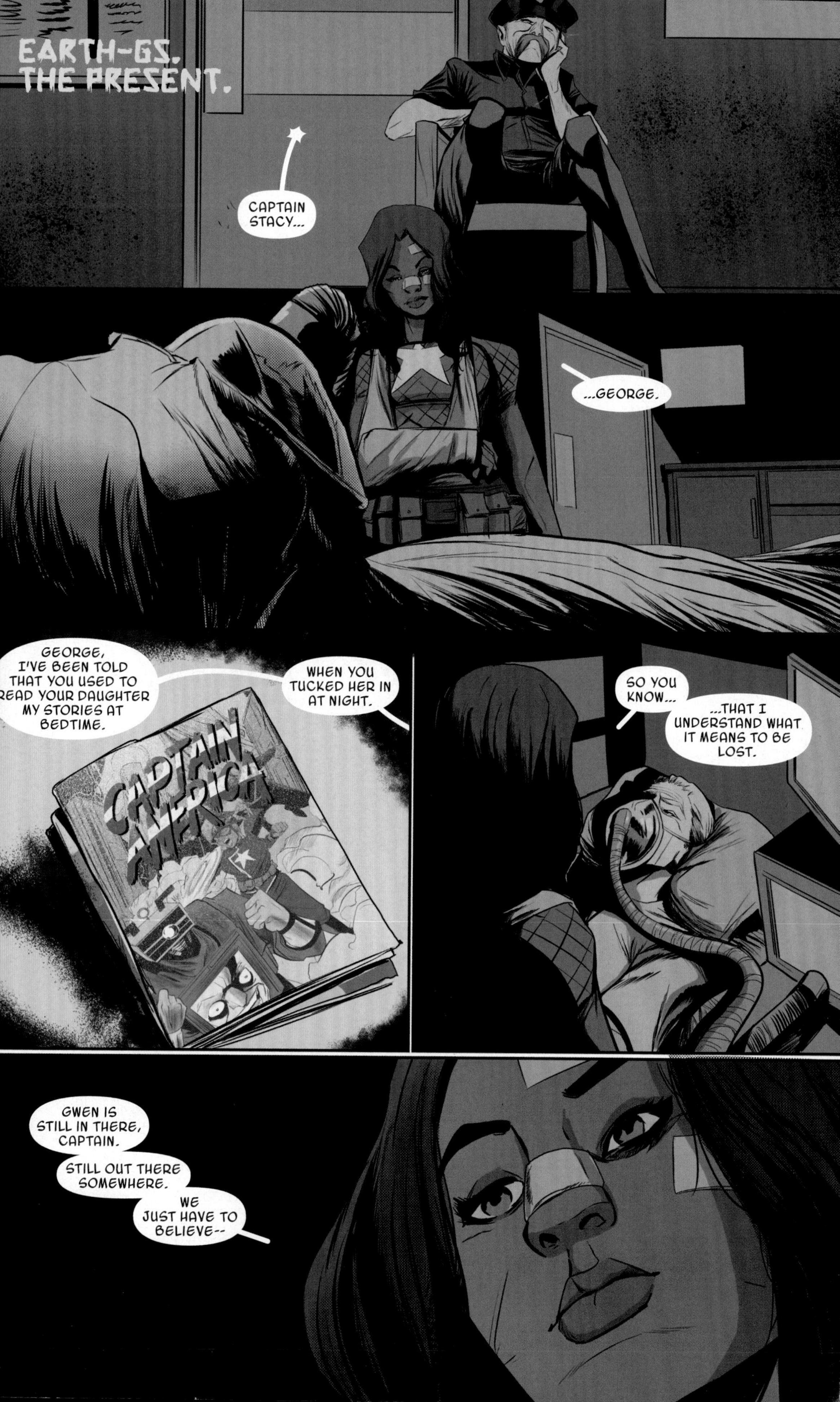
EARTH-65. THE PRESENT.
CAPTAIN STACY...
...GEORGE.
GEORGE, I'VE BEEN TOLD THAT YOU USED TO READ YOUR DAUGHTER MY STORIES AT BEDTIME.
WHEN YOU TUCKED HER IN AT NIGHT.
CAPTAIN AMERICA
SO YOU KNOW...
...THAT I UNDERSTAND WHAT IT MEANS TO BE LOST.
GWEN IS STILL IN THERE, CAPTAIN.
STILL OUT THERE SOMEWHERE.
WE JUST HAVE TO BELIEVE--

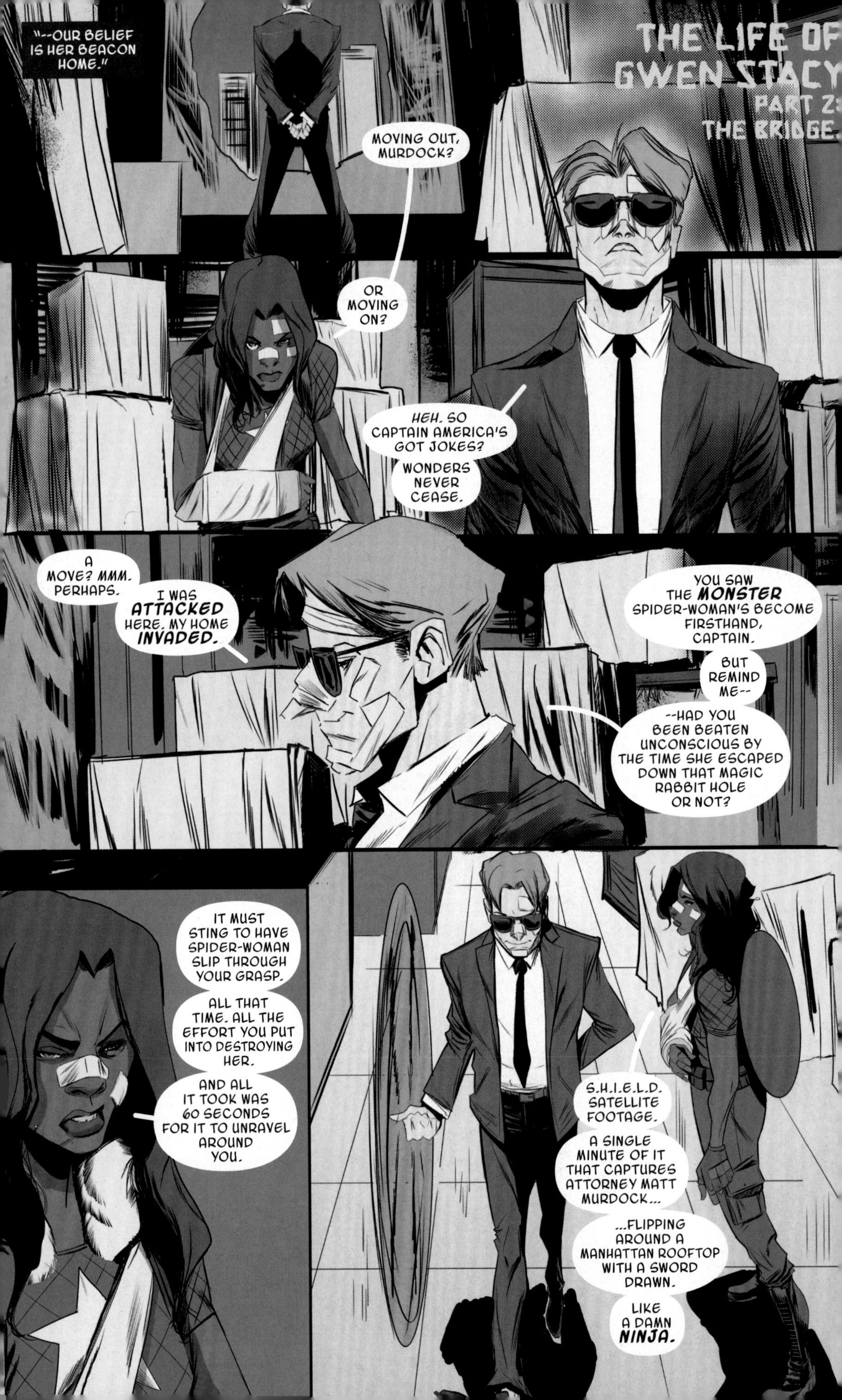
"--OUR BELIEF IS HER BEACON HOME."
THE LIFE OF GWEN STACY
PART 2: THE BRIDGE.
MOVING OUT, MURDOCK?
OR MOVING ON?
HEH. SO CAPTAIN AMERICA'S GOT JOKES?
WONDERS NEVER CEASE.
A MOVE? MMM. PERHAPS.
I WAS ATTACKED HERE. MY HOME INVADED.
YOU SAW THE MONSTER SPIDER-WOMAN'S BECOME FIRSTHAND, CAPTAIN.
BUT REMIND ME--
--HAD YOU BEEN BEATEN UNCONSCIOUS BY THE TIME SHE ESCAPED DOWN THAT MAGIC RABBIT HOLE OR NOT?
IT MUST STING TO HAVE SPIDER-WOMAN SLIP THROUGH YOUR GRASP.
ALL THAT TIME. ALL THE EFFORT YOU PUT INTO DESTROYING HER.
AND ALL IT TOOK WAS 60 SECONDS FOR IT TO UNRAVEL AROUND YOU.
S.H.I.E.L.D. SATELLITE FOOTAGE.
A SINGLE MINUTE OF IT THAT CAPTURES ATTORNEY MATT MURDOCK...
...FLIPPING AROUND A MANHATTAN ROOFTOP WITH A SWORD DRAWN.
LIKE A DAMN NINJA.

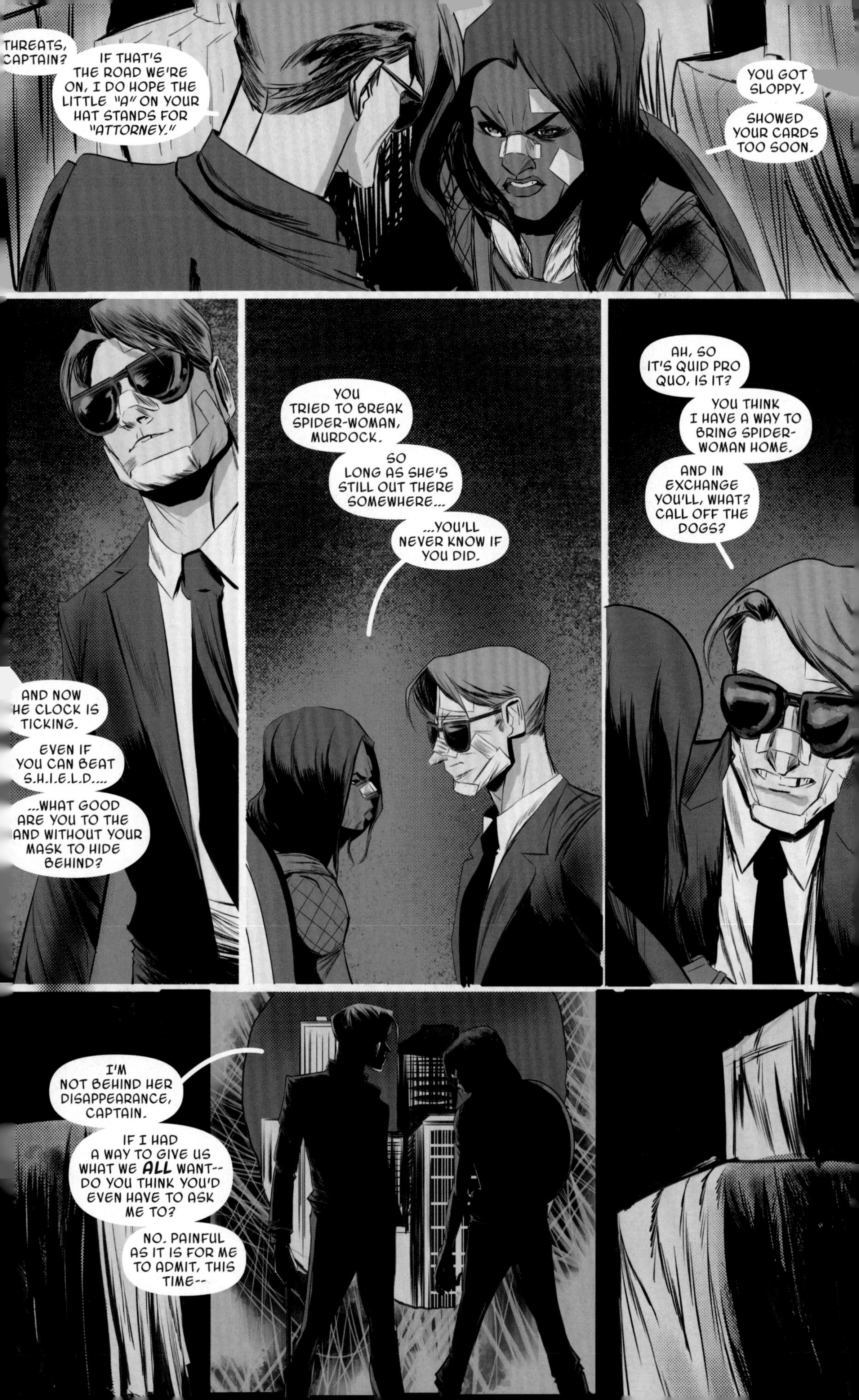
THREATS, CAPTAIN?
IF THAT'S THE ROAD WE'RE ON, I DO HOPE THE LITTLE "A" ON YOUR HAT STANDS FOR "ATTORNEY."
YOU GOT SLOPPY.
SHOWED YOUR CARDS TOO SOON.
AND NOW HE CLOCK IS TICKING.
EVEN IF YOU CAN BEAT S.H.I.E.L.D....
...WHAT GOOD ARE YOU TO THE AND WITHOUT YOUR MASK TO HIDE BEHIND?
YOU TRIED TO BREAK SPIDER-WOMAN, MURDOCK.
SO LONG AS SHE'S STILL OUT THERE SOMEWHERE...
...YOU'LL NEVER KNOW IF YOU DID.
AH, SO IT'S QUID PRO QUO, IS IT?
YOU THINK I HAVE A WAY TO BRING SPIDER-WOMAN HOME.
AND IN EXCHANGE YOU'LL, WHAT? CALL OFF THE DOGS?
I'M NOT BEHIND HER DISAPPEARANCE, CAPTAIN.
IF I HAD A WAY TO GIVE US WHAT WE ALL WANT-- DO YOU THINK YOU'D EVEN HAVE TO ASK ME TO?
NO. PAINFUL AS IT IS FOR ME TO ADMIT, THIS TIME--

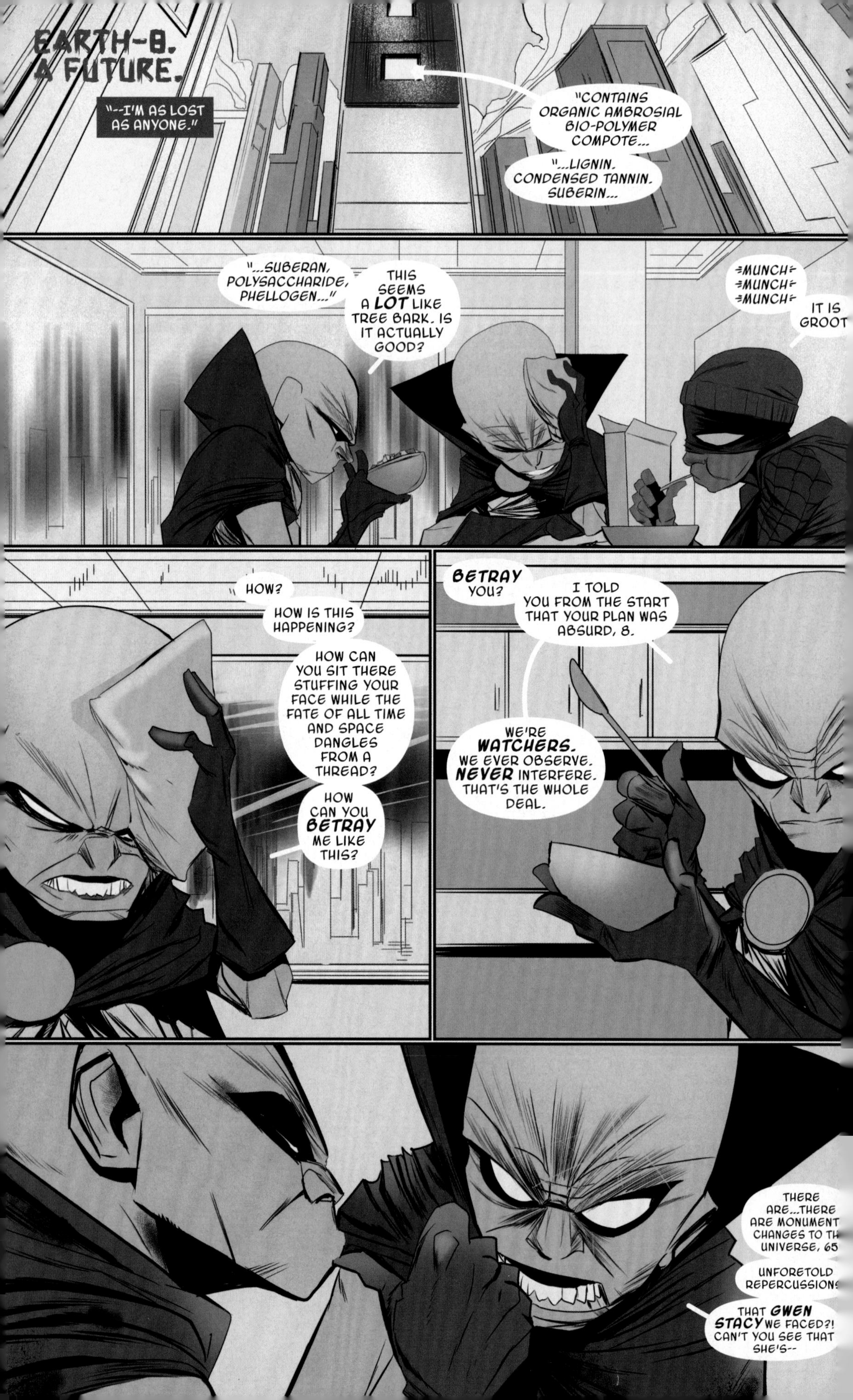
EARTH-8.
A FUTURE.
"--I'M AS LOST AS ANYONE."
"CONTAINS ORGANIC AMBROSIAL BIO-POLYMER COMPOTE...
"...LIGNIN. CONDENSED TANNIN. SUBERIN...
"...SUBERAN, POLYSACCHARIDE, PHELLOGEN..."
THIS SEEMS A LOT LIKE TREE BARK. IS IT ACTUALLY GOOD?
=MUNCH= =MUNCH= =MUNCH=
IT IS GROOT
HOW?
HOW IS THIS HAPPENING?
HOW CAN YOU SIT THERE STUFFING YOUR FACE WHILE THE FATE OF ALL TIME AND SPACE DANGLES FROM A THREAD?
HOW CAN YOU BETRAY ME LIKE THIS?
BETRAY YOU?
I TOLD YOU FROM THE START THAT YOUR PLAN WAS ABSURD, 8.
WE'RE WATCHERS. WE EVER OBSERVE. NEVER INTERFERE. THAT'S THE WHOLE DEAL.
THERE ARE...THERE ARE MONUMENT CHANGES TO TH UNIVERSE, 65
UNFORETOLD REPERCUSSIONS
THAT GWEN STACY WE FACED?! CAN'T YOU SEE THAT SHE'S--

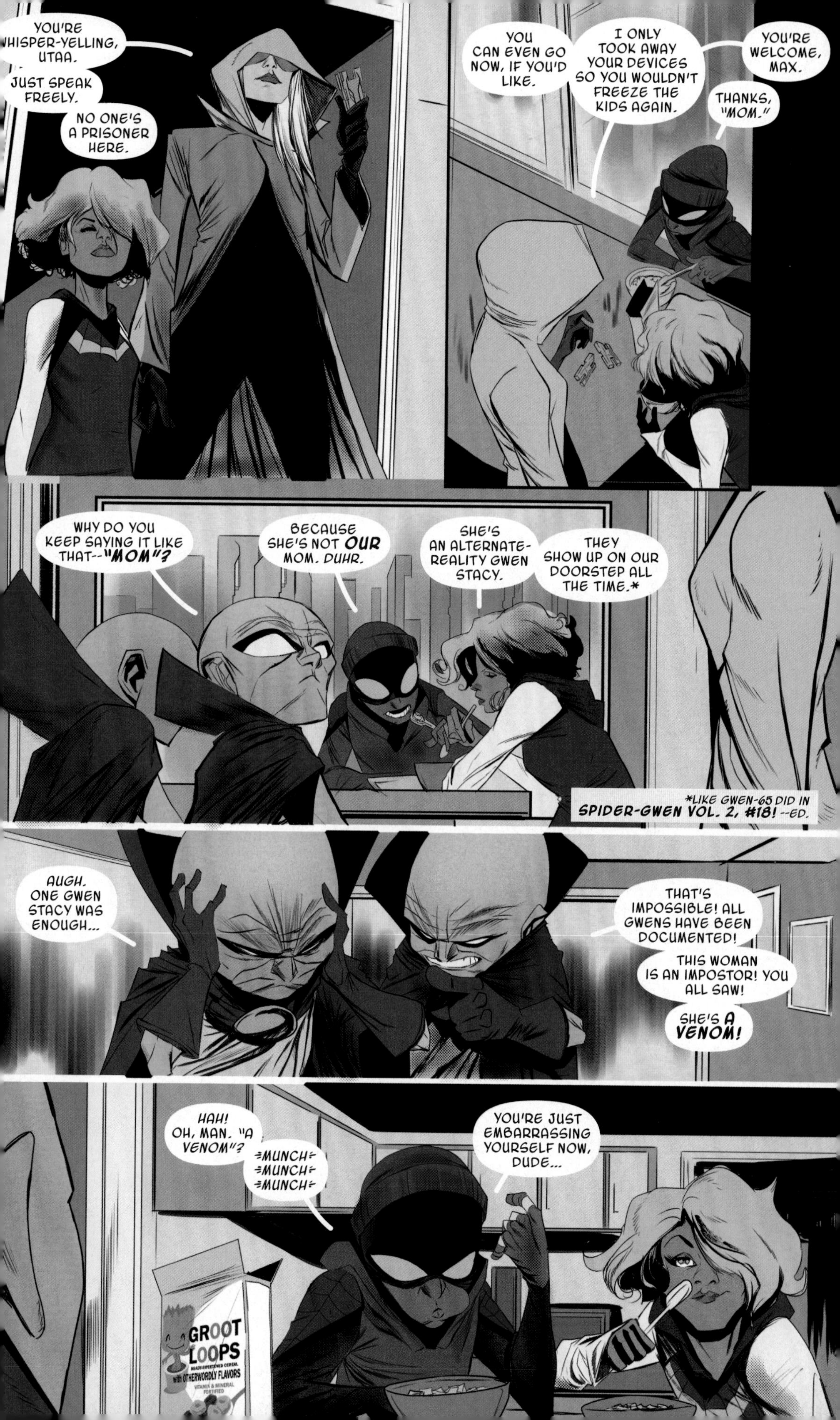
YOU'RE WHISPER-YELLING, UTAA.
JUST SPEAK FREELY.
NO ONE'S A PRISONER HERE.
YOU CAN EVEN GO NOW, IF YOU'D LIKE.
I ONLY TOOK AWAY YOUR DEVICES SO YOU WOULDN'T FREEZE THE KIDS AGAIN.
YOU'RE WELCOME, MAX.
THANKS, "MOM."
WHY DO YOU KEEP SAYING IT LIKE THAT--"MOM"?
BECAUSE SHE'S NOT OUR MOM. DUHR.
SHE'S AN ALTERNATE-REALITY GWEN STACY.
THEY SHOW UP ON OUR DOORSTEP ALL THE TIME.*
*LIKE GWEN-65 DID IN SPIDER-GWEN VOL. 2, #18! --ED.
AUGH. ONE GWEN STACY WAS ENOUGH...
THAT'S IMPOSSIBLE! ALL GWENS HAVE BEEN DOCUMENTED!
THIS WOMAN IS AN IMPOSTOR! YOU ALL SAW!
SHE'S A VENOM!
HAH! OH, MAN. "A VENOM"?
=MUNCH= =MUNCH= =MUNCH=
YOU'RE JUST EMBARRASSING YOURSELF NOW, DUDE...
GROOT LOOPS
with OTHERWORDLY FLAVORS

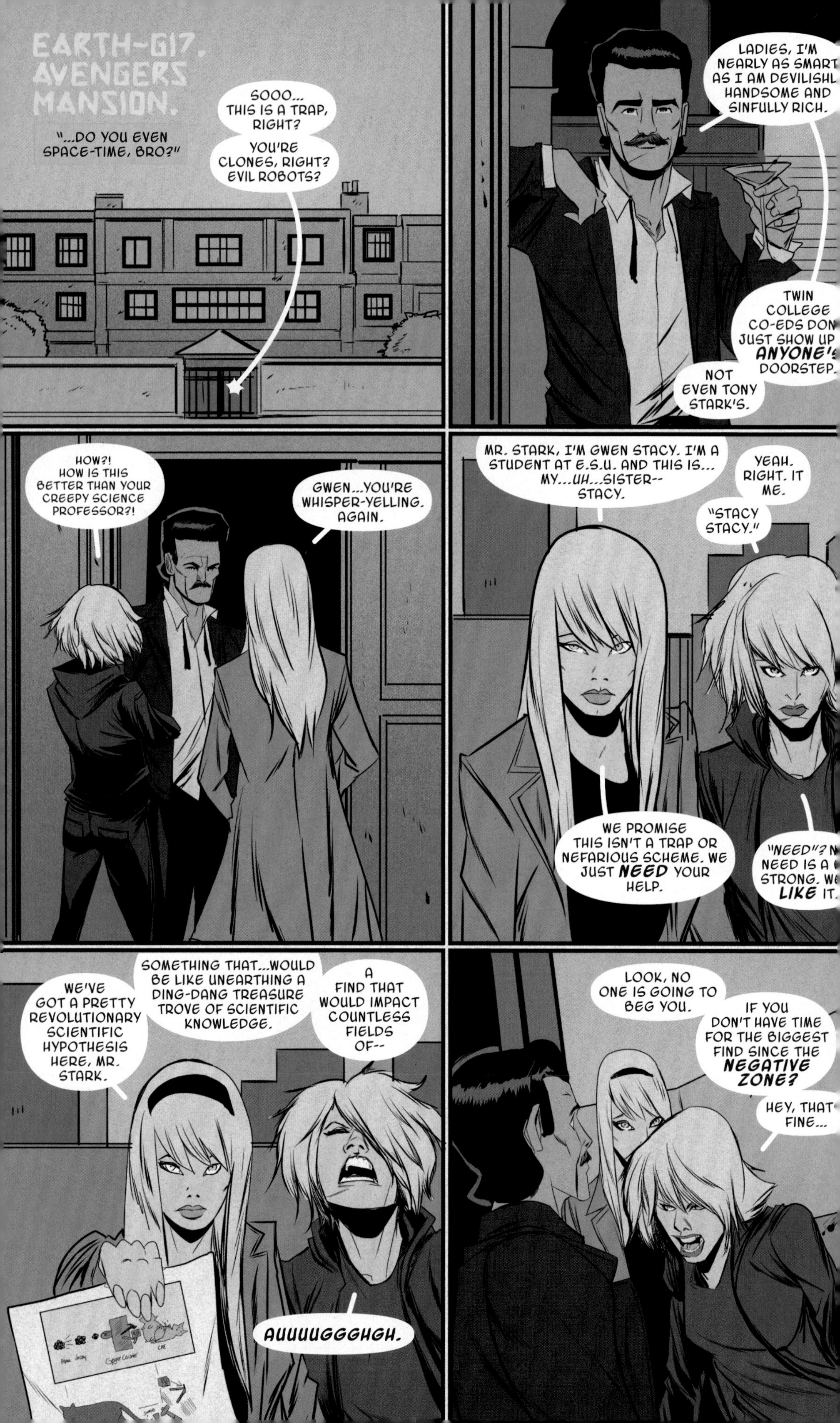
EARTH-G17. AVENGERS MANSION.
"...DO YOU EVEN SPACE-TIME, BRO?"
SOOO... THIS IS A TRAP, RIGHT?
YOU'RE CLONES, RIGHT? EVIL ROBOTS?
LADIES, I'M NEARLY AS SMART AS I AM DEVILISHL HANDSOME AND SINFULLY RICH.
TWIN COLLEGE CO-EDS DON JUST SHOW UP ANYONE' DOORSTEP.
NOT EVEN TONY STARK'S.
HOW?! HOW IS THIS BETTER THAN YOUR CREEPY SCIENCE PROFESSOR?!
GWEN...YOU'RE WHISPER-YELLING. AGAIN.
MR. STARK, I'M GWEN STACY. I'M A STUDENT AT E.S.U. AND THIS IS... MY...UH...SISTER-- STACY.
YEAH. RIGHT. IT ME.
"STACY STACY."
WE PROMISE THIS ISN'T A TRAP OR NEFARIOUS SCHEME. WE JUST NEED YOUR HELP.
"NEED"? N NEED IS A STRONG. W LIKE IT.
WE'VE GOT A PRETTY REVOLUTIONARY SCIENTIFIC HYPOTHESIS HERE, MR. STARK.
SOMETHING THAT...WOULD BE LIKE UNEARTHING A DING-DANG TREASURE TROVE OF SCIENTIFIC KNOWLEDGE.
A FIND THAT WOULD IMPACT COUNTLESS FIELDS OF--
AUUUUGGGHGH.
LOOK, NO ONE IS GOING TO BEG YOU.
IF YOU DON'T HAVE TIME FOR THE BIGGEST FIND SINCE THE NEGATIVE ZONE?
HEY, THAT FINE...

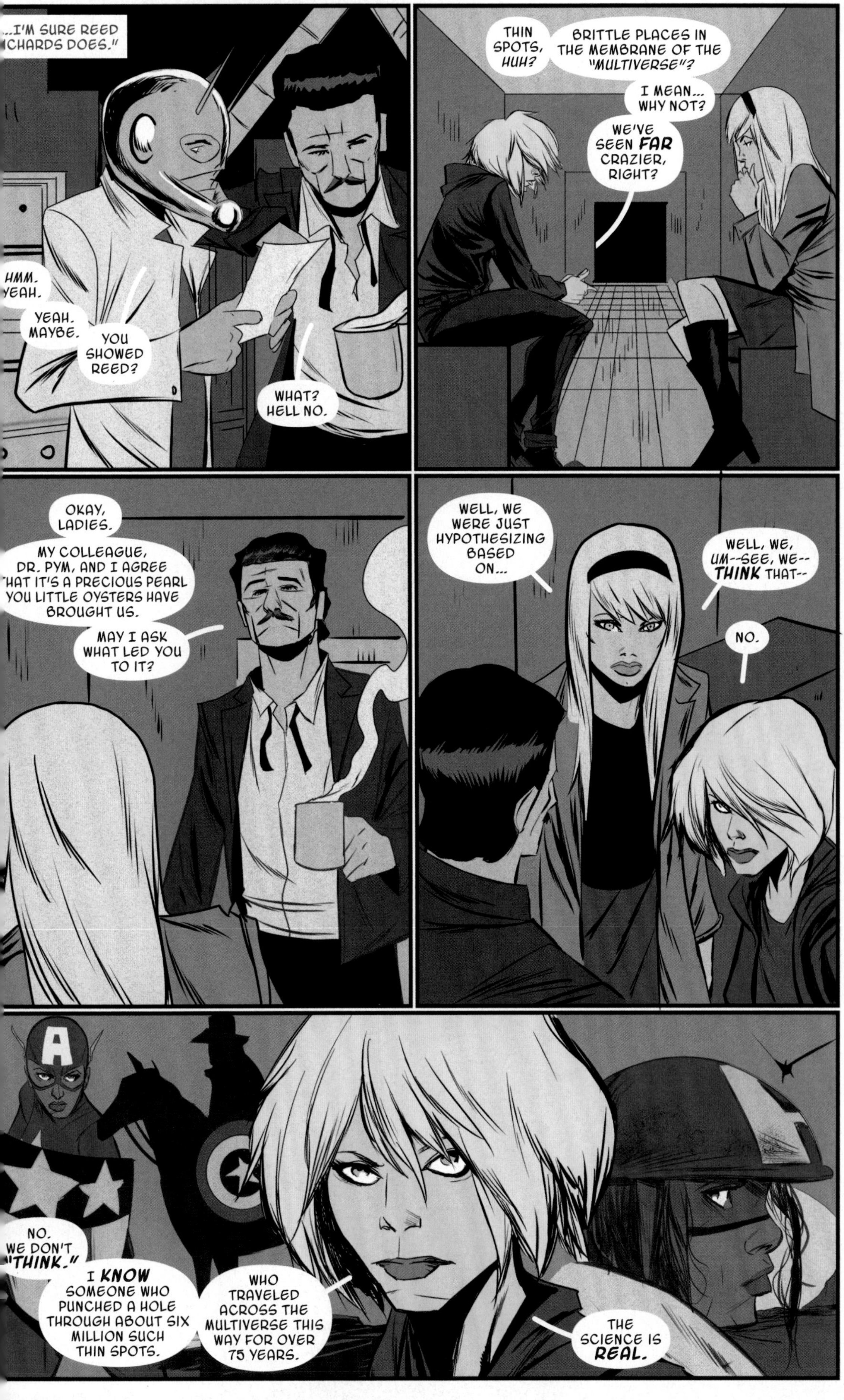

...I'M SURE REED
CHARDS DOES."
HMM. YEAH.
YEAH. MAYBE.
YOU SHOWED REED?
WHAT? HELL NO.
THIN SPOTS, HUH?
BRITTLE PLACES IN THE MEMBRANE OF THE "MULTIVERSE"?
I MEAN... WHY NOT?
WE'VE SEEN FAR CRAZIER, RIGHT?
OKAY, LADIES.
MY COLLEAGUE, DR. PYM, AND I AGREE THAT IT'S A PRECIOUS PEARL YOU LITTLE OYSTERS HAVE BROUGHT US.
MAY I ASK WHAT LED YOU TO IT?
WELL, WE WERE JUST HYPOTHESIZING BASED ON...
WELL, WE, UM--SEE, WE--THINK THAT--
NO.
NO. WE DON'T "THINK."
I KNOW SOMEONE WHO PUNCHED A HOLE THROUGH ABOUT SIX MILLION SUCH THIN SPOTS.
WHO TRAVELED ACROSS THE MULTIVERSE THIS WAY FOR OVER 75 YEARS.
THE SCIENCE IS REAL.

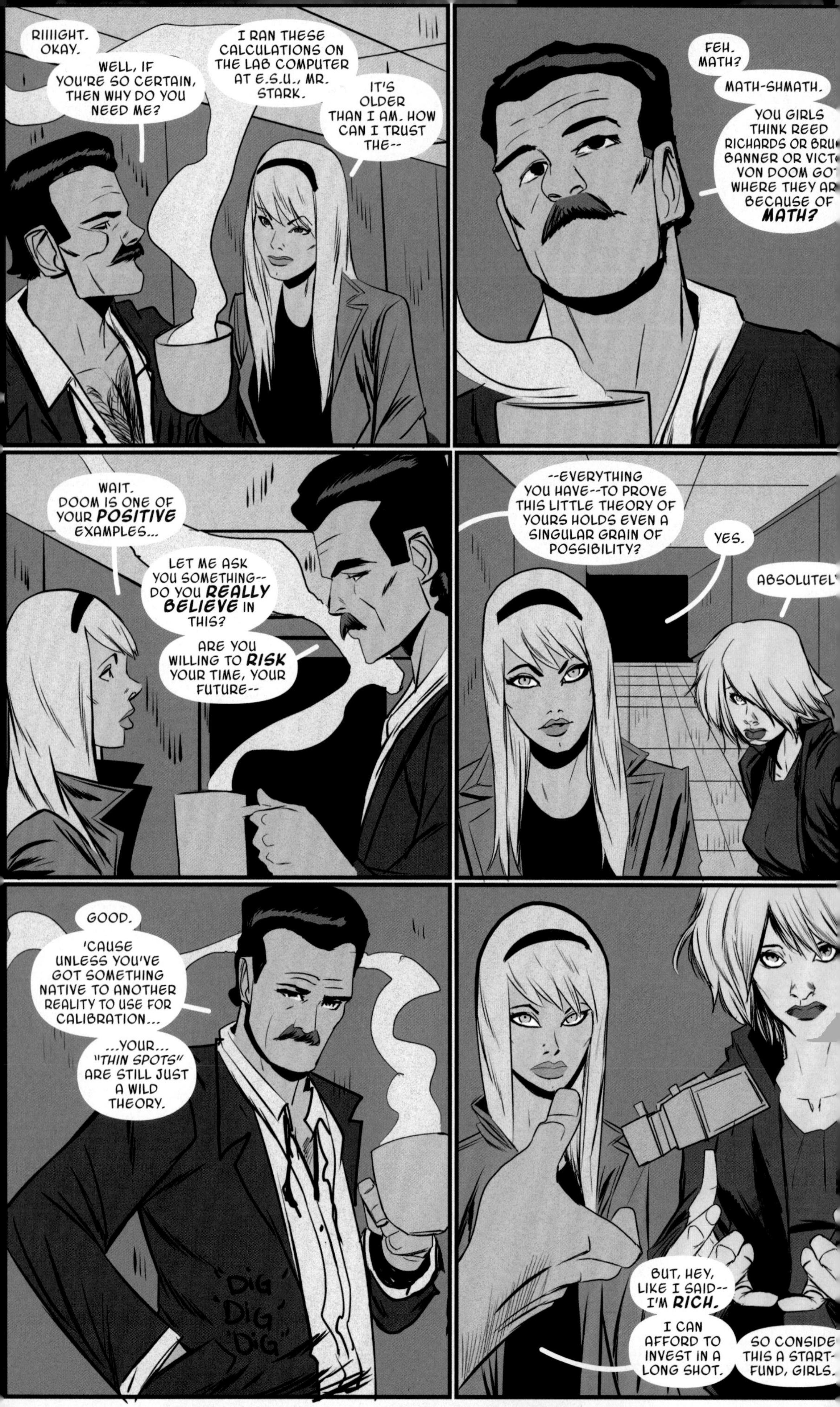
RIIIIGHT. OKAY.
WELL, IF YOU'RE SO CERTAIN, THEN WHY DO YOU NEED ME?
I RAN THESE CALCULATIONS ON THE LAB COMPUTER AT E.S.U., MR. STARK.
IT'S OLDER THAN I AM. HOW CAN I TRUST THE--
FEH. MATH?
MATH-SHMATH.
YOU GIRLS THINK REED RICHARDS OR BRU BANNER OR VICT VON DOOM GOT WHERE THEY AR BECAUSE OF MATH?
WAIT. DOOM IS ONE OF YOUR POSITIVE EXAMPLES...
LET ME ASK YOU SOMETHING-- DO YOU REALLY BELIEVE IN THIS?
ARE YOU WILLING TO RISK YOUR TIME, YOUR FUTURE--
--EVERYTHING YOU HAVE--TO PROVE THIS LITTLE THEORY OF YOURS HOLDS EVEN A SINGULAR GRAIN OF POSSIBILITY?
YES.
ABSOLUTEL
GOOD.
'CAUSE UNLESS YOU'VE GOT SOMETHING NATIVE TO ANOTHER REALITY TO USE FOR CALIBRATION...
...YOUR... "THIN SPOTS" ARE STILL JUST A WILD THEORY.
DIG DIG DIG
BUT, HEY, LIKE I SAID-- I'M RICH.
I CAN AFFORD TO INVEST IN A LONG SHOT.
SO CONSIDE THIS A START- FUND, GIRLS.

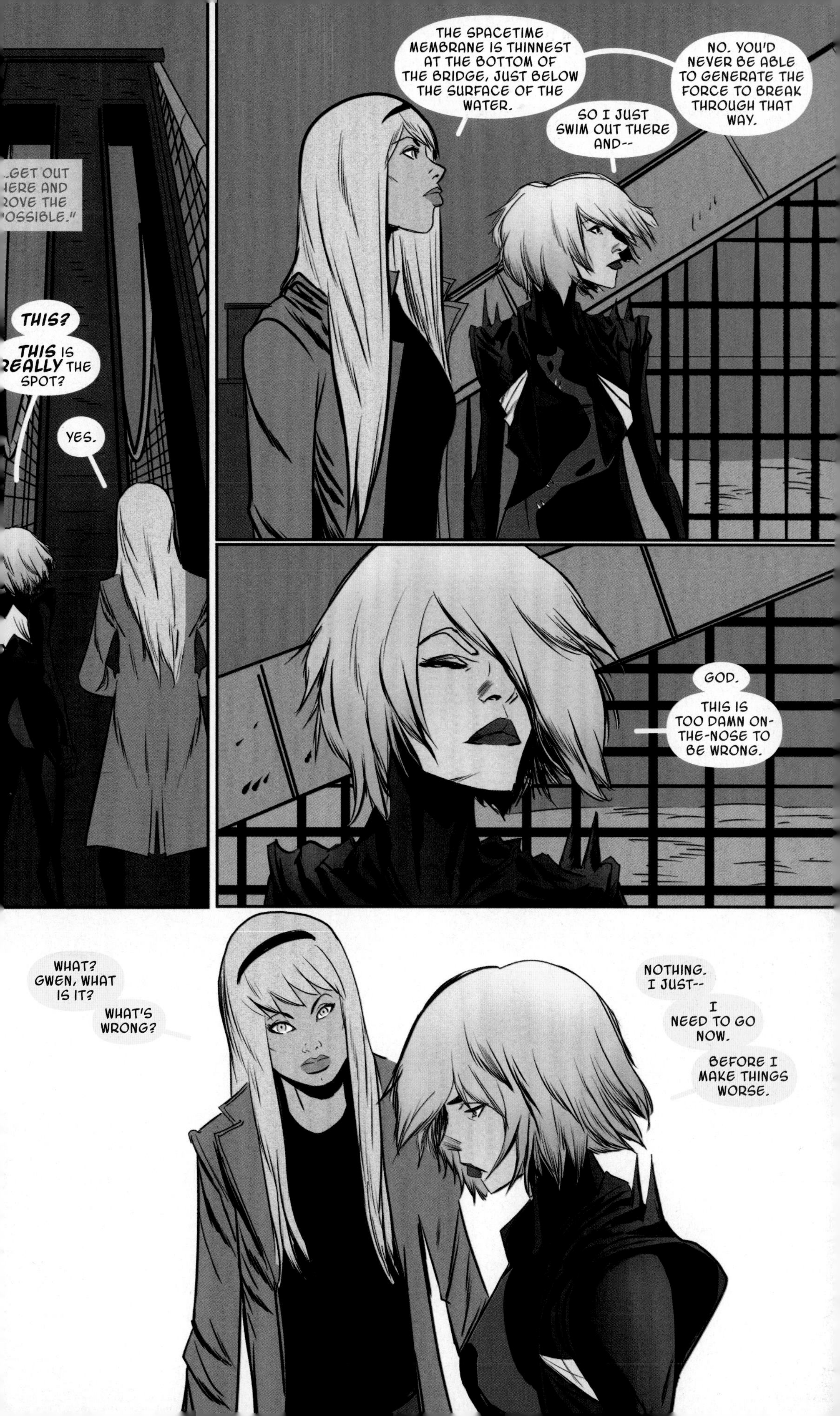
...GET OUT
HERE AND
PROVE THE
POSSIBLE."
THIS?
THIS IS REALLY THE SPOT?
YES.
THE SPACETIME MEMBRANE IS THINNEST AT THE BOTTOM OF THE BRIDGE, JUST BELOW THE SURFACE OF THE WATER.
SO I JUST SWIM OUT THERE AND--
NO. YOU'D NEVER BE ABLE TO GENERATE THE FORCE TO BREAK THROUGH THAT WAY.
GOD.
THIS IS TOO DAMN ON-THE-NOSE TO BE WRONG.
WHAT? GWEN, WHAT IS IT?
WHAT'S WRONG?
NOTHING. I JUST--
I NEED TO GO NOW.
BEFORE I MAKE THINGS WORSE.

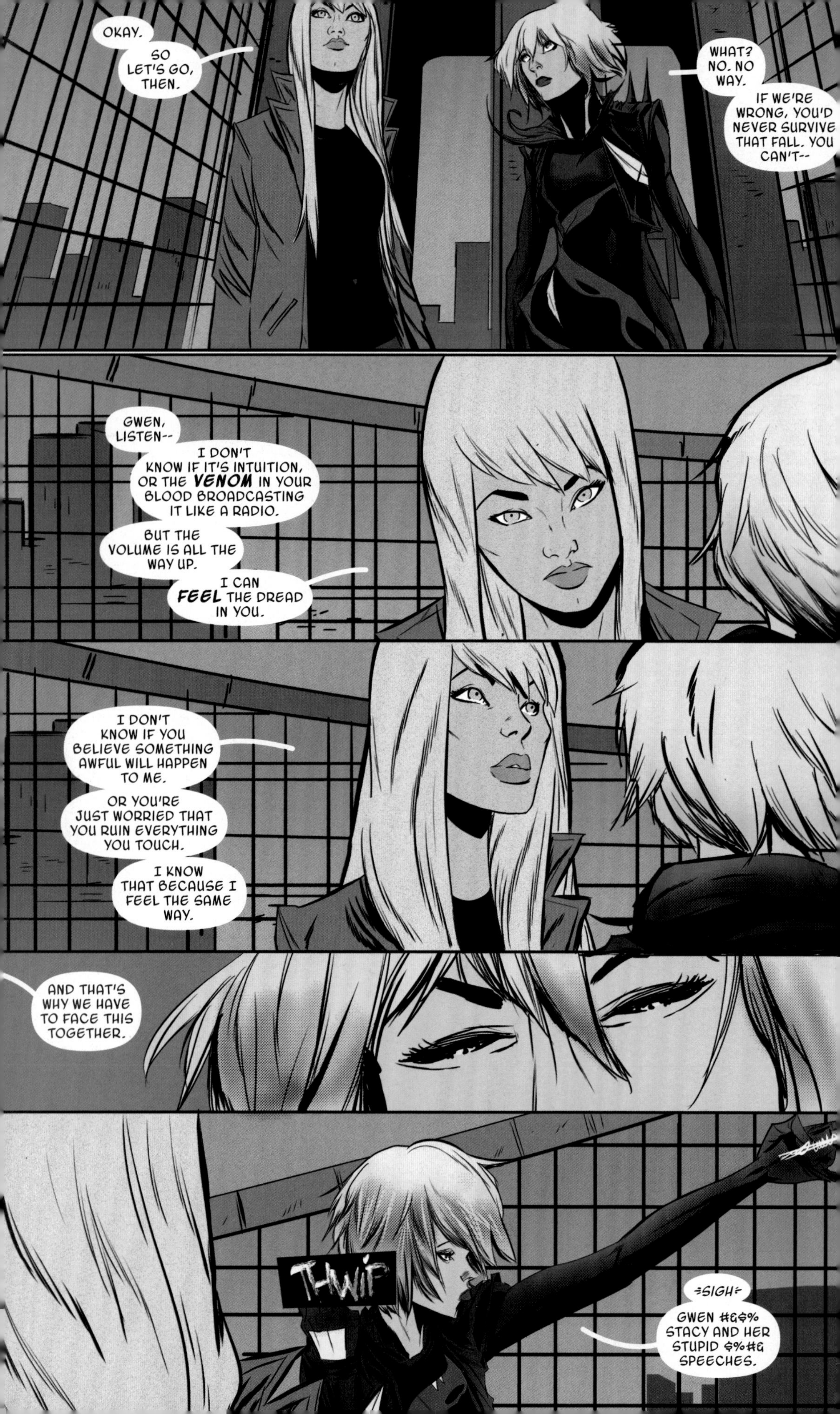

OKAY.
SO LET'S GO, THEN.
WHAT? NO. NO WAY.
IF WE'RE WRONG, YOU'D NEVER SURVIVE THAT FALL. YOU CAN'T--
GWEN, LISTEN--
I DON'T KNOW IF IT'S INTUITION, OR THE VENOM IN YOUR BLOOD BROADCASTING IT LIKE A RADIO.
BUT THE VOLUME IS ALL THE WAY UP.
I CAN FEEL THE DREAD IN YOU.
I DON'T KNOW IF YOU BELIEVE SOMETHING AWFUL WILL HAPPEN TO ME.
OR YOU'RE JUST WORRIED THAT YOU RUIN EVERYTHING YOU TOUCH.
I KNOW THAT BECAUSE I FEEL THE SAME WAY.
AND THAT'S WHY WE HAVE TO FACE THIS TOGETHER.
THWIP
=SIGH=
GWEN #&$% STACY AND HER STUPID $%#& SPEECHES.

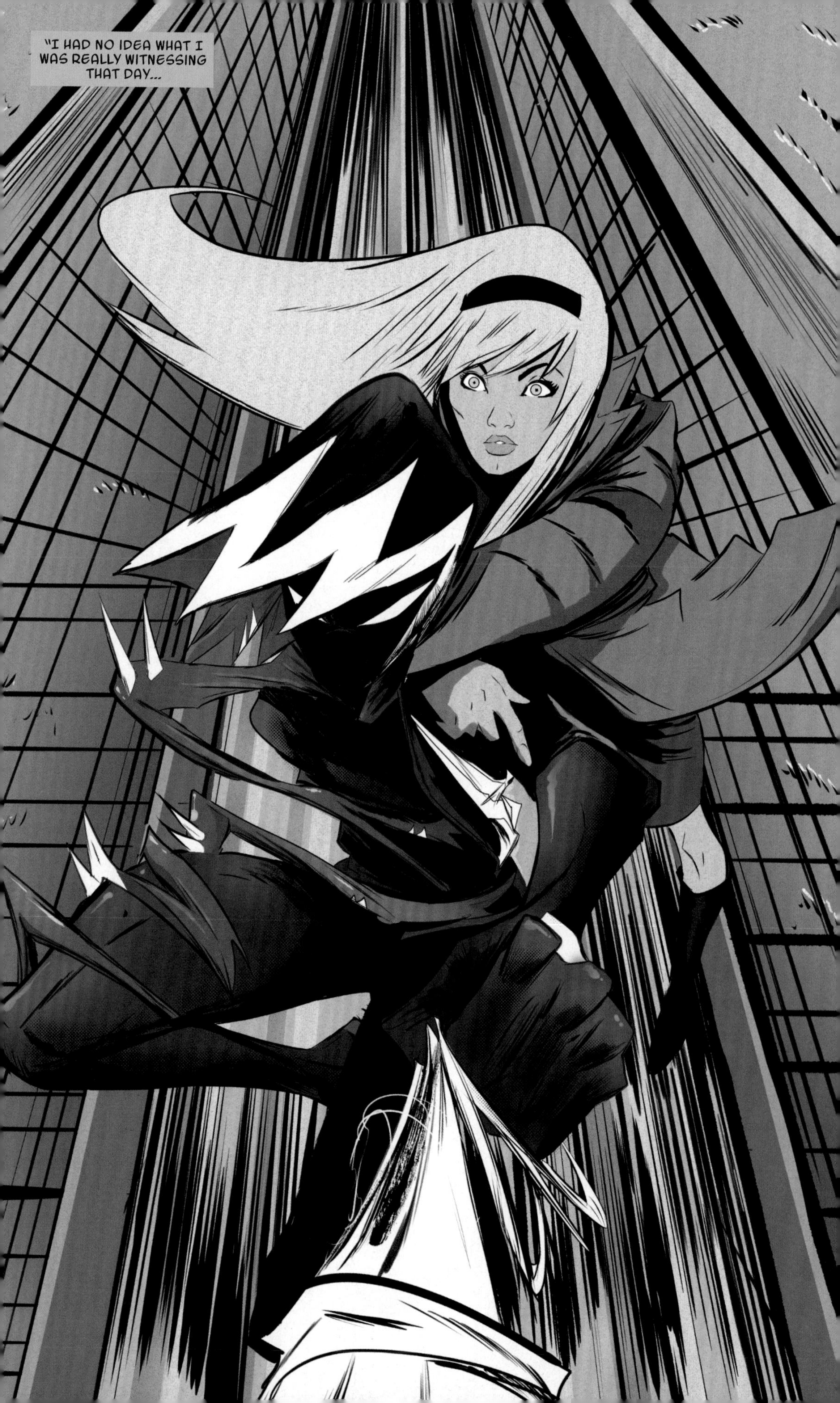
"I HAD NO IDEA WHAT I WAS REALLY WITNESSING THAT DAY...

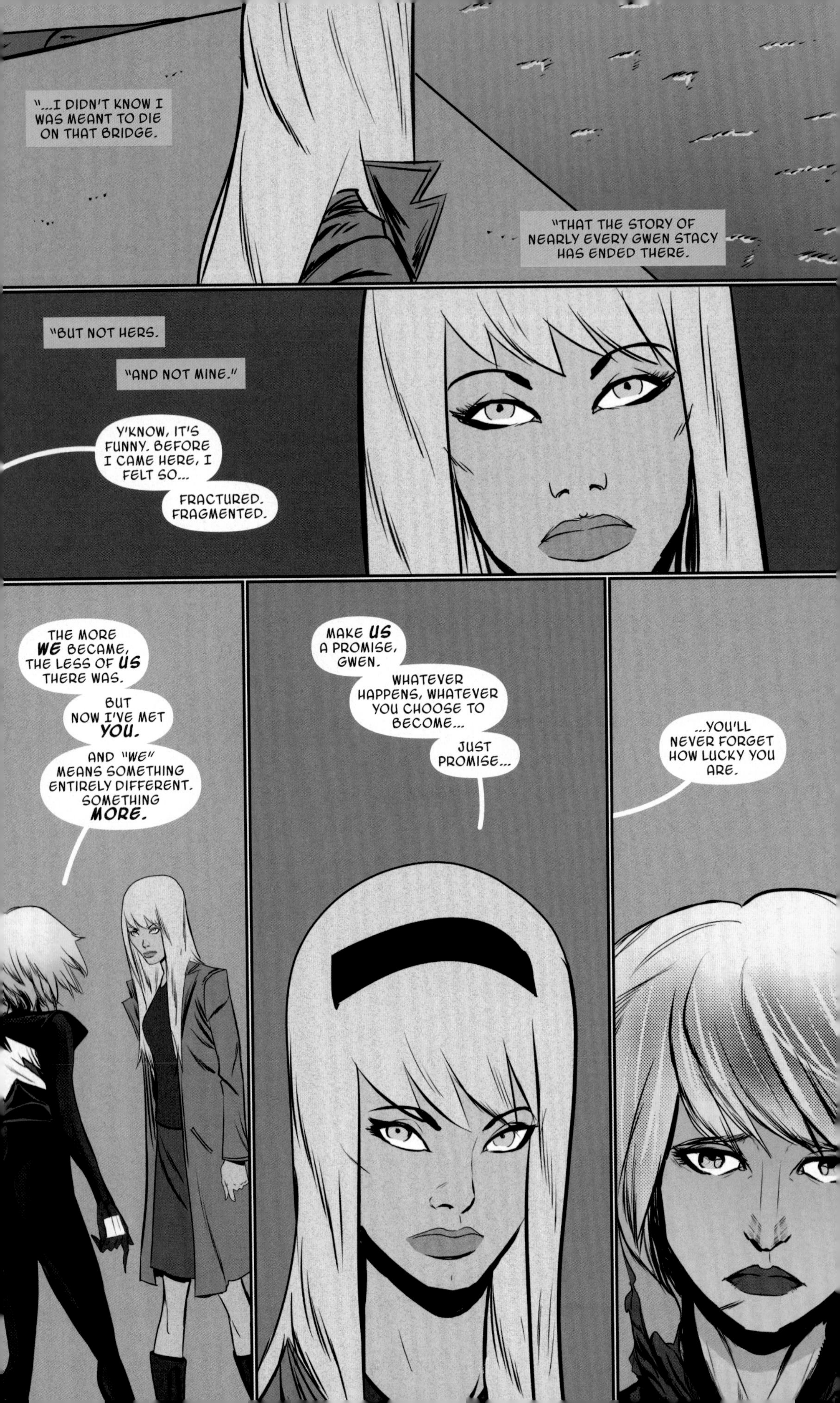
"...I DIDN'T KNOW I WAS MEANT TO DIE ON THAT BRIDGE.
"THAT THE STORY OF NEARLY EVERY GWEN STACY HAS ENDED THERE.
"BUT NOT HERS.
"AND NOT MINE."
Y'KNOW, IT'S FUNNY. BEFORE I CAME HERE, I FELT SO...
FRACTURED. FRAGMENTED.
THE MORE WE BECAME, THE LESS OF US THERE WAS.
BUT NOW I'VE MET YOU.
AND "WE" MEANS SOMETHING ENTIRELY DIFFERENT. SOMETHING MORE.
MAKE US A PROMISE, GWEN.
WHATEVER HAPPENS, WHATEVER YOU CHOOSE TO BECOME...
JUST PROMISE...
...YOU'LL NEVER FORGET HOW LUCKY YOU ARE.

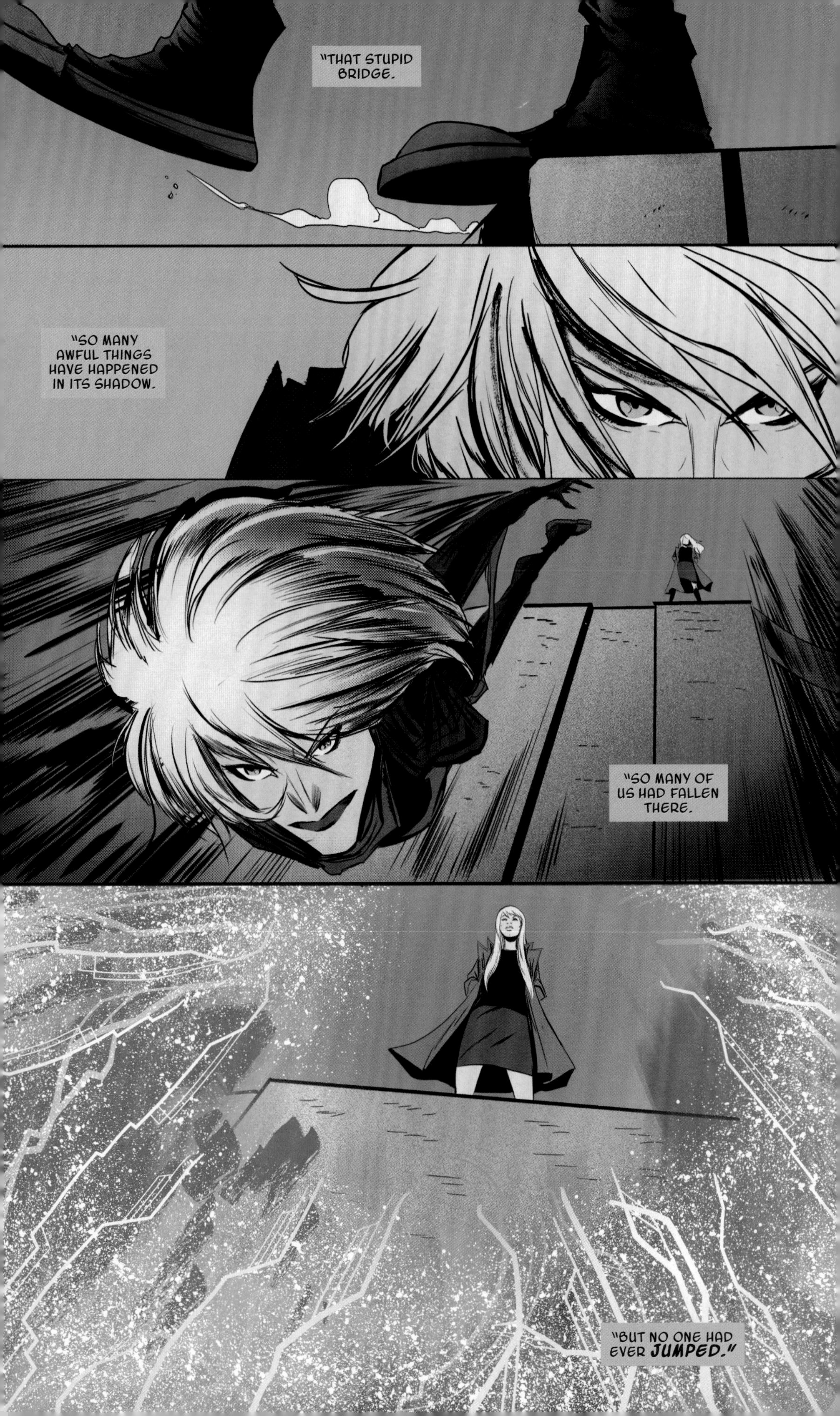
"THAT STUPID BRIDGE.
"SO MANY AWFUL THINGS HAVE HAPPENED IN ITS SHADOW.
"SO MANY OF US HAD FALLEN THERE.
"BUT NO ONE HAD EVER JUMPED."

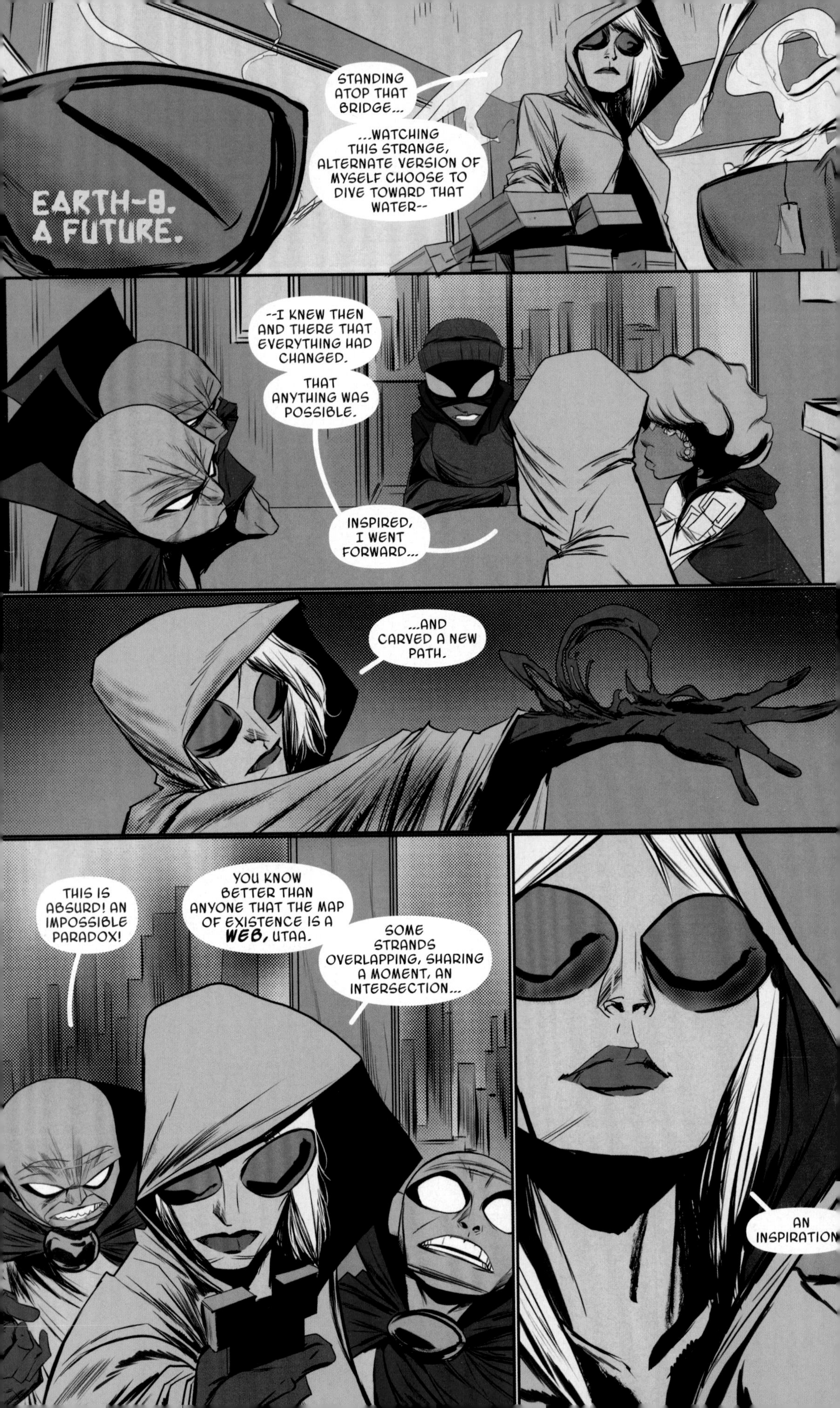
EARTH-8. A FUTURE.
STANDING ATOP THAT BRIDGE...
...WATCHING THIS STRANGE, ALTERNATE VERSION OF MYSELF CHOOSE TO DIVE TOWARD THAT WATER--
--I KNEW THEN AND THERE THAT EVERYTHING HAD CHANGED.
THAT ANYTHING WAS POSSIBLE.
INSPIRED, I WENT FORWARD...
...AND CARVED A NEW PATH.
THIS IS ABSURD! AN IMPOSSIBLE PARADOX!
YOU KNOW BETTER THAN ANYONE THAT THE MAP OF EXISTENCE IS A WEB, UTAA.
SOME STRANDS OVERLAPPING, SHARING A MOMENT, AN INTERSECTION...
AN INSPIRATION

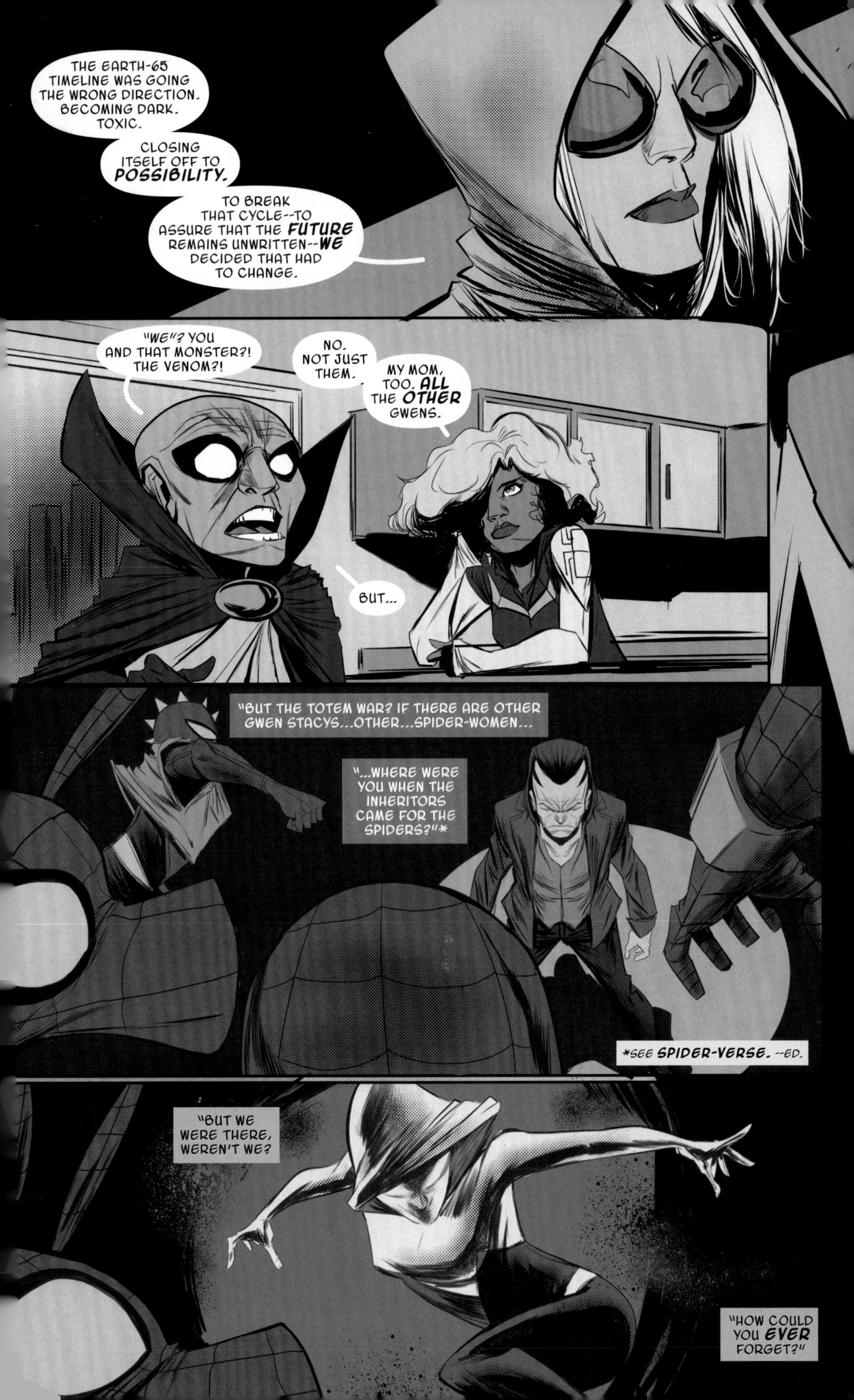
THE EARTH-65 TIMELINE WAS GOING THE WRONG DIRECTION. BECOMING DARK. TOXIC.
CLOSING ITSELF OFF TO POSSIBILITY.
TO BREAK THAT CYCLE--TO ASSURE THAT THE FUTURE REMAINS UNWRITTEN--WE DECIDED THAT HAD TO CHANGE.
"WE"? YOU AND THAT MONSTER?! THE VENOM?!
NO. NOT JUST THEM.
MY MOM, TOO. ALL THE OTHER GWENS.
BUT...
"BUT THE TOTEM WAR? IF THERE ARE OTHER GWEN STACYS...OTHER...SPIDER-WOMEN...
"...WHERE WERE YOU WHEN THE INHERITORS CAME FOR THE SPIDERS?"*
*SEE SPIDER-VERSE. --ED.
"BUT WE WERE THERE, WEREN'T WE?
"HOW COULD YOU EVER FORGET?"

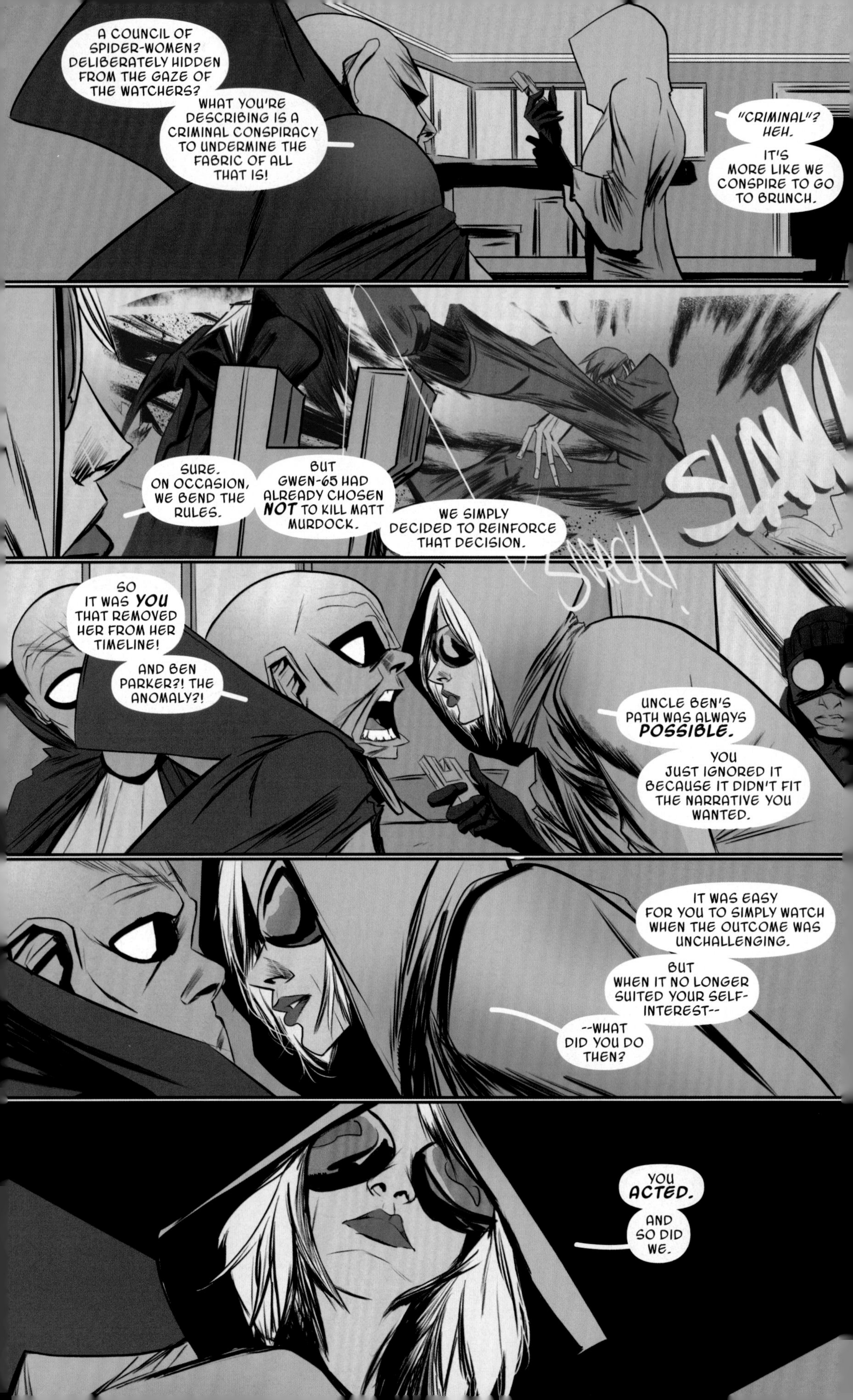
A COUNCIL OF SPIDER-WOMEN? DELIBERATELY HIDDEN FROM THE GAZE OF THE WATCHERS?
WHAT YOU'RE DESCRIBING IS A CRIMINAL CONSPIRACY TO UNDERMINE THE FABRIC OF ALL THAT IS!
"CRIMINAL"? HEH.
IT'S MORE LIKE WE CONSPIRE TO GO TO BRUNCH.
SURE. ON OCCASION, WE BEND THE RULES.
BUT GWEN-65 HAD ALREADY CHOSEN NOT TO KILL MATT MURDOCK.
WE SIMPLY DECIDED TO REINFORCE THAT DECISION.
SLAM
SMACK!
SO IT WAS YOU THAT REMOVED HER FROM HER TIMELINE!
AND BEN PARKER?! THE ANOMALY?!
UNCLE BEN'S PATH WAS ALWAYS POSSIBLE.
YOU JUST IGNORED IT BECAUSE IT DIDN'T FIT THE NARRATIVE YOU WANTED.
IT WAS EASY FOR YOU TO SIMPLY WATCH WHEN THE OUTCOME WAS UNCHALLENGING.
BUT WHEN IT NO LONGER SUITED YOUR SELF-INTEREST--
--WHAT DID YOU DO THEN?
YOU ACTED.
AND SO DID WE.

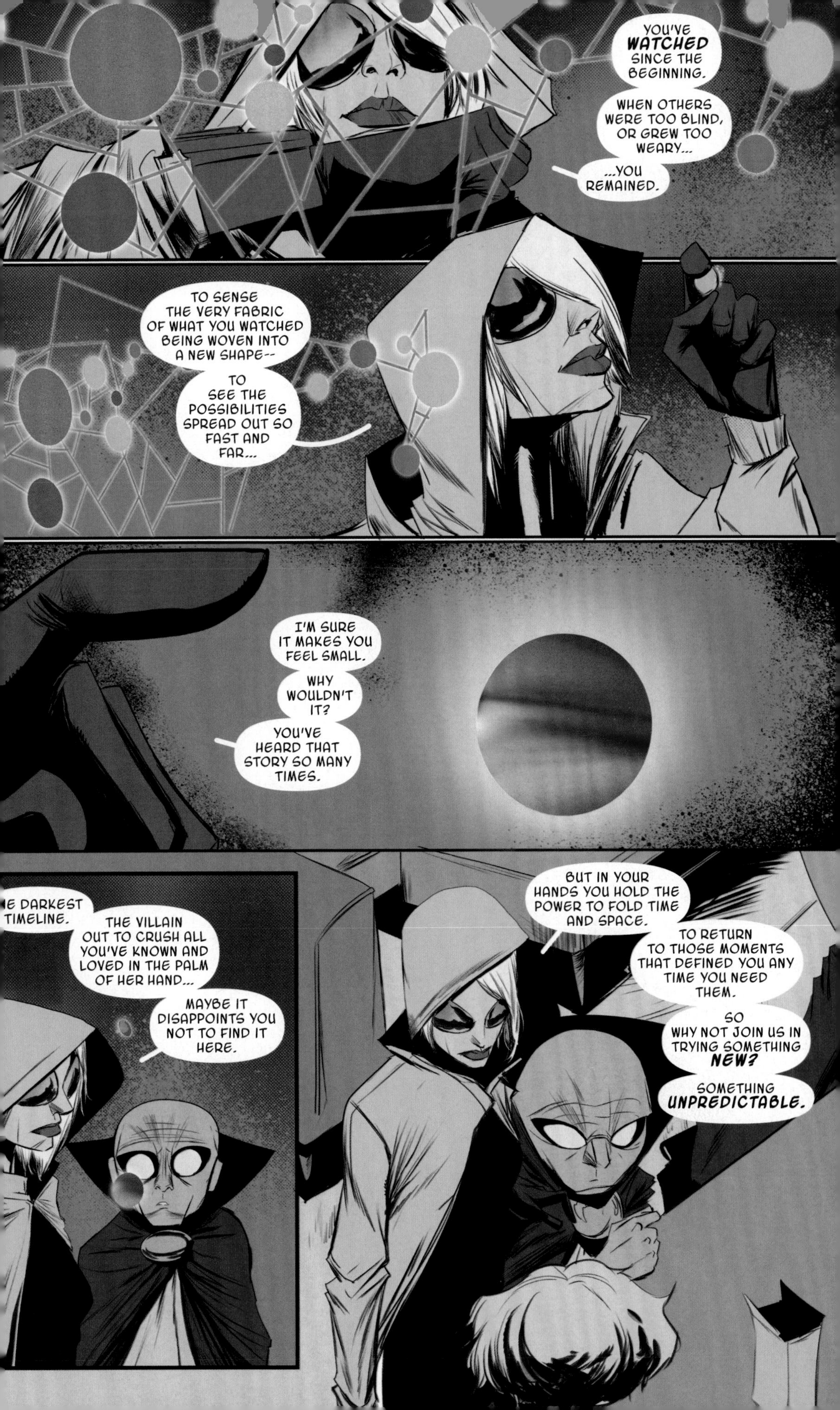
YOU'VE WATCHED SINCE THE BEGINNING.
WHEN OTHERS WERE TOO BLIND, OR GREW TOO WEARY...
...YOU REMAINED.
TO SENSE THE VERY FABRIC OF WHAT YOU WATCHED BEING WOVEN INTO A NEW SHAPE--
TO SEE THE POSSIBILITIES SPREAD OUT SO FAST AND FAR...
I'M SURE IT MAKES YOU FEEL SMALL.
WHY WOULDN'T IT?
YOU'VE HEARD THAT STORY SO MANY TIMES.
E DARKEST TIMELINE.
THE VILLAIN OUT TO CRUSH ALL YOU'VE KNOWN AND LOVED IN THE PALM OF HER HAND...
MAYBE IT DISAPPOINTS YOU NOT TO FIND IT HERE.
BUT IN YOUR HANDS YOU HOLD THE POWER TO FOLD TIME AND SPACE.
TO RETURN TO THOSE MOMENTS THAT DEFINED YOU ANY TIME YOU NEED THEM.
SO WHY NOT JOIN US IN TRYING SOMETHING NEW?
SOMETHING UNPREDICTABLE.

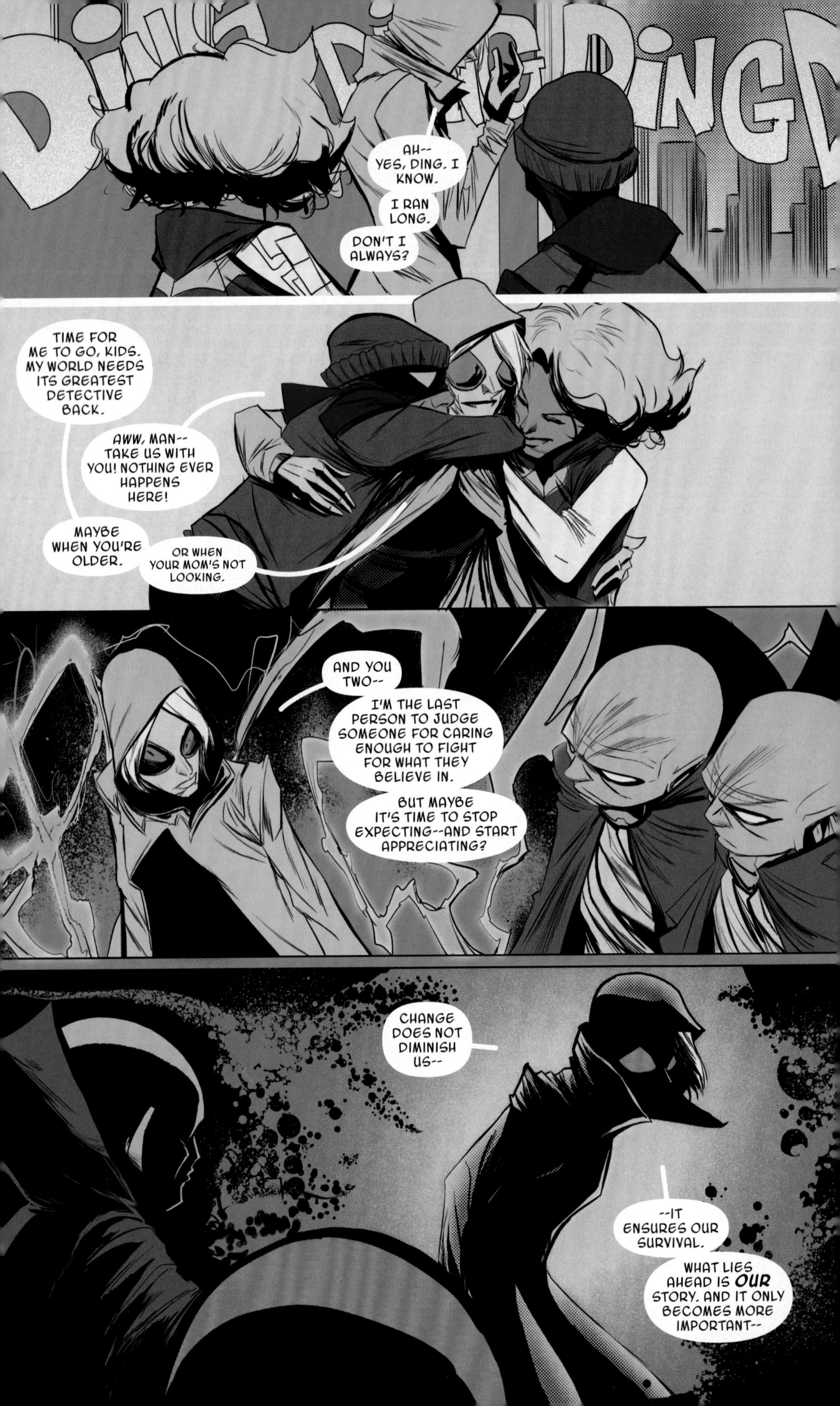
DING DING DING
AH-- YES, DING. I KNOW.
I RAN LONG.
DON'T I ALWAYS?
TIME FOR ME TO GO, KIDS. MY WORLD NEEDS ITS GREATEST DETECTIVE BACK.
AWW, MAN-- TAKE US WITH YOU! NOTHING EVER HAPPENS HERE!
MAYBE WHEN YOU'RE OLDER.
OR WHEN YOUR MOM'S NOT LOOKING.
AND YOU TWO--
I'M THE LAST PERSON TO JUDGE SOMEONE FOR CARING ENOUGH TO FIGHT FOR WHAT THEY BELIEVE IN.
BUT MAYBE IT'S TIME TO STOP EXPECTING--AND START APPRECIATING?
CHANGE DOES NOT DIMINISH US--
--IT ENSURES OUR SURVIVAL.
WHAT LIES AHEAD IS OUR STORY. AND IT ONLY BECOMES MORE IMPORTANT--

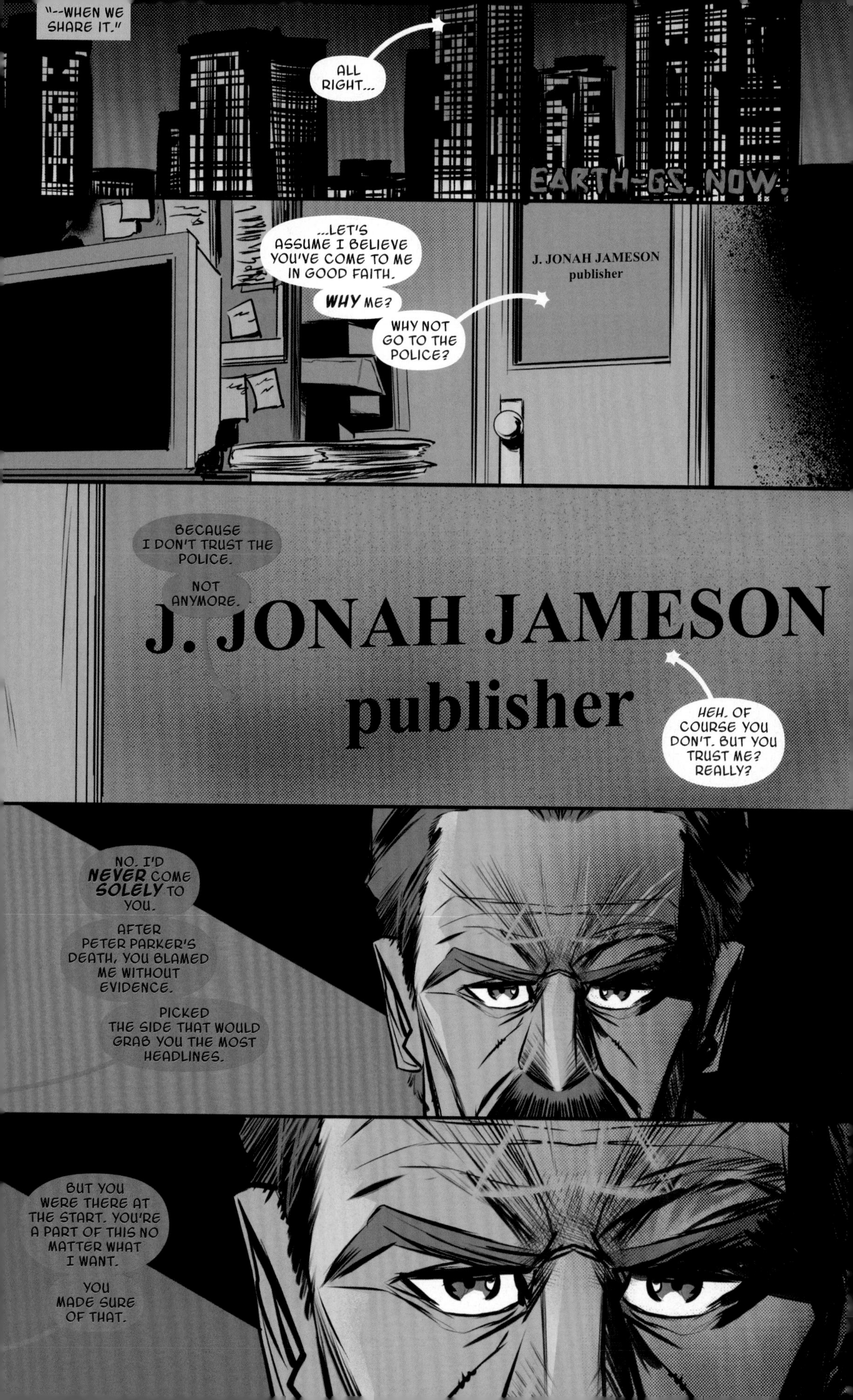
"--WHEN WE SHARE IT."
ALL RIGHT...
EARTH-65. NOW.
...LET'S ASSUME I BELIEVE YOU'VE COME TO ME IN GOOD FAITH.
WHY ME?
WHY NOT GO TO THE POLICE?
J. JONAH JAMESON publisher
BECAUSE I DON'T TRUST THE POLICE.
NOT ANYMORE.
J. JONAH JAMESON publisher
HEH. OF COURSE YOU DON'T. BUT YOU TRUST ME? REALLY?
NO. I'D NEVER COME SOLELY TO YOU.
AFTER PETER PARKER'S DEATH, YOU BLAMED ME WITHOUT EVIDENCE.
PICKED THE SIDE THAT WOULD GRAB YOU THE MOST HEADLINES.
BUT YOU WERE THERE AT THE START. YOU'RE A PART OF THIS NO MATTER WHAT I WANT.
YOU MADE SURE OF THAT.

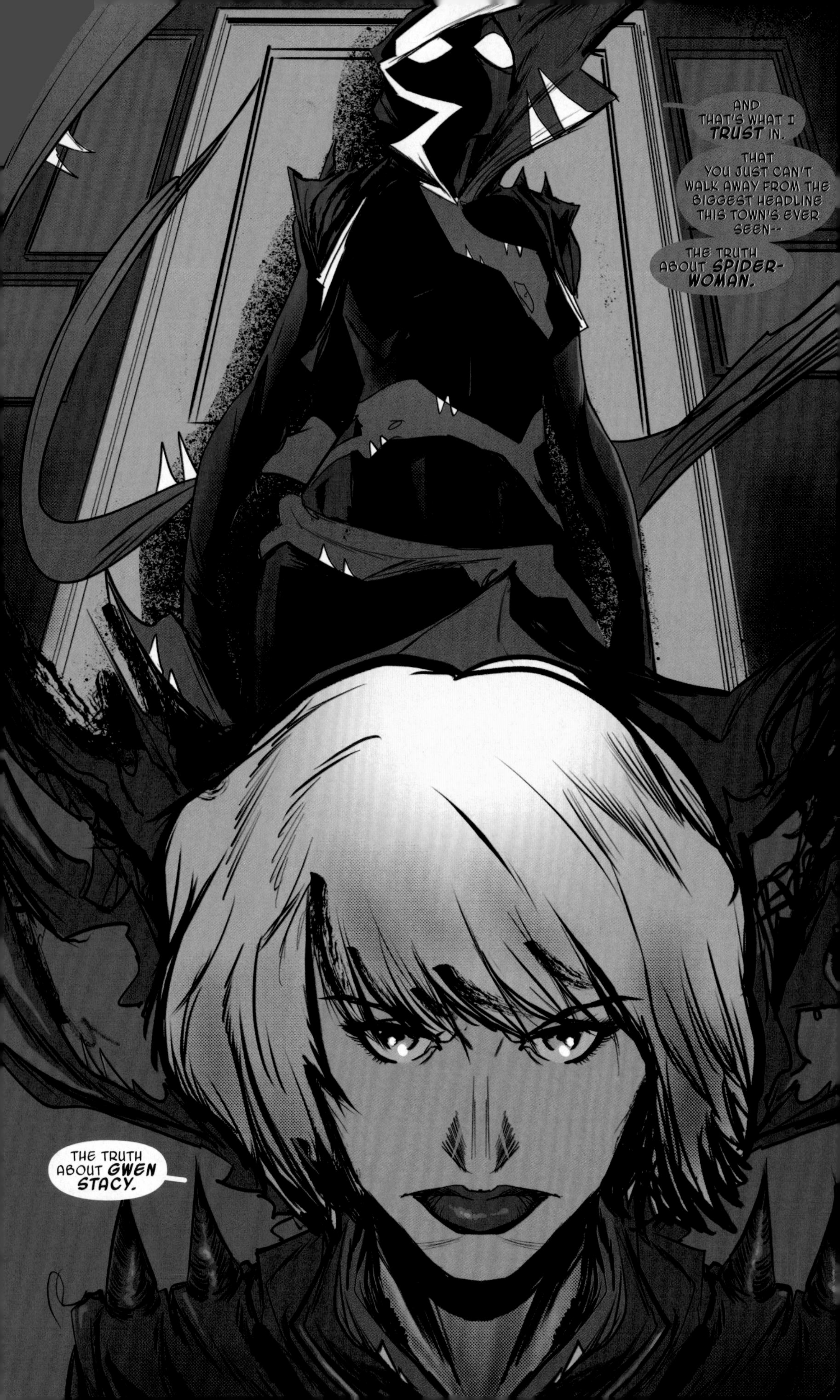
AND THAT'S WHAT I TRUST IN.
THAT YOU JUST CAN'T WALK AWAY FROM THE BIGGEST HEADLINE THIS TOWN'S EVER SEEN--
THE TRUTH ABOUT SPIDER-WOMAN.
THE TRUTH ABOUT GWEN STACY.

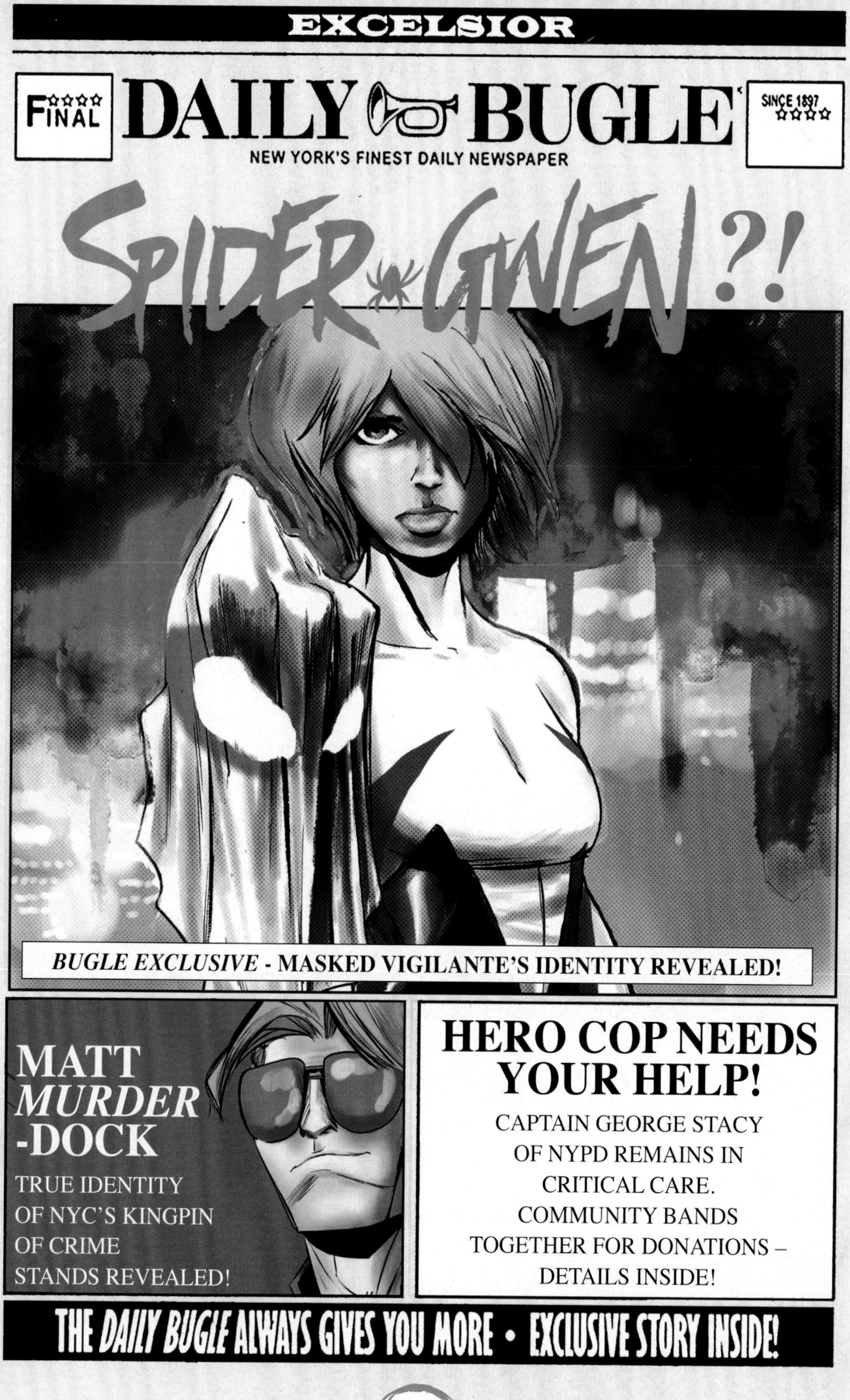
EXCELSIOR
FINAL
DAILY BUGLE
SINCE 1897
NEW YORK'S FINEST DAILY NEWSPAPER
SPIDER-GWEN?!
BUGLE EXCLUSIVE - MASKED VIGILANTE'S IDENTITY REVEALED!
MATT MURDER-DOCK
TRUE IDENTITY OF NYC'S KINGPIN OF CRIME STANDS REVEALED!
HERO COP NEEDS YOUR HELP!
CAPTAIN GEORGE STACY OF NYPD REMAINS IN CRITICAL CARE. COMMUNITY BANDS TOGETHER FOR DONATIONS – DETAILS INSIDE!
THE DAILY BUGLE ALWAYS GIVES YOU MORE • EXCLUSIVE STORY INSIDE!

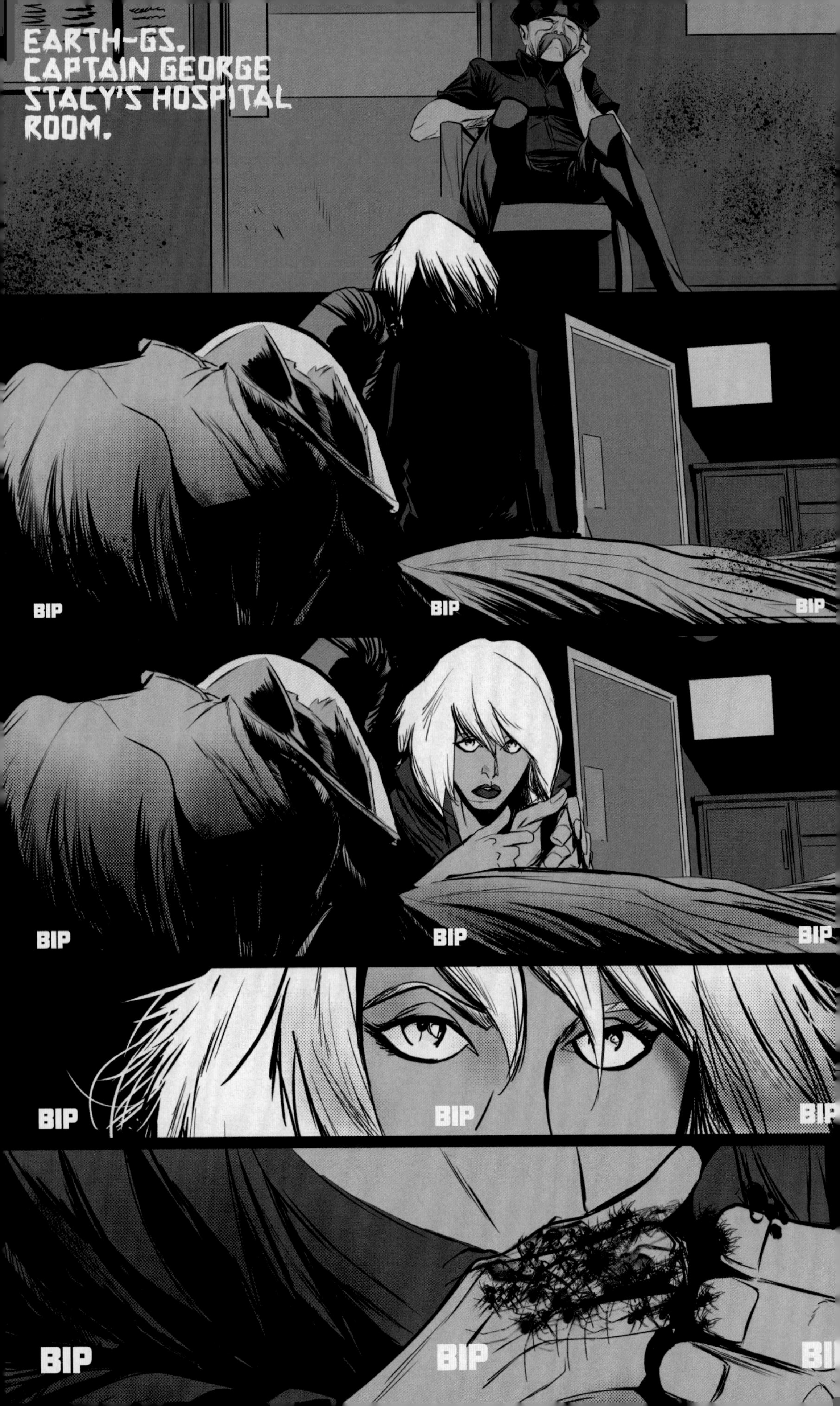
EARTH-65. CAPTAIN GEORGE STACY'S HOSPITAL ROOM.
BIP
BIP
BIP
BIP
BIP
BIP
BIP
BIP
BIP
BIP
BIP

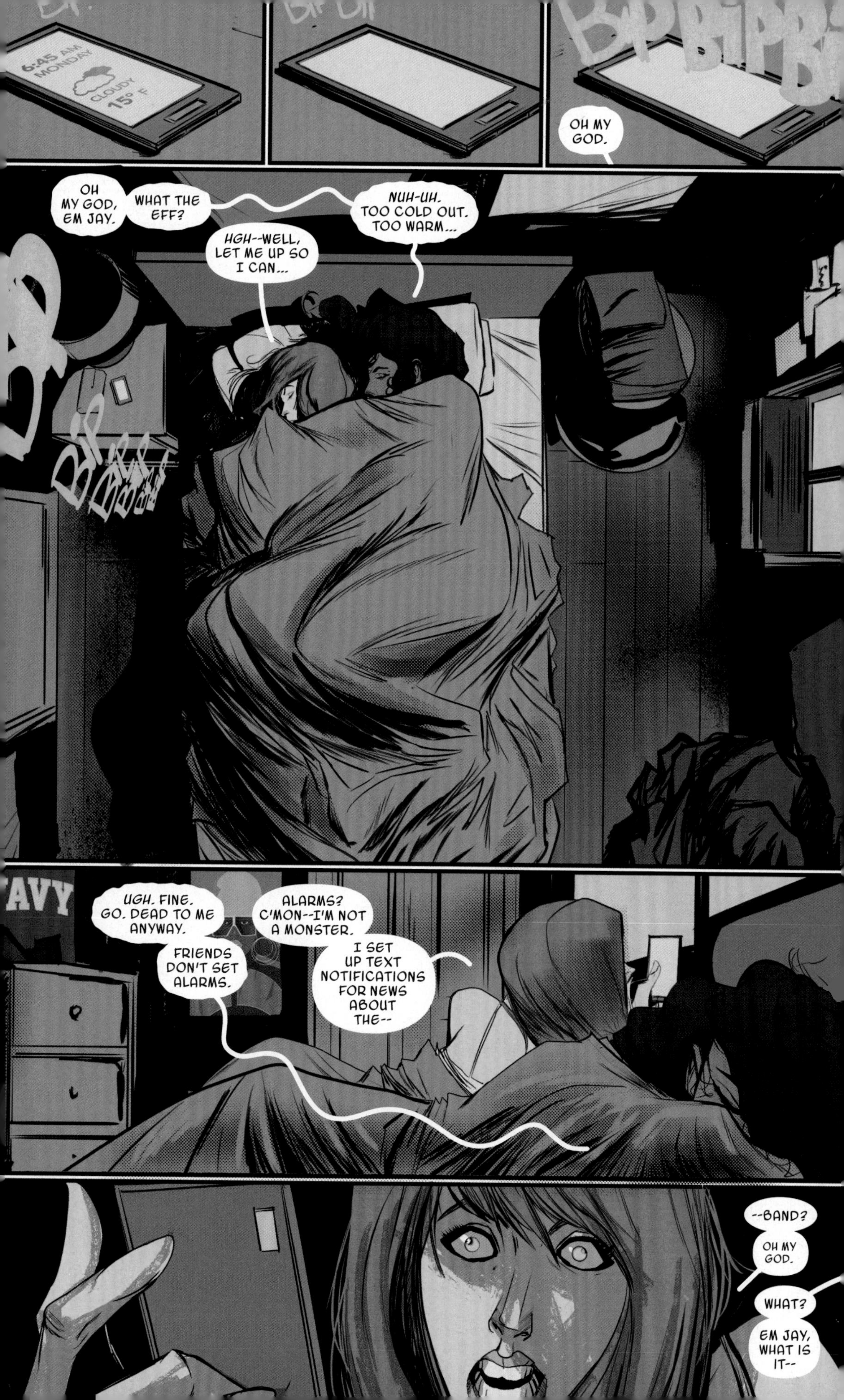
6:45 AM
MONDAY
CLOUDY
15° F
OH MY GOD.
OH MY GOD, EM JAY.
WHAT THE EFF?
UGH--WELL, LET ME UP SO I CAN...
NUH-UH. TOO COLD OUT. TOO WARM...
UGH. FINE. GO. DEAD TO ME ANYWAY.
FRIENDS DON'T SET ALARMS.
ALARMS? C'MON--I'M NOT A MONSTER.
I SET UP TEXT NOTIFICATIONS FOR NEWS ABOUT THE--
--BAND?
OH MY GOD.
WHAT?
EM JAY, WHAT IS IT--

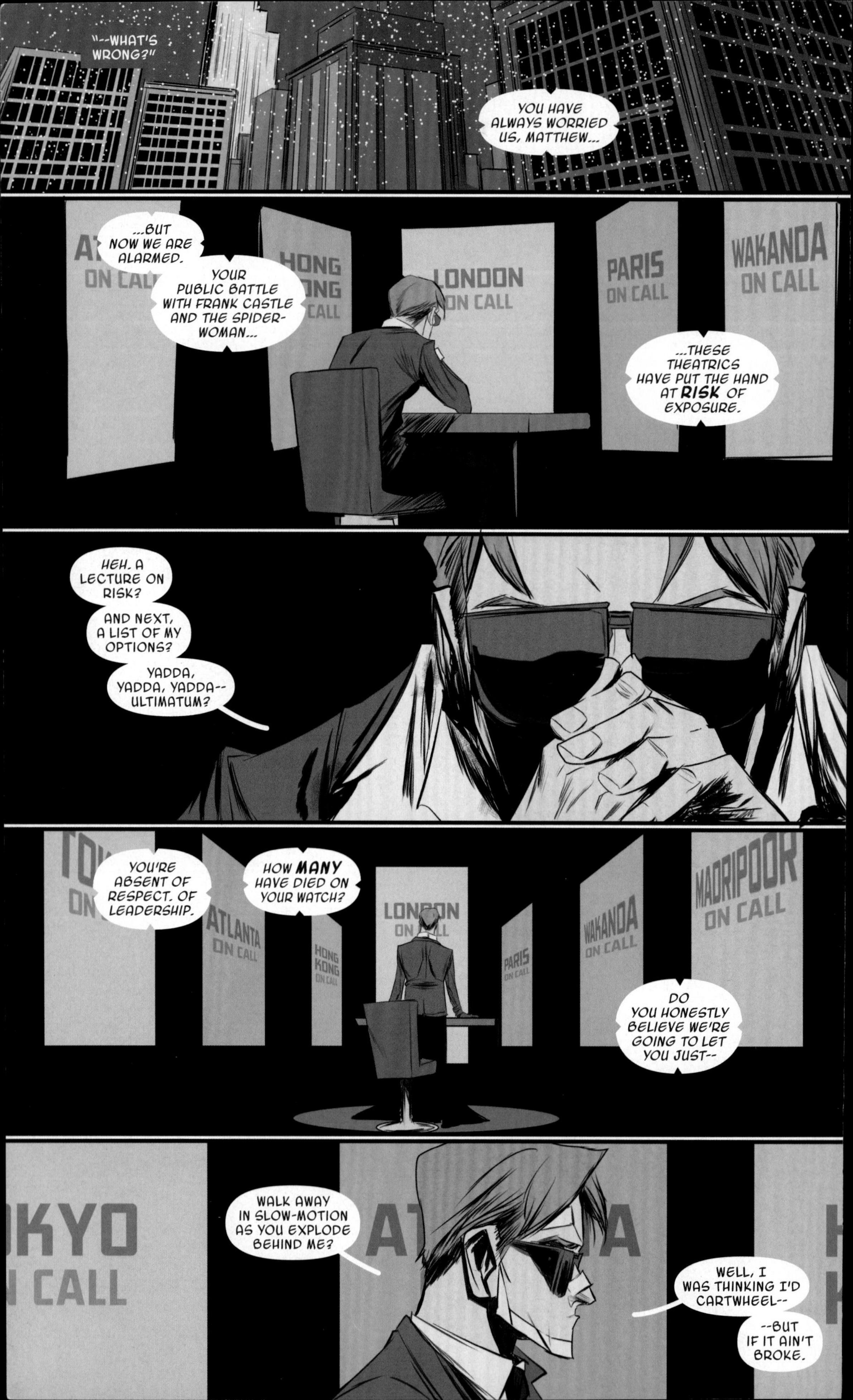
"--WHAT'S WRONG?"
YOU HAVE ALWAYS WORRIED US, MATTHEW...
...BUT NOW WE ARE ALARMED.
YOUR PUBLIC BATTLE WITH FRANK CASTLE AND THE SPIDER-WOMAN...
HONG KONG ON CALL
LONDON ON CALL
PARIS ON CALL
WAKANDA ON CALL
...THESE THEATRICS HAVE PUT THE HAND AT RISK OF EXPOSURE.
HEH. A LECTURE ON RISK?
AND NEXT, A LIST OF MY OPTIONS?
YADDA, YADDA, YADDA-- ULTIMATUM?
YOU'RE ABSENT OF RESPECT. OF LEADERSHIP.
HOW MANY HAVE DIED ON YOUR WATCH?
LONDON ON CALL
ATLANTA ON CALL
HONG KONG ON CALL
PARIS ON CALL
WAKANDA ON CALL
MADRIPOOR ON CALL
DO YOU HONESTLY BELIEVE WE'RE GOING TO LET YOU JUST--
WALK AWAY IN SLOW-MOTION AS YOU EXPLODE BEHIND ME?
WELL, I WAS THINKING I'D CARTWHEEL--
--BUT IF IT AIN'T BROKE.

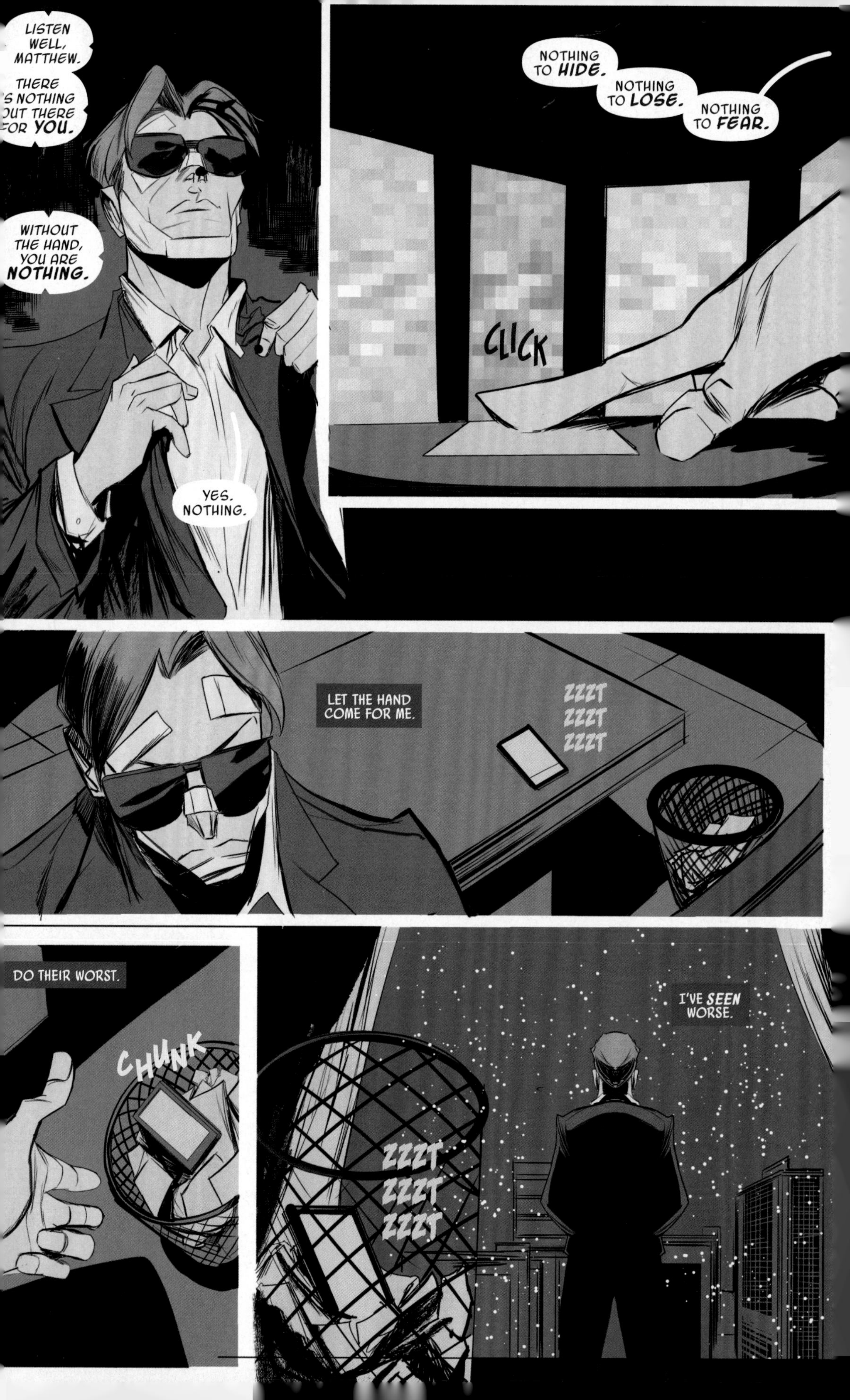
LISTEN WELL, MATTHEW.
THERE 'S NOTHING OUT THERE FOR YOU.
WITHOUT THE HAND, YOU ARE NOTHING.
YES. NOTHING.
NOTHING TO HIDE.
NOTHING TO LOSE.
NOTHING TO FEAR.
CLICK
LET THE HAND COME FOR ME.
ZZZT ZZZT ZZZT
DO THEIR WORST.
CHUNK
ZZZT ZZZT ZZZT
I'VE SEEN WORSE.

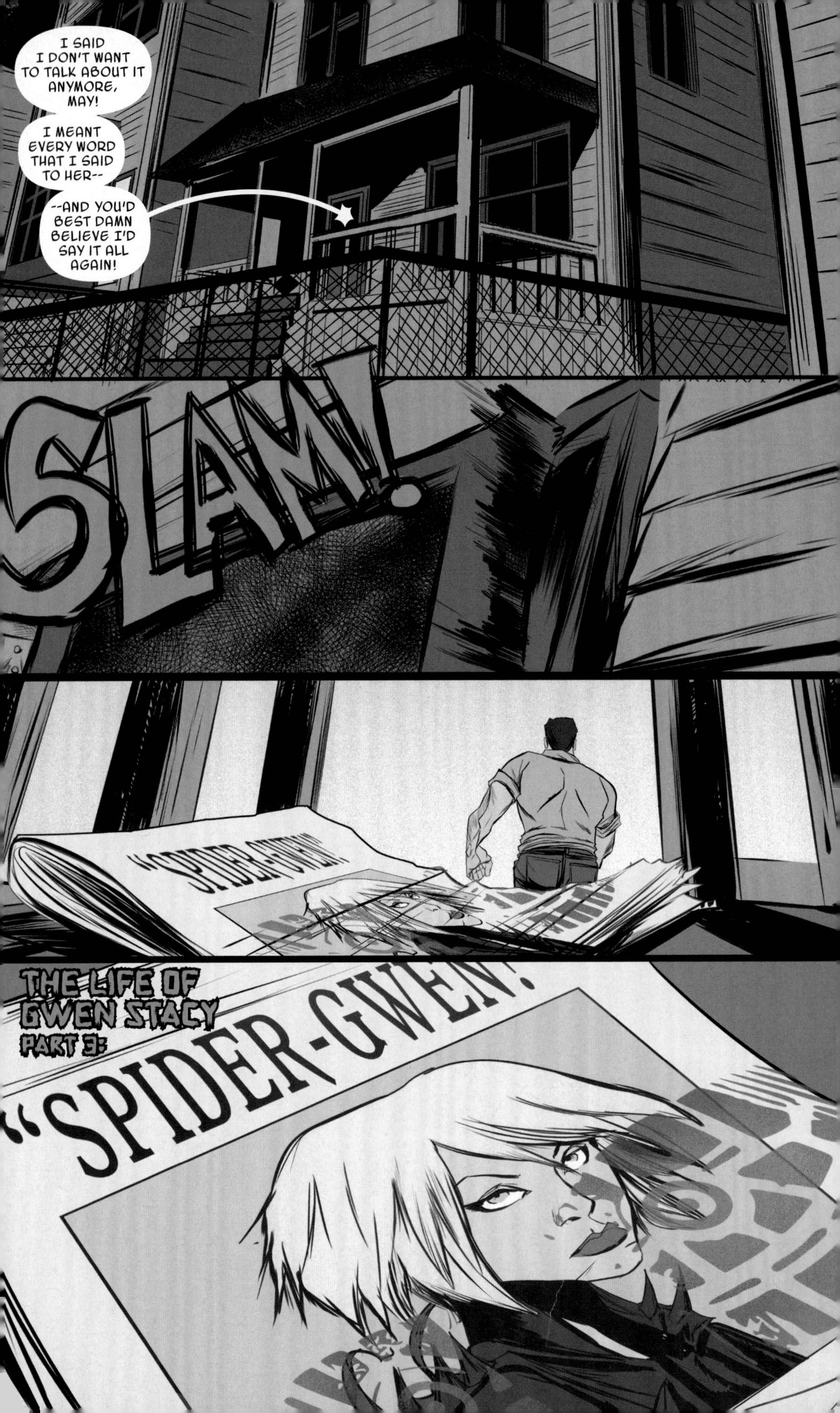
I SAID I DON'T WANT TO TALK ABOUT IT ANYMORE, MAY!
I MEANT EVERY WORD THAT I SAID TO HER--
--AND YOU'D BEST DAMN BELIEVE I'D SAY IT ALL AGAIN!
SLAM!
"SPIDER-GWEN!"
THE LIFE OF GWEN STACY PART 3:
"SPIDER-GWEN!"

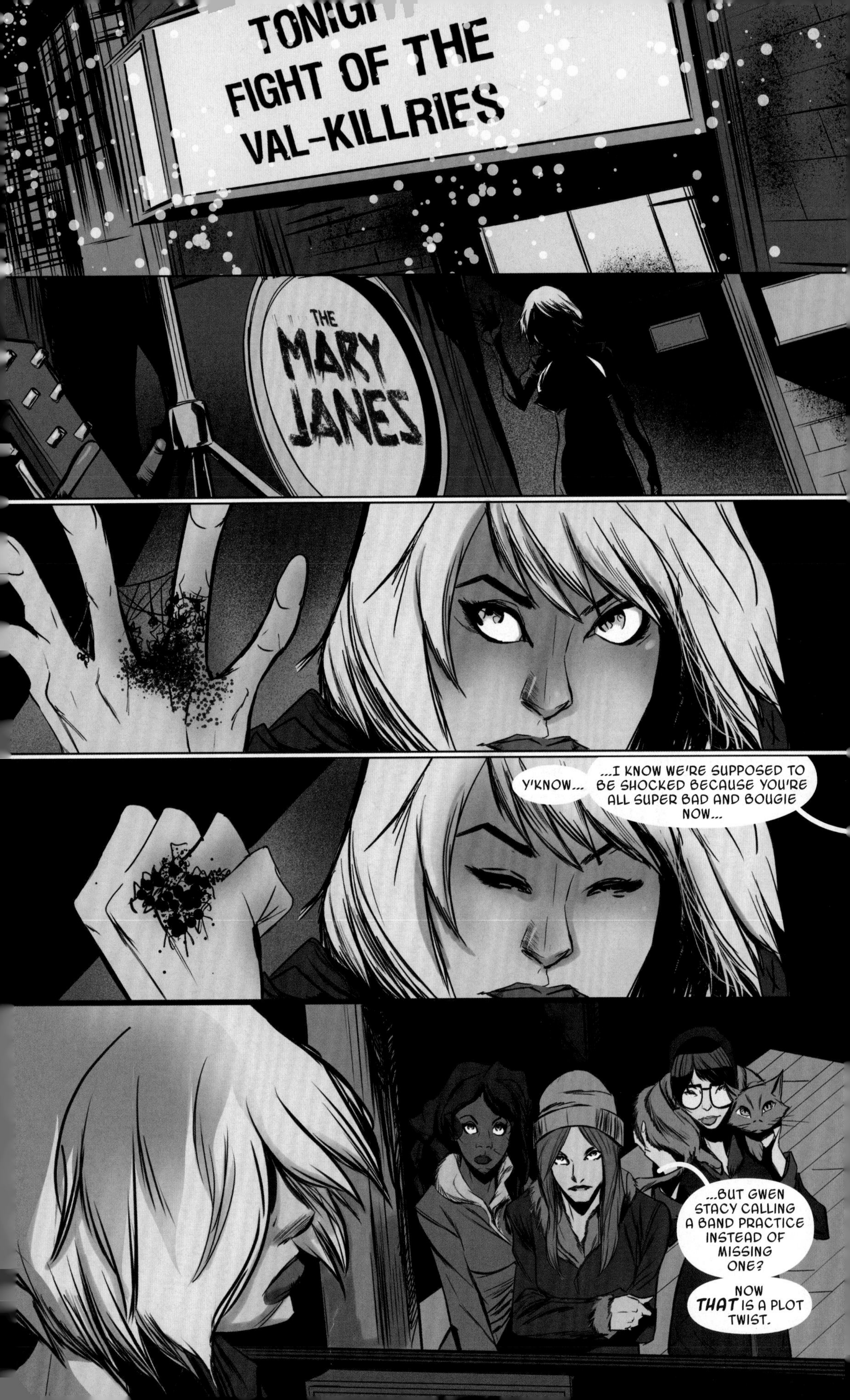
TONIG
FIGHT OF THE
VAL-KILLRIES
THE MARY JANES
Y'KNOW...
...I KNOW WE'RE SUPPOSED TO BE SHOCKED BECAUSE YOU'RE ALL SUPER BAD AND BOUGIE NOW...
...BUT GWEN STACY CALLING A BAND PRACTICE INSTEAD OF MISSING ONE?
NOW *THAT* IS A PLOT TWIST.

HEY.

WE MISSED YOU, TOO, NERD.

WHOA. YOU SLIMED ME WITH YOUR VENOM GOOP.

WELL, AT LEAST I THOUGHT IT WAS GOOP. IT'S MORE LIKE...

GUMMY SPIDERS. A BLANKET OF TINY, GUMMY SPIDERS.

IS--IS IT DANGEROUS?

YES.

NO, I MEAN...

ALL I KNOW IS WHEN I INPUT ANGER, OR FEAR, OR PAIN--

TOO MUCH AND IT'S LIKE A DAM BURSTS. A FLOOD OF EMOTIONS THAT I'VE--

THAT WE'VE NEVER HAD BEFORE.

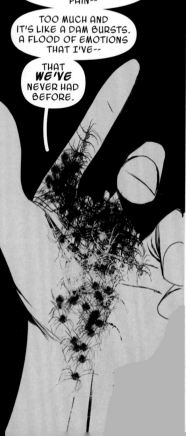

SO WAS IT ALIEN EMOTIONS THAT OVERCAME YOU WHEN YOU TOLD JONAH JAMESON EVERYTHING?

YEAH. YOU MIGHT AS WELL HAVE GONE ON SECRET WARS WITH RICK JONES.

YEAH. ABOUT THAT...

I-- I KNOW I LOOK CRAZY, REVEALING MYSELF.

LIKE I HAVEN'T THOUGHT ANY OF THIS THROUGH.

BUT YOU HAVE TO UNDERSTAND, ALL I'VE DONE IS THINK.

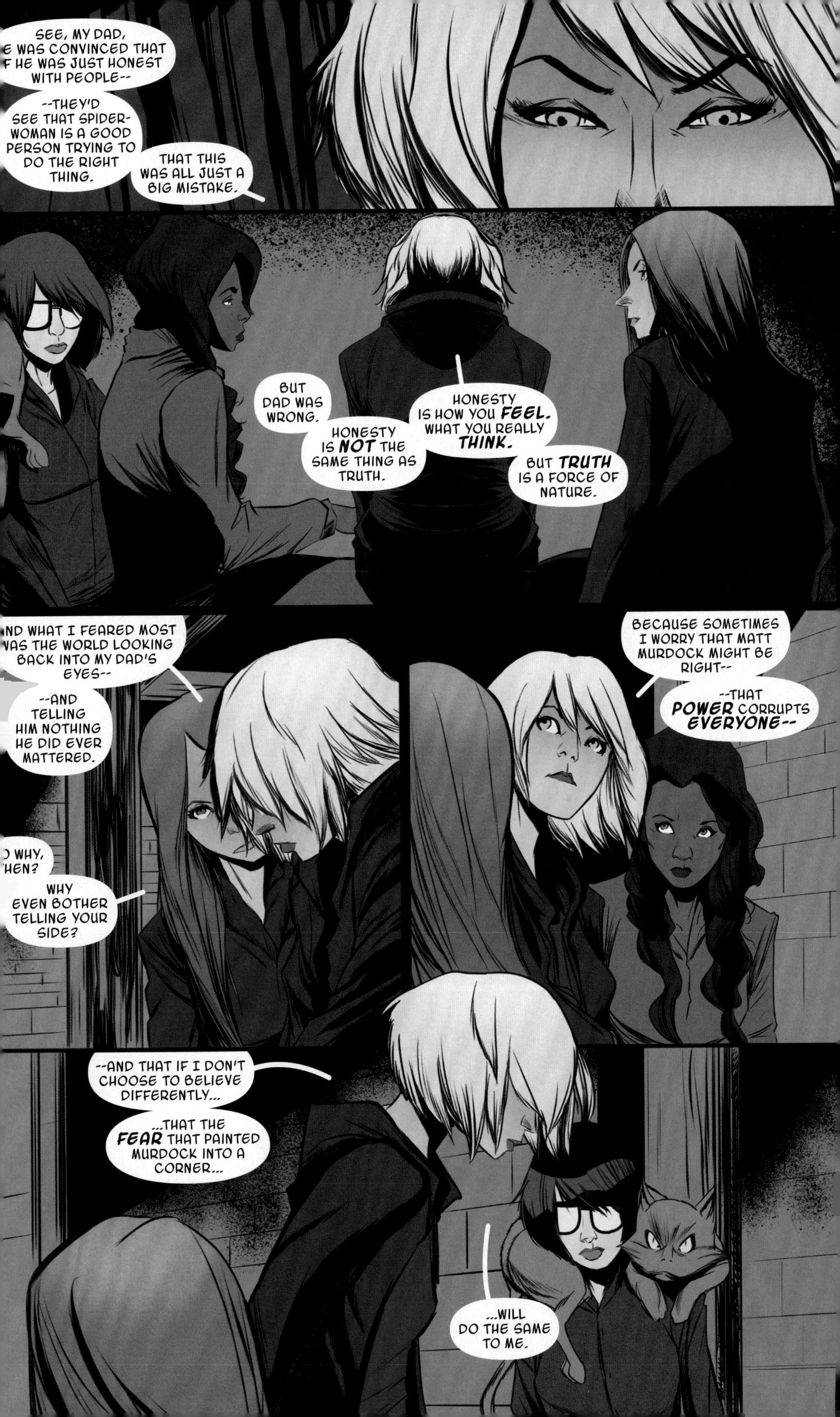
SEE, MY DAD, E WAS CONVINCED THAT F HE WAS JUST HONEST WITH PEOPLE--
--THEY'D SEE THAT SPIDER-WOMAN IS A GOOD PERSON TRYING TO DO THE RIGHT THING.
THAT THIS WAS ALL JUST A BIG MISTAKE.
BUT DAD WAS WRONG.
HONESTY IS NOT THE SAME THING AS TRUTH.
HONESTY IS HOW YOU FEEL. WHAT YOU REALLY THINK.
BUT TRUTH IS A FORCE OF NATURE.
ND WHAT I FEARED MOST VAS THE WORLD LOOKING BACK INTO MY DAD'S EYES--
--AND TELLING HIM NOTHING HE DID EVER MATTERED.
WHY, HEN?
WHY EVEN BOTHER TELLING YOUR SIDE?
BECAUSE SOMETIMES I WORRY THAT MATT MURDOCK MIGHT BE RIGHT--
--THAT POWER CORRUPTS EVERYONE--
--AND THAT IF I DON'T CHOOSE TO BELIEVE DIFFERENTLY...
...THAT THE FEAR THAT PAINTED MURDOCK INTO A CORNER...
...WILL DO THE SAME TO ME.

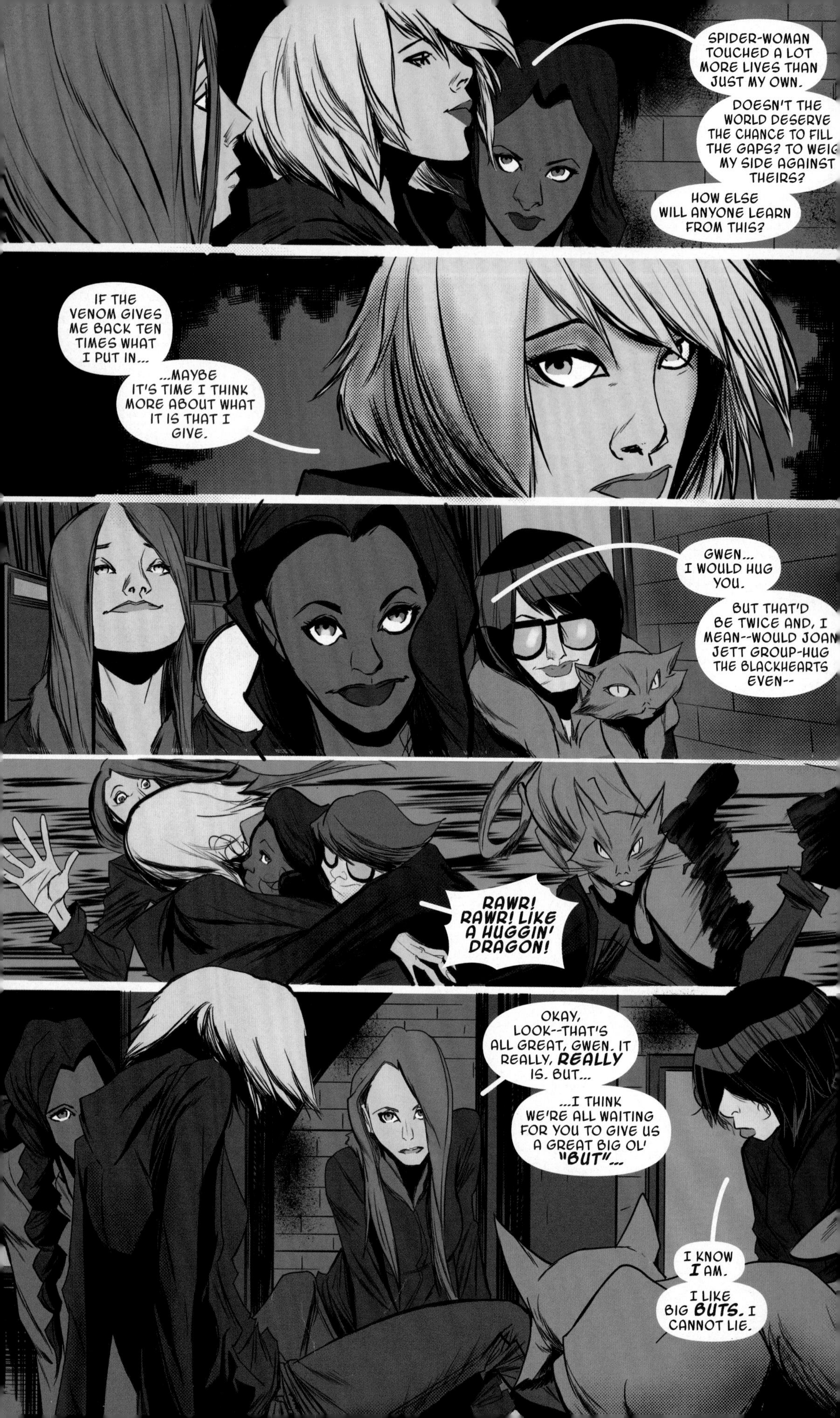
SPIDER-WOMAN TOUCHED A LOT MORE LIVES THAN JUST MY OWN.
DOESN'T THE WORLD DESERVE THE CHANCE TO FILL THE GAPS? TO WEIG MY SIDE AGAINST THEIRS?
HOW ELSE WILL ANYONE LEARN FROM THIS?
IF THE VENOM GIVES ME BACK TEN TIMES WHAT I PUT IN...
...MAYBE IT'S TIME I THINK MORE ABOUT WHAT IT IS THAT I GIVE.
GWEN... I WOULD HUG YOU.
BUT THAT'D BE TWICE AND, I MEAN--WOULD JOAN JETT GROUP-HUG THE BLACKHEARTS EVEN--
RAWR! RAWR! LIKE A HUGGIN' DRAGON!
OKAY, LOOK--THAT'S ALL GREAT, GWEN. IT REALLY, REALLY IS. BUT...
...I THINK WE'RE ALL WAITING FOR YOU TO GIVE US A GREAT BIG OL' "BUT"...
I KNOW I AM.
I LIKE BIG BUTS. I CANNOT LIE.

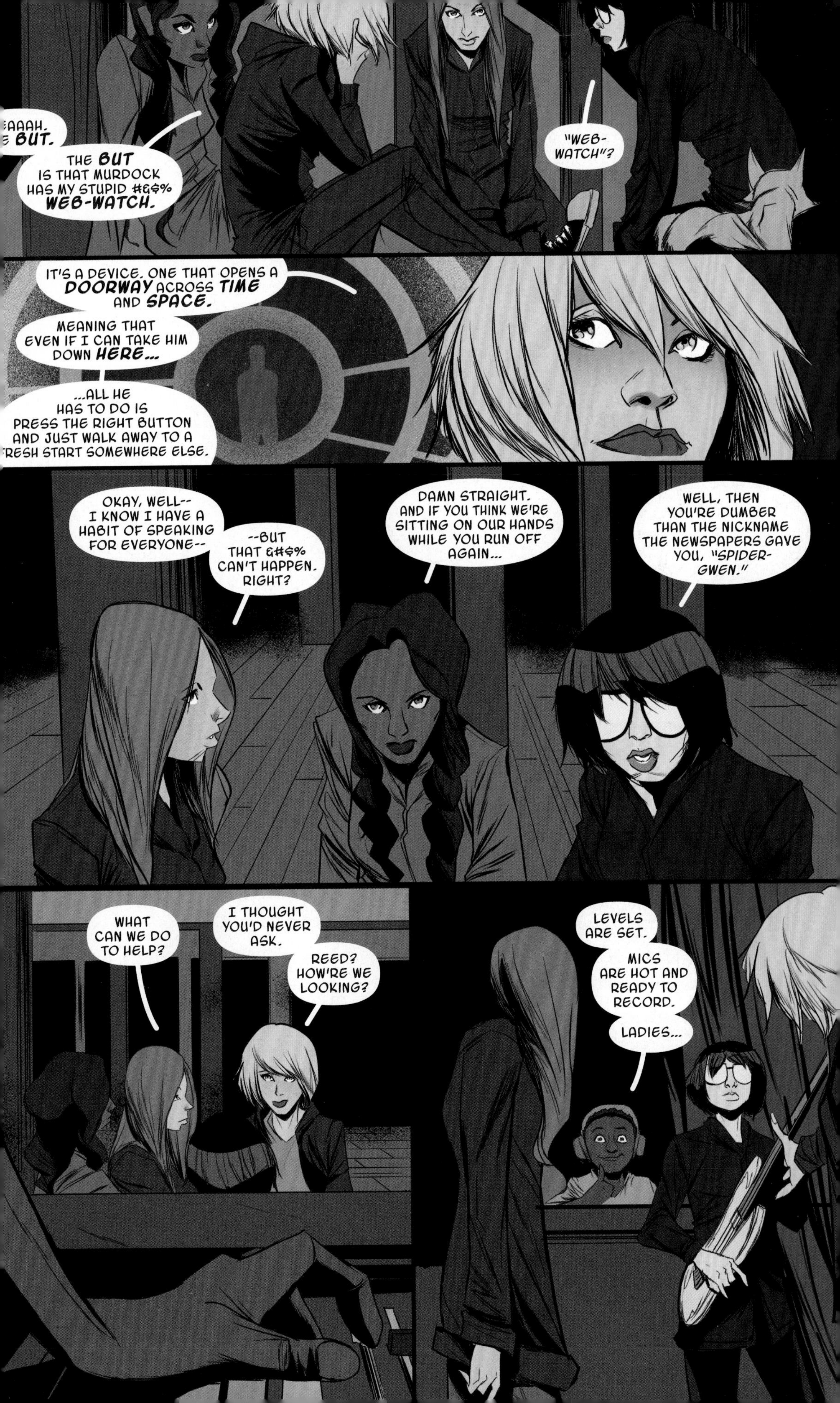

EAAAH.
E BUT.
THE BUT IS THAT MURDOCK HAS MY STUPID #&$% WEB-WATCH.
"WEB-WATCH"?
IT'S A DEVICE. ONE THAT OPENS A DOORWAY ACROSS TIME AND SPACE.
MEANING THAT EVEN IF I CAN TAKE HIM DOWN HERE...
...ALL HE HAS TO DO IS PRESS THE RIGHT BUTTON AND JUST WALK AWAY TO A RESH START SOMEWHERE ELSE.
OKAY, WELL-- I KNOW I HAVE A HABIT OF SPEAKING FOR EVERYONE--
--BUT THAT &#$% CAN'T HAPPEN. RIGHT?
DAMN STRAIGHT. AND IF YOU THINK WE'RE SITTING ON OUR HANDS WHILE YOU RUN OFF AGAIN...
WELL, THEN YOU'RE DUMBER THAN THE NICKNAME THE NEWSPAPERS GAVE YOU, "SPIDER-GWEN."
WHAT CAN WE DO TO HELP?
I THOUGHT YOU'D NEVER ASK.
REED? HOW'RE WE LOOKING?
LEVELS ARE SET.
MICS ARE HOT AND READY TO RECORD.
LADIES...

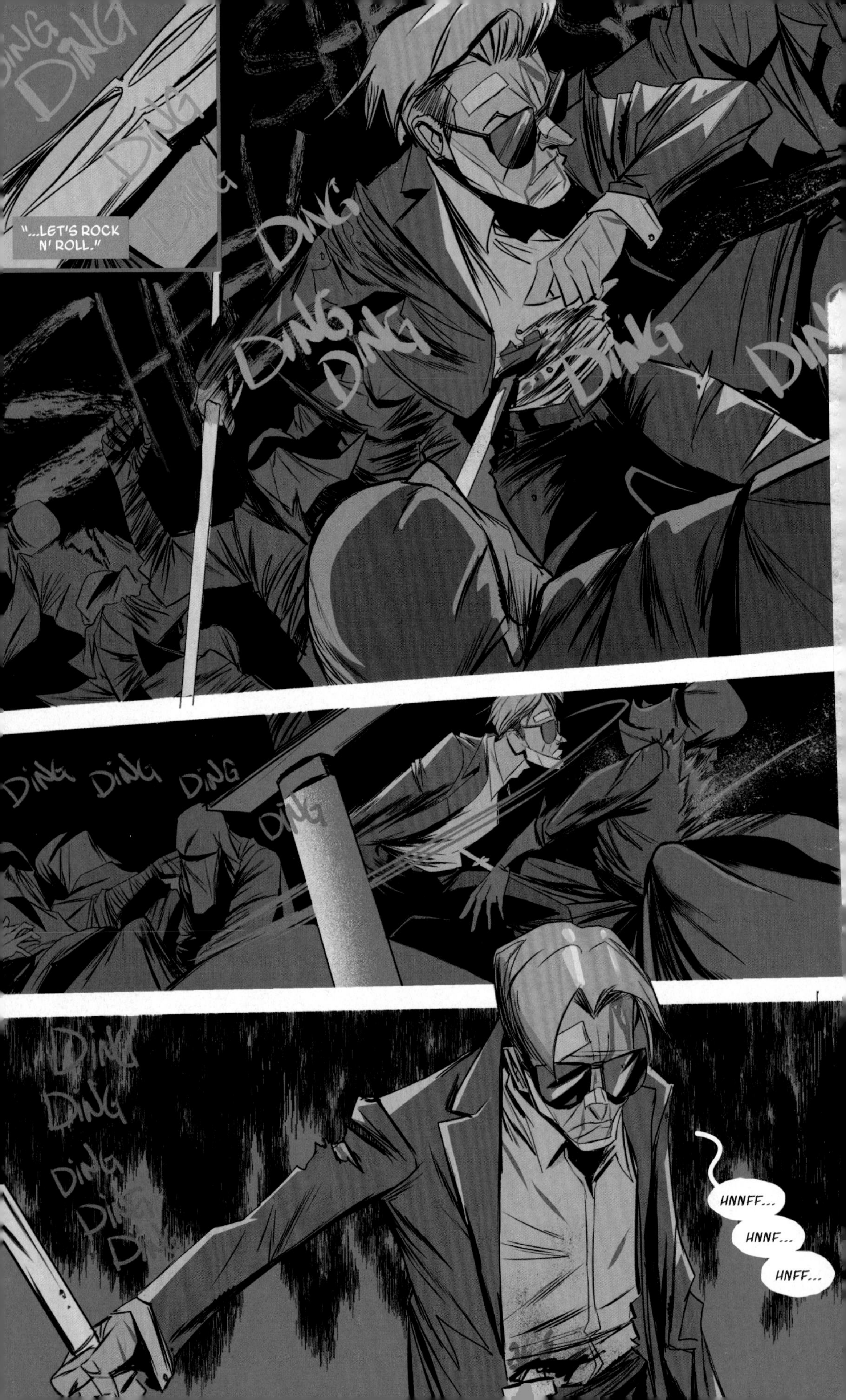
DING DING
DING
DING
"...LET'S ROCK N' ROLL."
DING
DING DING
DING
DING
DING DING DING
DING
DING
DING
DING
DING
HNNFF...
HNNF...
HNFF...

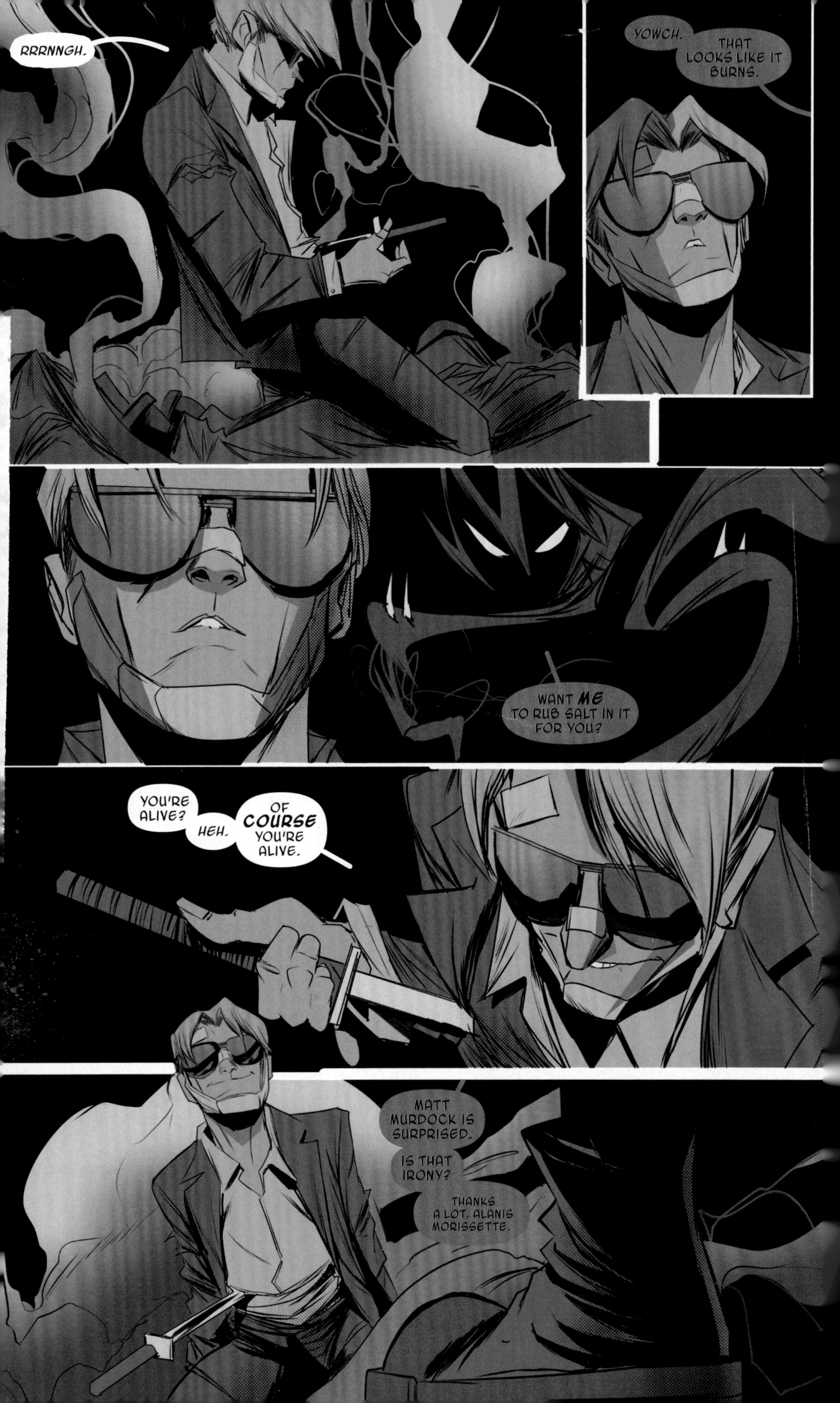
RRRNNGH.
YOWCH.
THAT LOOKS LIKE IT BURNS.
WANT ME TO RUB SALT IN IT FOR YOU?
YOU'RE ALIVE?
HEH.
OF COURSE YOU'RE ALIVE.
MATT MURDOCK IS SURPRISED.
IS THAT IRONY?
THANKS A LOT, ALANIS MORISSETTE.

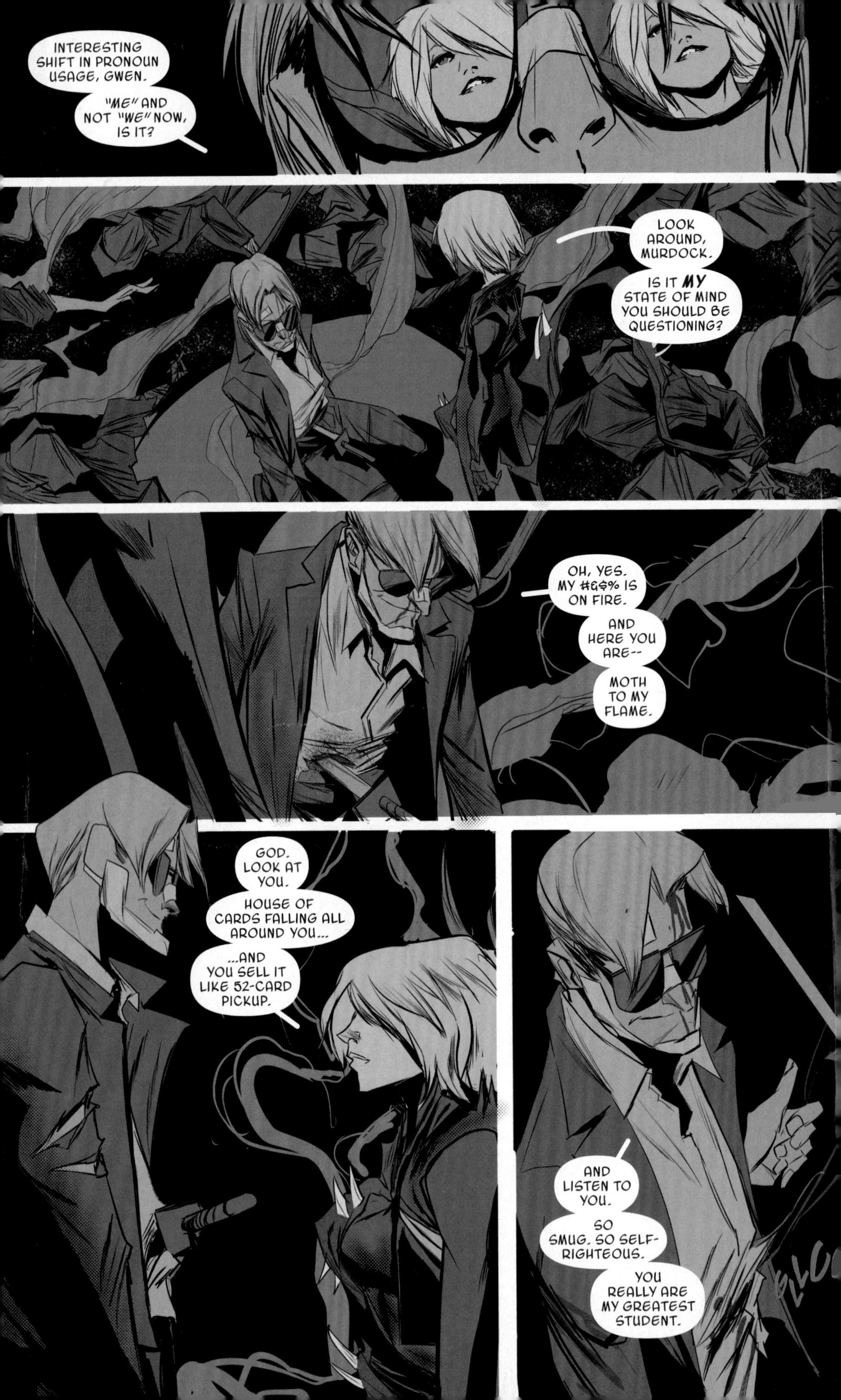

INTERESTING SHIFT IN PRONOUN USAGE, GWEN.
"ME" AND NOT "WE" NOW, IS IT?
LOOK AROUND, MURDOCK.
IS IT **MY** STATE OF MIND YOU SHOULD BE QUESTIONING?
OH, YES. MY #G$% IS ON FIRE.
AND HERE YOU ARE--
MOTH TO MY FLAME.
GOD. LOOK AT YOU.
HOUSE OF CARDS FALLING ALL AROUND YOU...
...AND YOU SELL IT LIKE 52-CARD PICKUP.
AND LISTEN TO YOU.
SO SMUG. SO SELF-RIGHTEOUS.
YOU REALLY ARE MY GREATEST STUDENT.

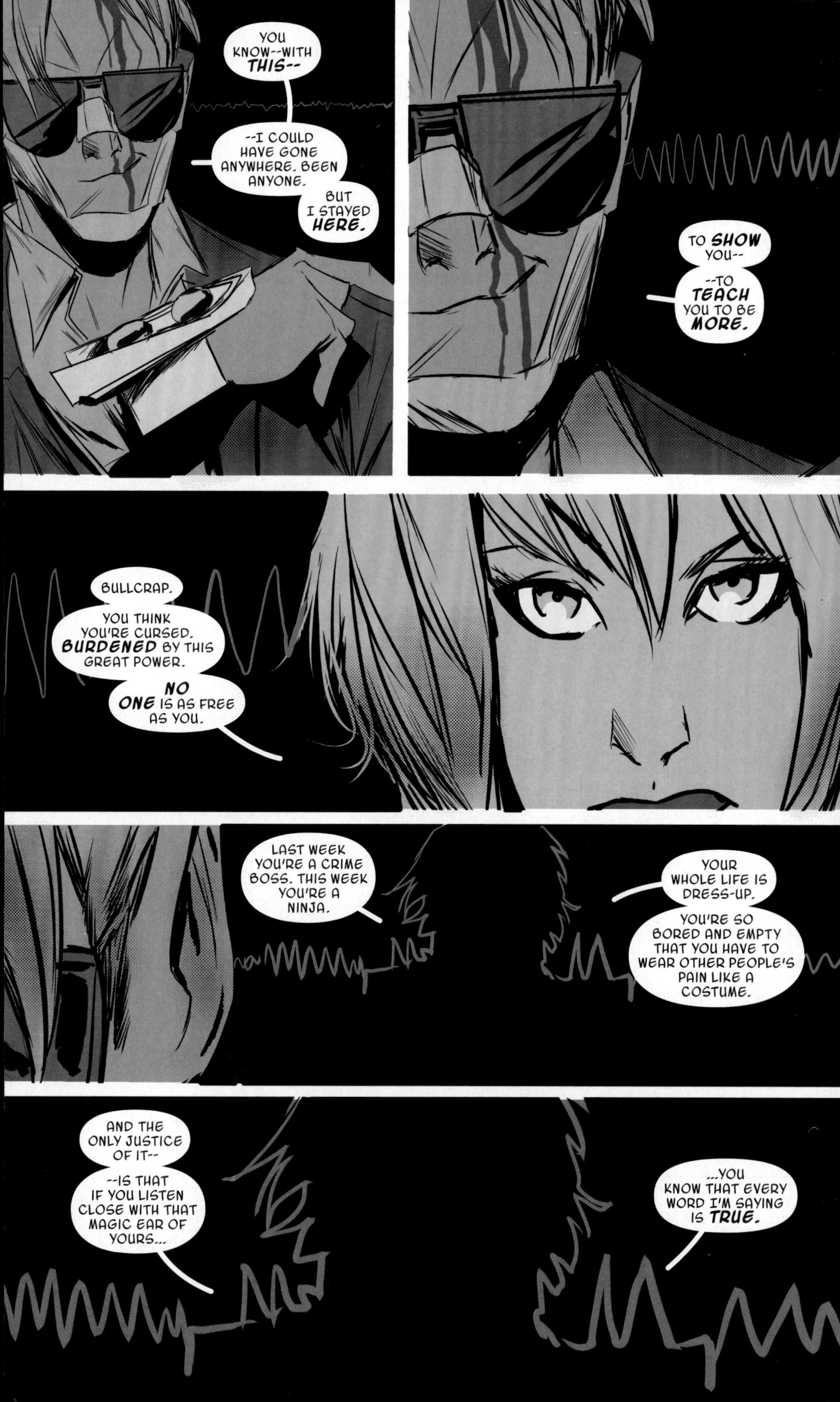
YOU KNOW--WITH THIS--
--I COULD HAVE GONE ANYWHERE. BEEN ANYONE.
BUT I STAYED HERE.
TO SHOW YOU--
--TO TEACH YOU TO BE MORE.
BULLCRAP.
YOU THINK YOU'RE CURSED. BURDENED BY THIS GREAT POWER.
NO ONE IS AS FREE AS YOU.
LAST WEEK YOU'RE A CRIME BOSS. THIS WEEK YOU'RE A NINJA.
YOUR WHOLE LIFE IS DRESS-UP.
YOU'RE SO BORED AND EMPTY THAT YOU HAVE TO WEAR OTHER PEOPLE'S PAIN LIKE A COSTUME.
AND THE ONLY JUSTICE OF IT--
--IS THAT IF YOU LISTEN CLOSE WITH THAT MAGIC EAR OF YOURS...
...YOU KNOW THAT EVERY WORD I'M SAYING IS TRUE.

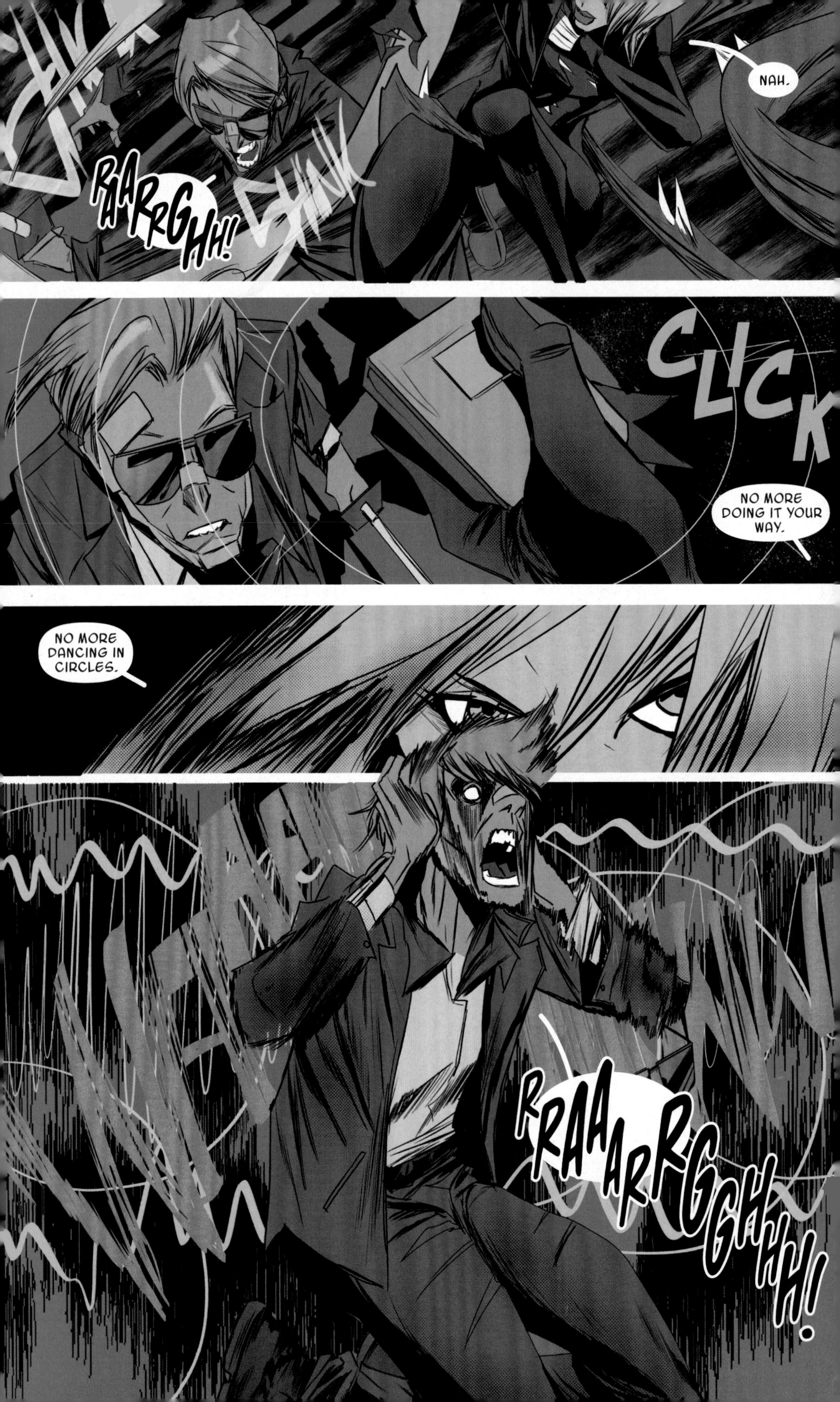

RAARRGHH!
CHINK
NAH.
CLICK
NO MORE DOING IT YOUR WAY.
NO MORE DANCING IN CIRCLES.
RRAAARRGHHH!

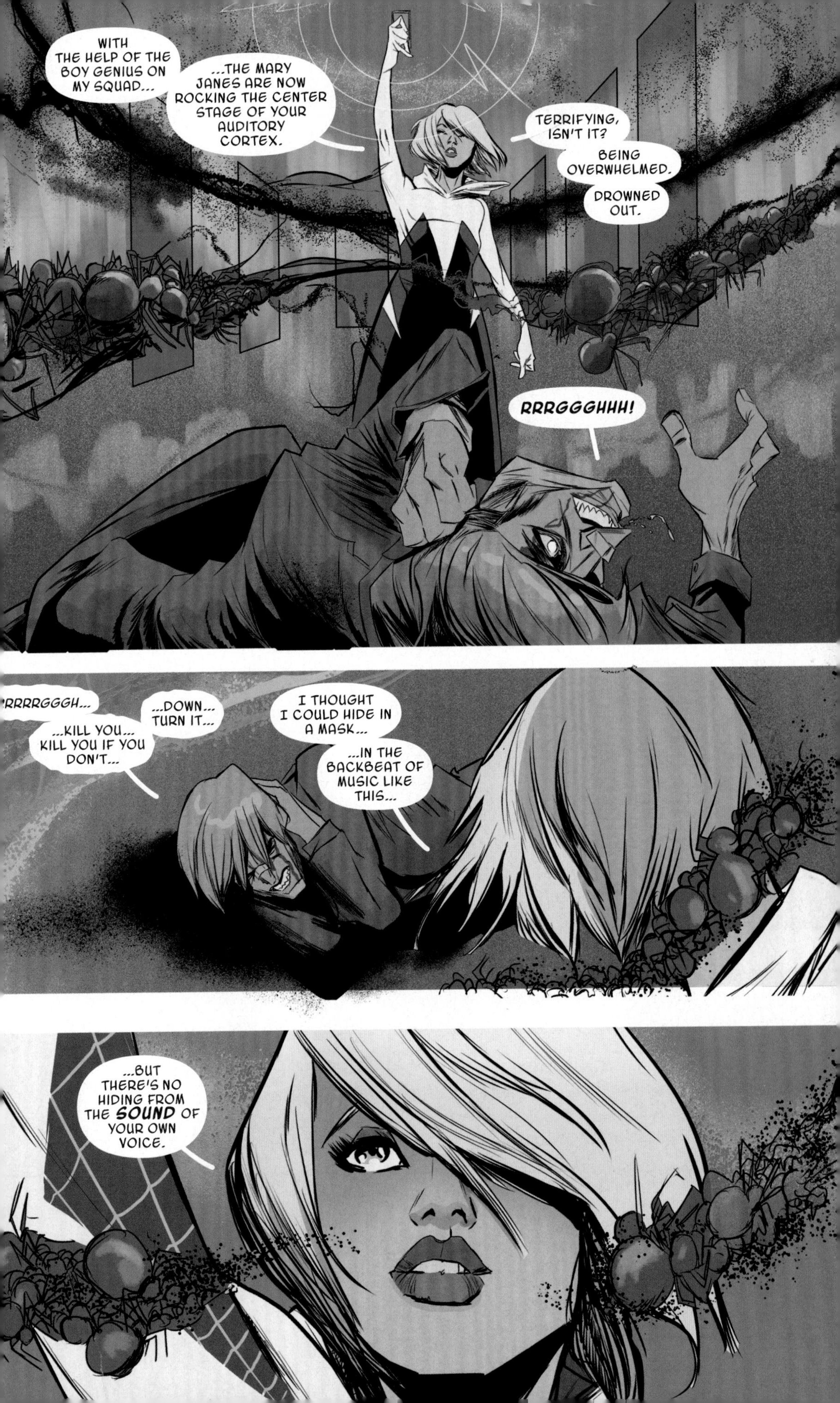
WITH THE HELP OF THE BOY GENIUS ON MY SQUAD...
...THE MARY JANES ARE NOW ROCKING THE CENTER STAGE OF YOUR AUDITORY CORTEX.
TERRIFYING, ISN'T IT?
BEING OVERWHELMED.
DROWNED OUT.
RRRGGGHHH!
RRRRGGGH...
...KILL YOU... KILL YOU IF YOU DON'T...
...DOWN... TURN IT...
I THOUGHT I COULD HIDE IN A MASK...
...IN THE BACKBEAT OF MUSIC LIKE THIS...
...BUT THERE'S NO HIDING FROM THE SOUND OF YOUR OWN VOICE.

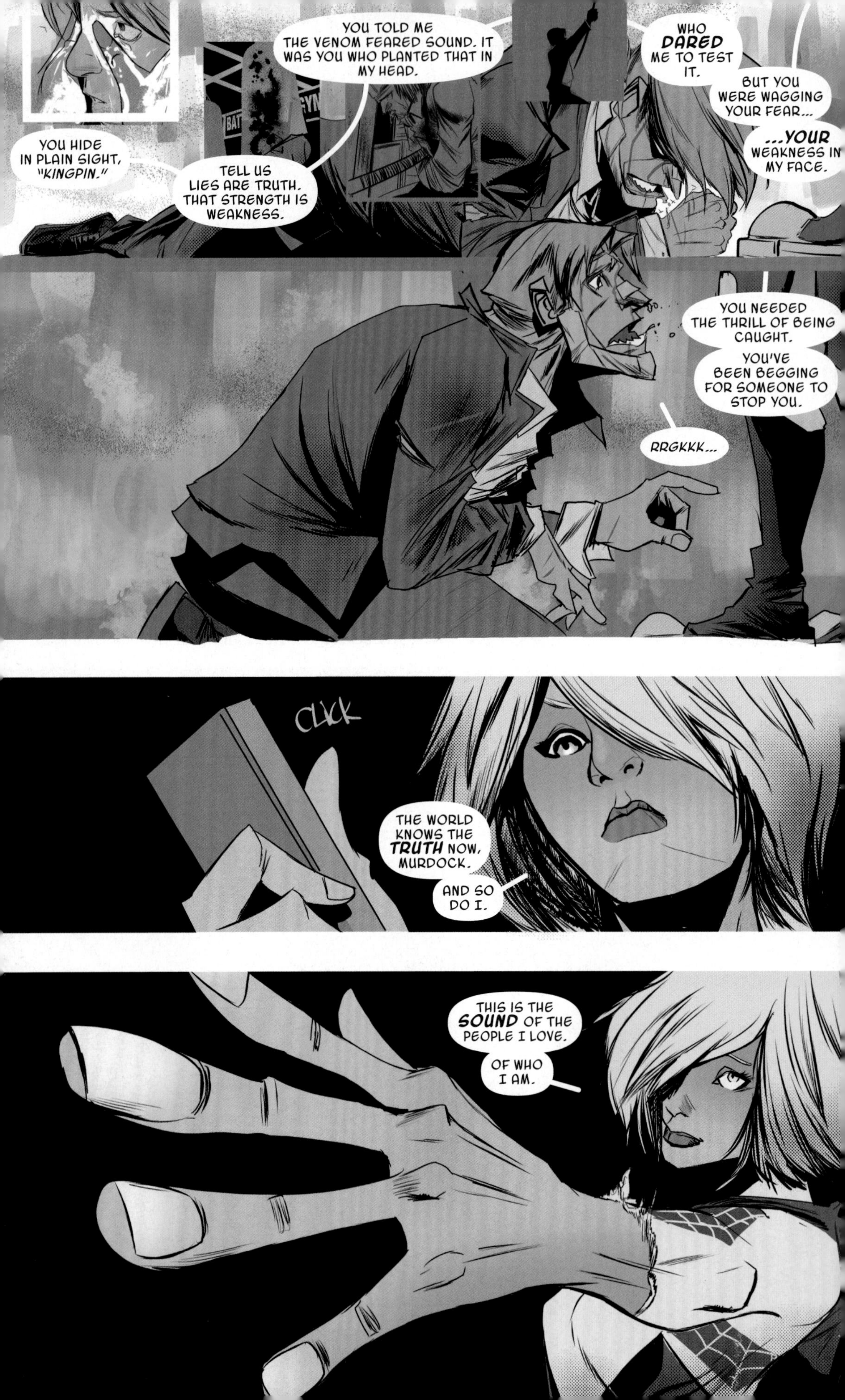
YOU HIDE IN PLAIN SIGHT, "KINGPIN."
TELL US LIES ARE TRUTH. THAT STRENGTH IS WEAKNESS.
YOU TOLD ME THE VENOM FEARED SOUND. IT WAS YOU WHO PLANTED THAT IN MY HEAD.
WHO DARED ME TO TEST IT.
BUT YOU WERE WAGGING YOUR FEAR...
...YOUR WEAKNESS IN MY FACE.
YOU NEEDED THE THRILL OF BEING CAUGHT.
YOU'VE BEEN BEGGING FOR SOMEONE TO STOP YOU.
RRGKKK...
CLICK
THE WORLD KNOWS THE TRUTH NOW, MURDOCK.
AND SO DO I.
THIS IS THE SOUND OF THE PEOPLE I LOVE.
OF WHO I AM.

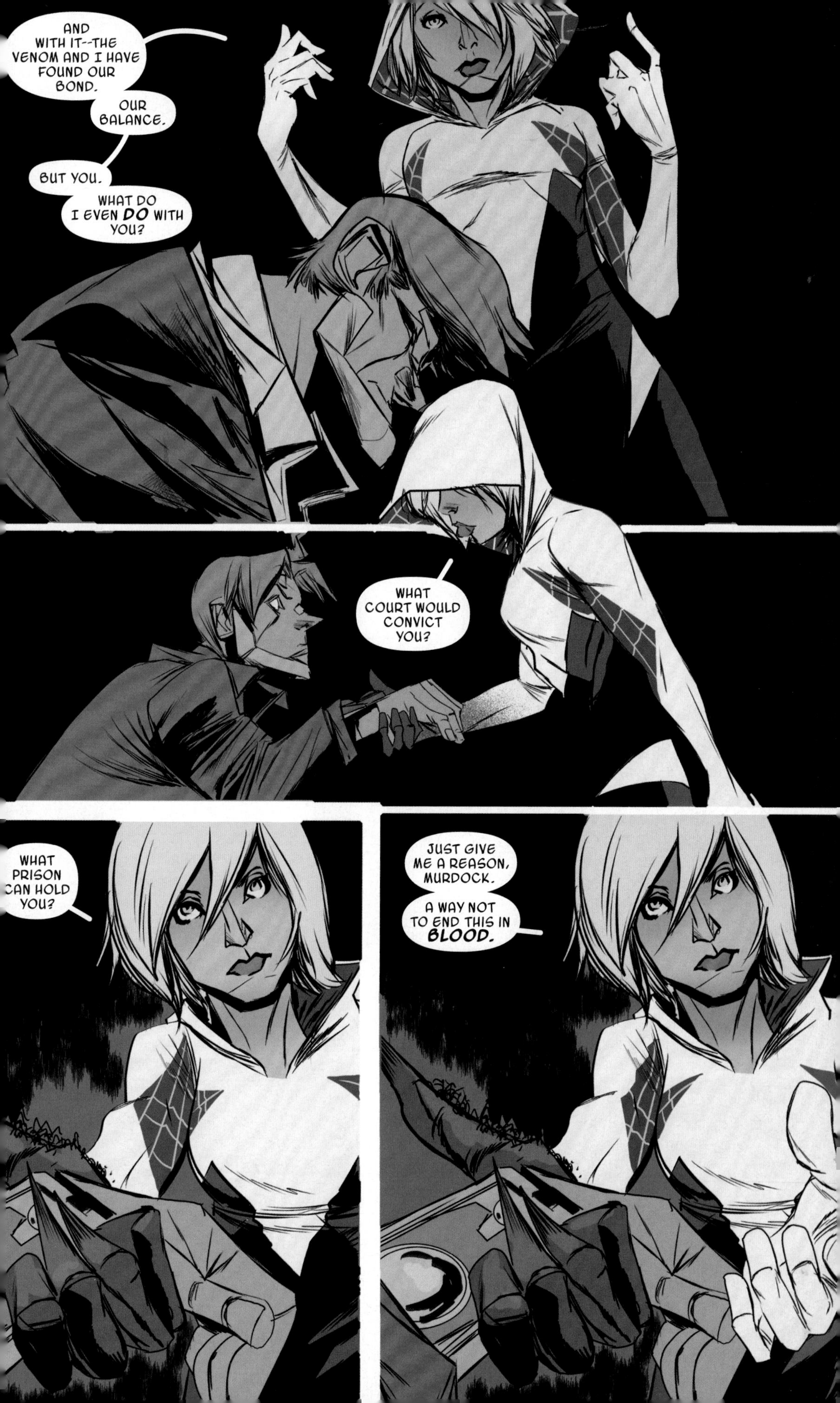
AND WITH IT--THE VENOM AND I HAVE FOUND OUR BOND.
OUR BALANCE.
BUT YOU.
WHAT DO I EVEN DO WITH YOU?
WHAT COURT WOULD CONVICT YOU?
WHAT PRISON CAN HOLD YOU?
JUST GIVE ME A REASON, MURDOCK.
A WAY NOT TO END THIS IN BLOOD.

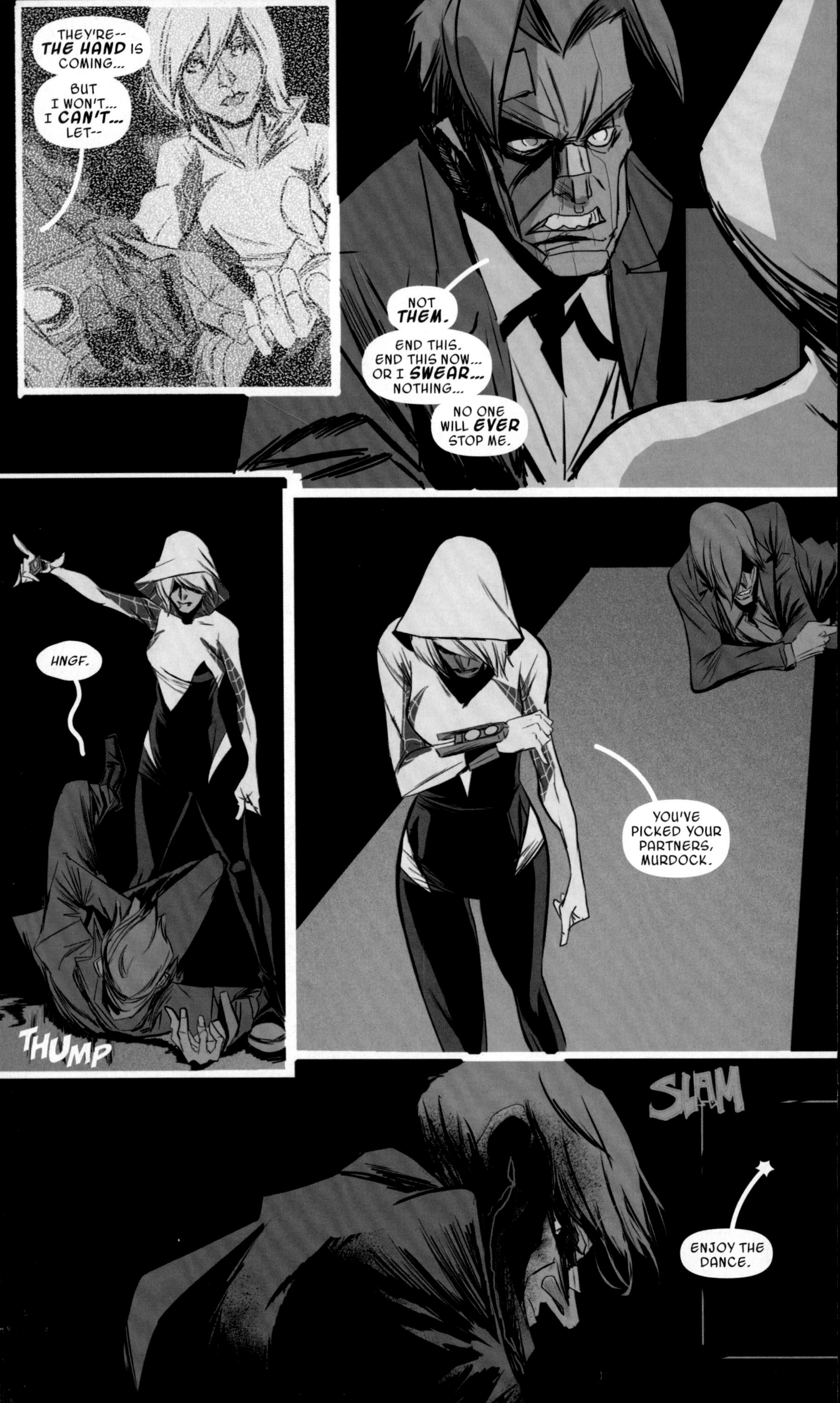
THEY'RE-- THE HAND IS COMING...
BUT I WON'T... I CAN'T... LET--
NOT THEM.
END THIS. END THIS NOW... OR I SWEAR... NOTHING...
NO ONE WILL EVER STOP ME.
HNGF.
THUMP
YOU'VE PICKED YOUR PARTNERS, MURDOCK.
SLAM
ENJOY THE DANCE.

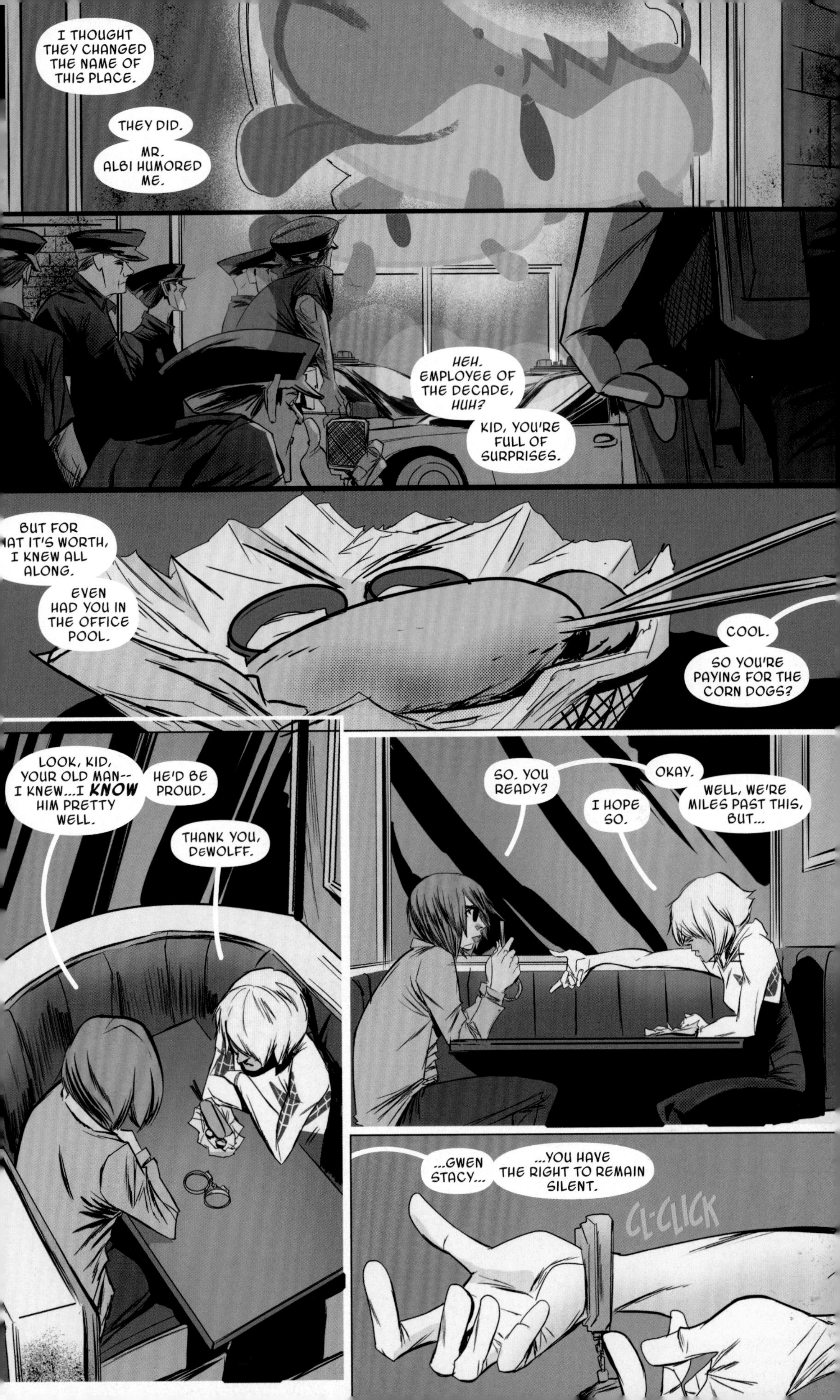
I THOUGHT THEY CHANGED THE NAME OF THIS PLACE.
THEY DID.
MR. ALBI HUMORED ME.
HEH. EMPLOYEE OF THE DECADE, HUH?
KID, YOU'RE FULL OF SURPRISES.
BUT FOR AT IT'S WORTH, I KNEW ALL ALONG.
EVEN HAD YOU IN THE OFFICE POOL.
COOL.
SO YOU'RE PAYING FOR THE CORN DOGS?
LOOK, KID, YOUR OLD MAN-- I KNEW...I **KNOW** HIM PRETTY WELL.
HE'D BE PROUD.
THANK YOU, DeWOLFF.
SO. YOU READY?
I HOPE SO.
OKAY.
WELL, WE'RE MILES PAST THIS, BUT...
...GWEN STACY...
...YOU HAVE THE RIGHT TO REMAIN SILENT.
CL-CLICK

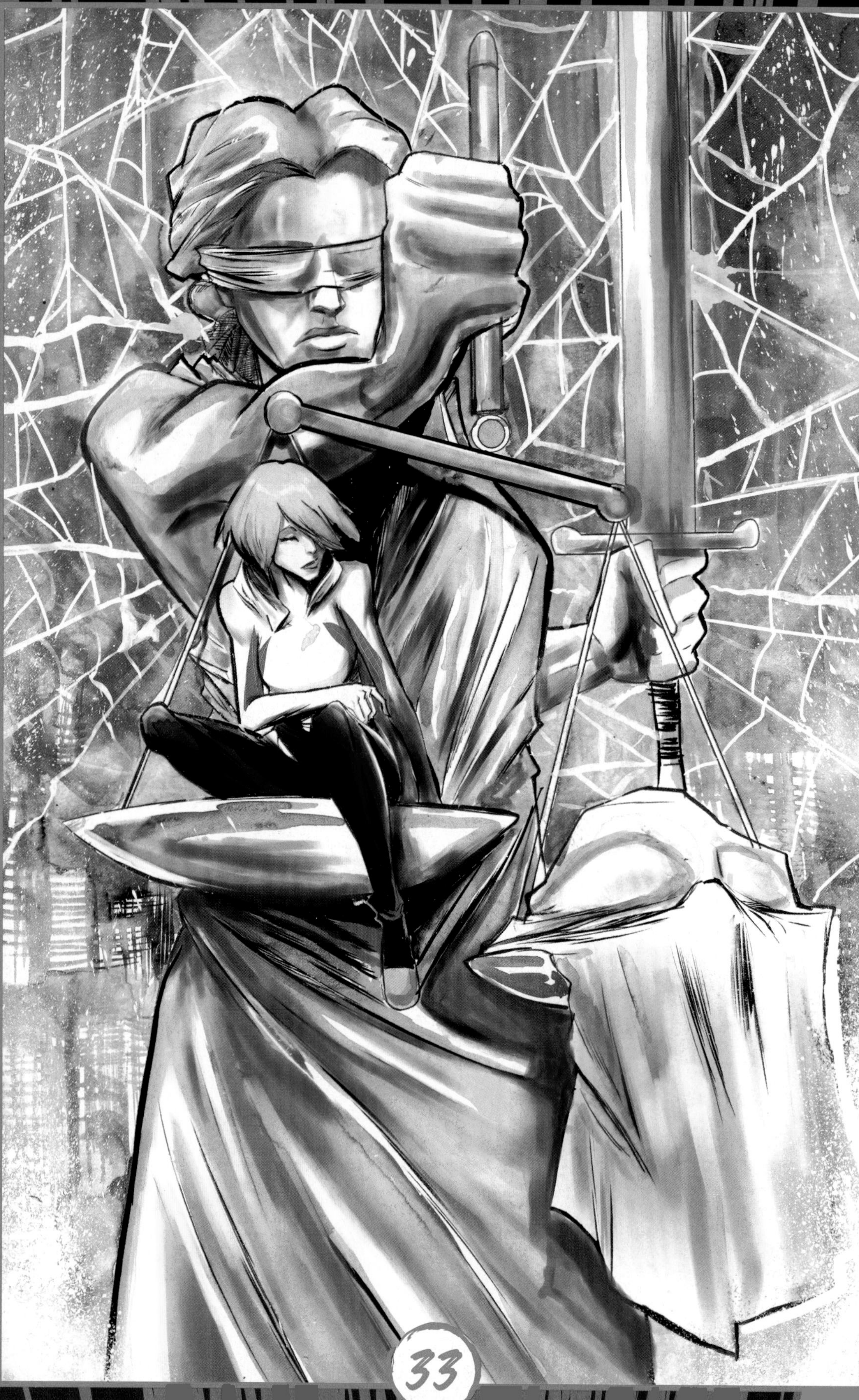

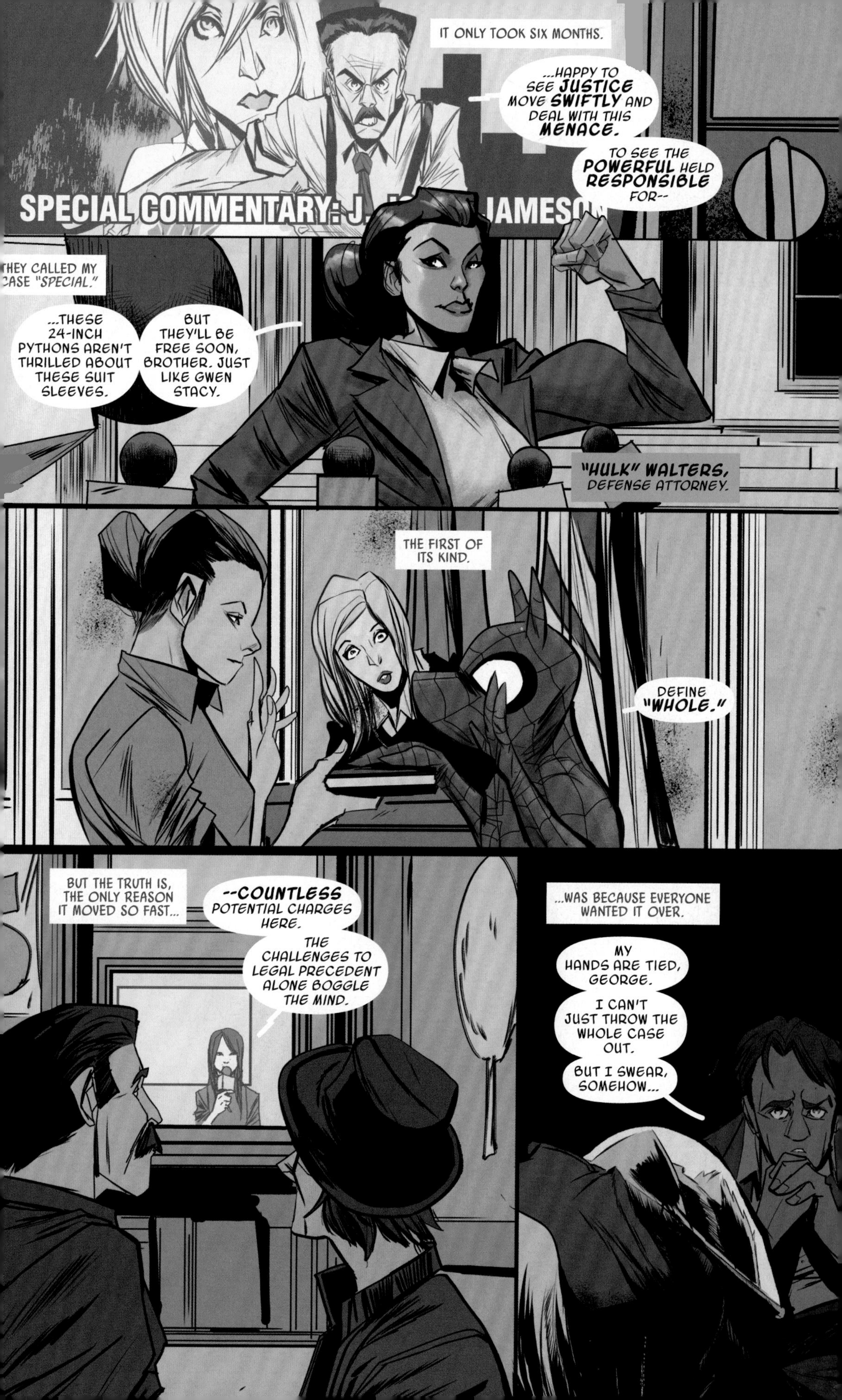

IT ONLY TOOK SIX MONTHS.
...HAPPY TO SEE JUSTICE MOVE SWIFTLY AND DEAL WITH THIS MENACE.
TO SEE THE POWERFUL HELD RESPONSIBLE FOR--
SPECIAL COMMENTARY: J. JAMESON
THEY CALLED MY CASE "SPECIAL."
...THESE 24-INCH PYTHONS AREN'T THRILLED ABOUT THESE SUIT SLEEVES.
BUT THEY'LL BE FREE SOON, BROTHER. JUST LIKE GWEN STACY.
"HULK" WALTERS, DEFENSE ATTORNEY.
THE FIRST OF ITS KIND.
DEFINE "WHOLE."
BUT THE TRUTH IS, THE ONLY REASON IT MOVED SO FAST...
--COUNTLESS POTENTIAL CHARGES HERE.
THE CHALLENGES TO LEGAL PRECEDENT ALONE BOGGLE THE MIND.
...WAS BECAUSE EVERYONE WANTED IT OVER.
MY HANDS ARE TIED, GEORGE.
I CAN'T JUST THROW THE WHOLE CASE OUT.
BUT I SWEAR, SOMEHOW...

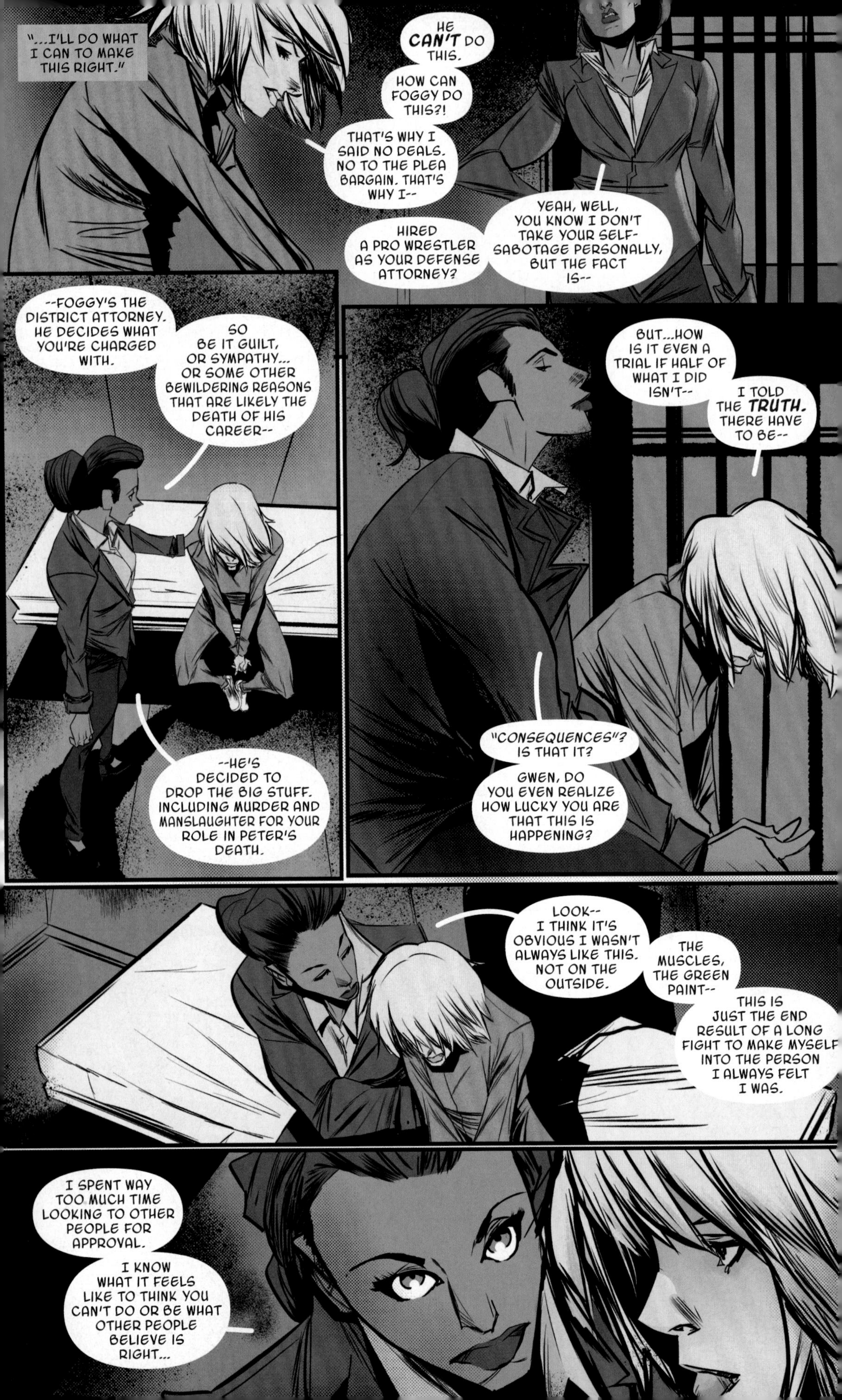
"...I'LL DO WHAT I CAN TO MAKE THIS RIGHT."
HE CAN'T DO THIS.
HOW CAN FOGGY DO THIS?!
THAT'S WHY I SAID NO DEALS. NO TO THE PLEA BARGAIN. THAT'S WHY I--
HIRED A PRO WRESTLER AS YOUR DEFENSE ATTORNEY?
YEAH, WELL, YOU KNOW I DON'T TAKE YOUR SELF-SABOTAGE PERSONALLY, BUT THE FACT IS--
--FOGGY'S THE DISTRICT ATTORNEY. HE DECIDES WHAT YOU'RE CHARGED WITH.
SO BE IT GUILT, OR SYMPATHY... OR SOME OTHER BEWILDERING REASONS THAT ARE LIKELY THE DEATH OF HIS CAREER--
--HE'S DECIDED TO DROP THE BIG STUFF. INCLUDING MURDER AND MANSLAUGHTER FOR YOUR ROLE IN PETER'S DEATH.
BUT...HOW IS IT EVEN A TRIAL IF HALF OF WHAT I DID ISN'T--
I TOLD THE TRUTH. THERE HAVE TO BE--
"CONSEQUENCES"? IS THAT IT?
GWEN, DO YOU EVEN REALIZE HOW LUCKY YOU ARE THAT THIS IS HAPPENING?
LOOK-- I THINK IT'S OBVIOUS I WASN'T ALWAYS LIKE THIS. NOT ON THE OUTSIDE.
THE MUSCLES, THE GREEN PAINT--
THIS IS JUST THE END RESULT OF A LONG FIGHT TO MAKE MYSELF INTO THE PERSON I ALWAYS FELT I WAS.
I SPENT WAY TOO MUCH TIME LOOKING TO OTHER PEOPLE FOR APPROVAL.
I KNOW WHAT IT FEELS LIKE TO THINK YOU CAN'T DO OR BE WHAT OTHER PEOPLE BELIEVE IS RIGHT...

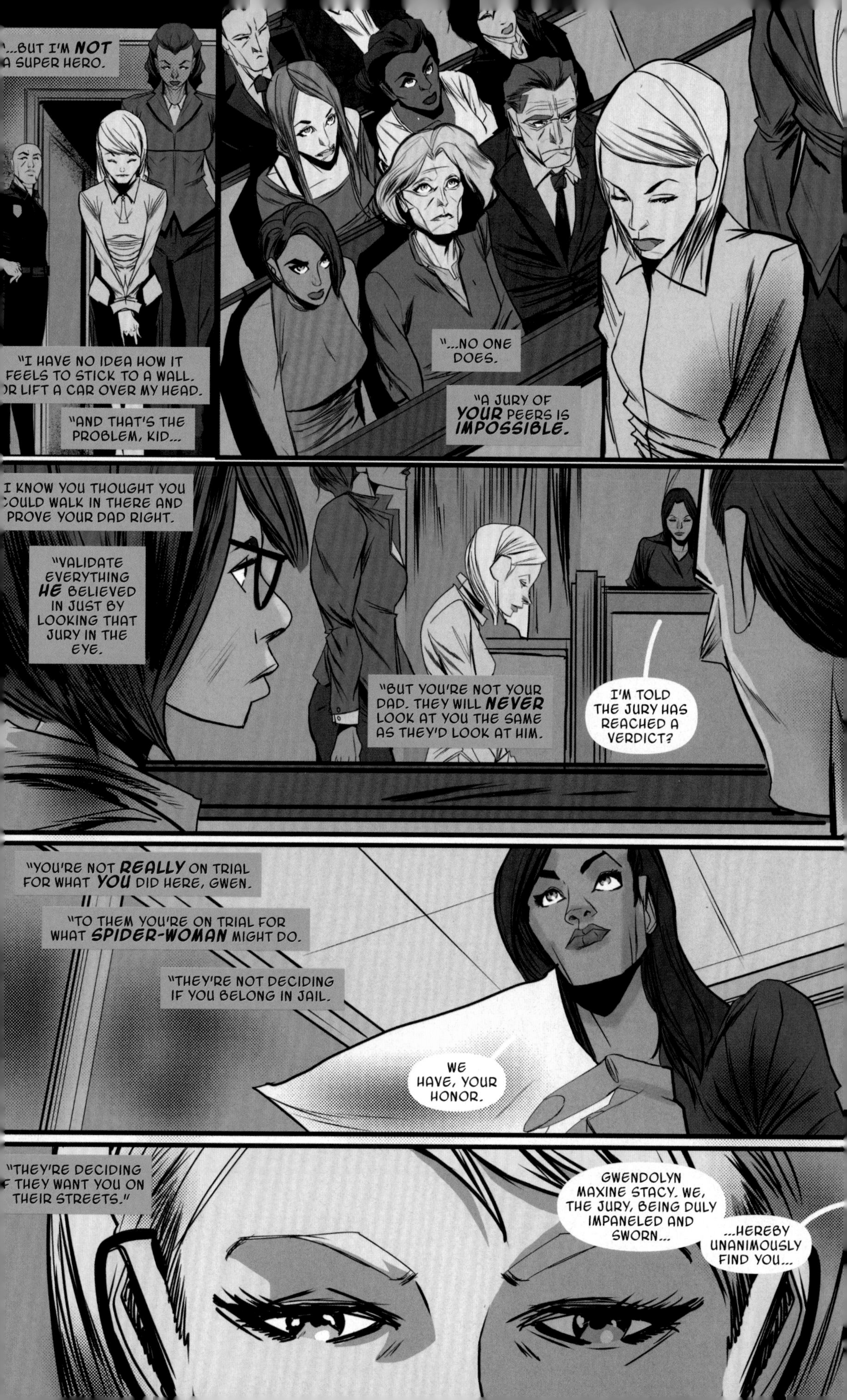

"...BUT I'M NOT A SUPER HERO.
"I HAVE NO IDEA HOW IT FEELS TO STICK TO A WALL. OR LIFT A CAR OVER MY HEAD.
"AND THAT'S THE PROBLEM, KID...
"...NO ONE DOES.
"A JURY OF YOUR PEERS IS IMPOSSIBLE.
I KNOW YOU THOUGHT YOU COULD WALK IN THERE AND PROVE YOUR DAD RIGHT.
"VALIDATE EVERYTHING HE BELIEVED IN JUST BY LOOKING THAT JURY IN THE EYE.
"BUT YOU'RE NOT YOUR DAD. THEY WILL NEVER LOOK AT YOU THE SAME AS THEY'D LOOK AT HIM.
I'M TOLD THE JURY HAS REACHED A VERDICT?
"YOU'RE NOT REALLY ON TRIAL FOR WHAT YOU DID HERE, GWEN.
"TO THEM YOU'RE ON TRIAL FOR WHAT SPIDER-WOMAN MIGHT DO.
"THEY'RE NOT DECIDING IF YOU BELONG IN JAIL.
WE HAVE, YOUR HONOR.
"THEY'RE DECIDING IF THEY WANT YOU ON THEIR STREETS."
GWENDOLYN MAXINE STACY. WE, THE JURY, BEING DULY IMPANELED AND SWORN...
...HEREBY UNANIMOUSLY FIND YOU...

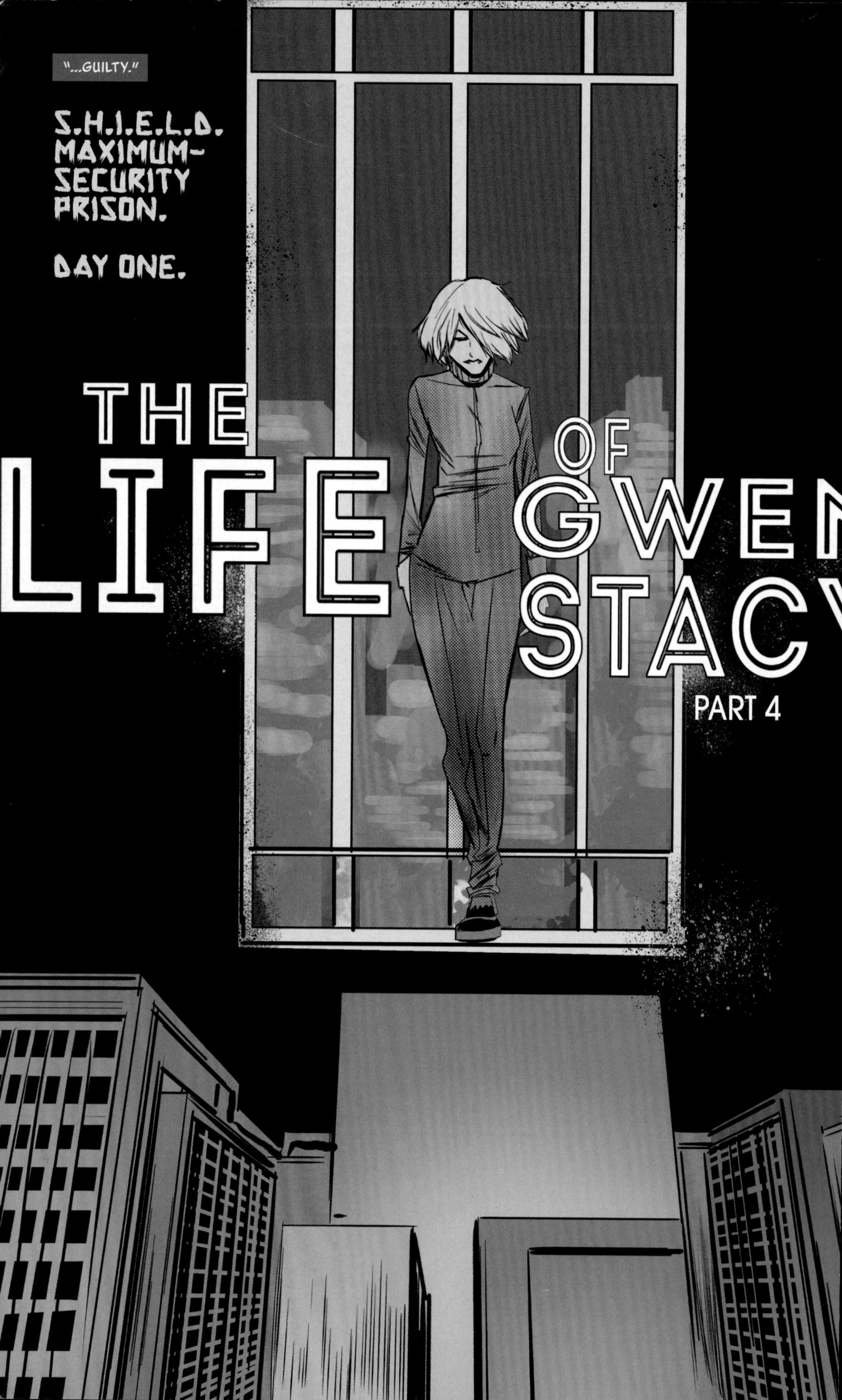
"...GUILTY."
S.H.I.E.L.D. MAXIMUM-SECURITY PRISON.
DAY ONE.
THE LIFE OF GWEN STACY
PART 4

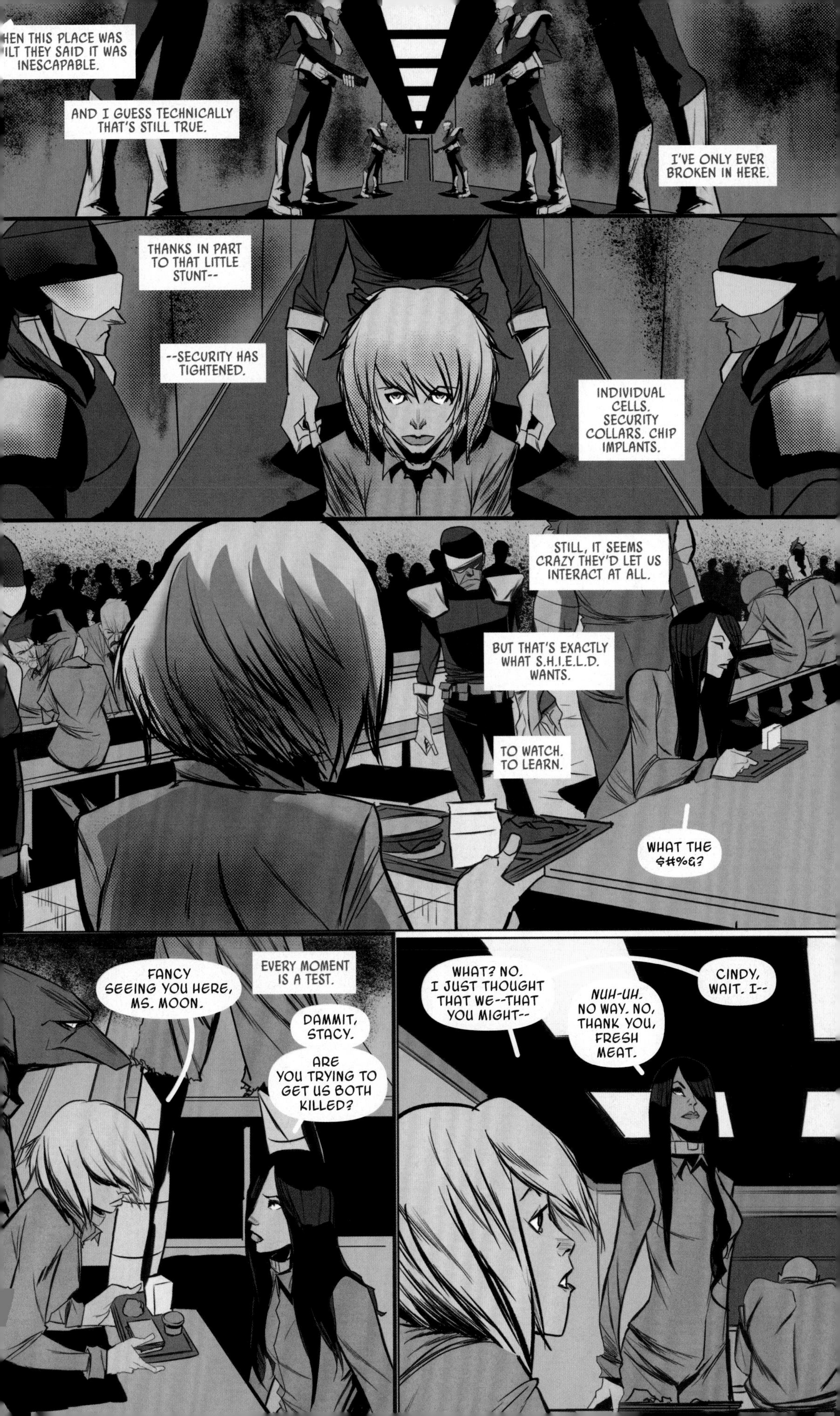
HEN THIS PLACE WAS
ILT THEY SAID IT WAS
INESCAPABLE.
AND I GUESS TECHNICALLY THAT'S STILL TRUE.
I'VE ONLY EVER BROKEN IN HERE.
THANKS IN PART TO THAT LITTLE STUNT--
--SECURITY HAS TIGHTENED.
INDIVIDUAL CELLS. SECURITY COLLARS. CHIP IMPLANTS.
STILL, IT SEEMS CRAZY THEY'D LET US INTERACT AT ALL.
BUT THAT'S EXACTLY WHAT S.H.I.E.L.D. WANTS.
TO WATCH. TO LEARN.
WHAT THE $#%&?
FANCY SEEING YOU HERE, MS. MOON.
EVERY MOMENT IS A TEST.
DAMMIT, STACY.
ARE YOU TRYING TO GET US BOTH KILLED?
WHAT? NO. I JUST THOUGHT THAT WE--THAT YOU MIGHT--
NUH-UH. NO WAY. NO, THANK YOU, FRESH MEAT.
CINDY, WAIT. I--

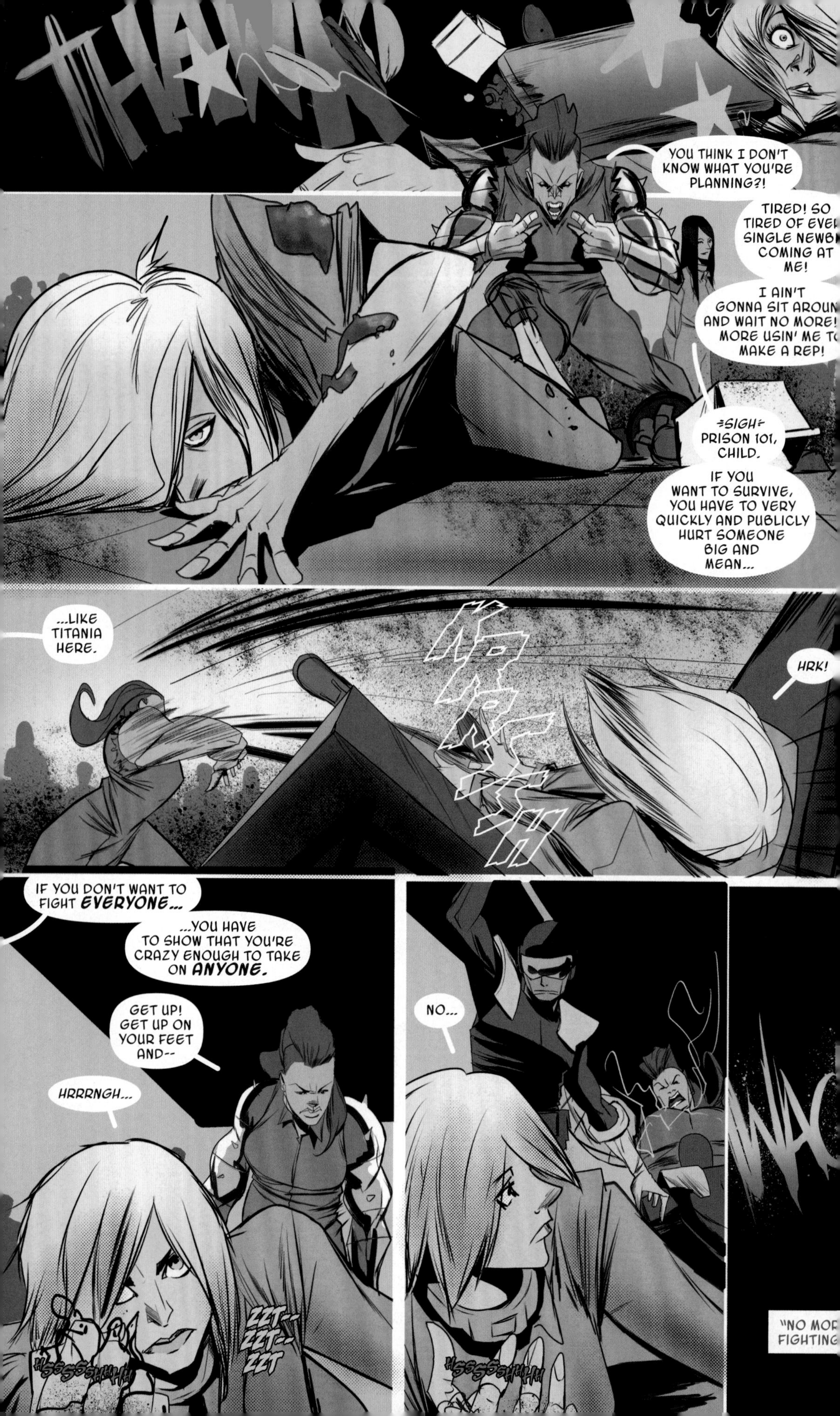
THWAK
YOU THINK I DON'T KNOW WHAT YOU'RE PLANNING?!
TIRED! SO TIRED OF EVE SINGLE NEWB COMING AT ME!
I AIN'T GONNA SIT AROU AND WAIT NO MORE! MORE USIN' ME T MAKE A REP!
=SIGH= PRISON 101, CHILD.
IF YOU WANT TO SURVIVE, YOU HAVE TO VERY QUICKLY AND PUBLICLY HURT SOMEONE BIG AND MEAN...
...LIKE TITANIA HERE.
KRASSH
HRK!
IF YOU DON'T WANT TO FIGHT EVERYONE...
...YOU HAVE TO SHOW THAT YOU'RE CRAZY ENOUGH TO TAKE ON ANYONE.
GET UP! GET UP ON YOUR FEET AND--
HRRRNGH...
ZZT-- ZZT-- ZZT
HSSSSSHHH
NO...
HSSSSSHHH
"NO MOR FIGHTING

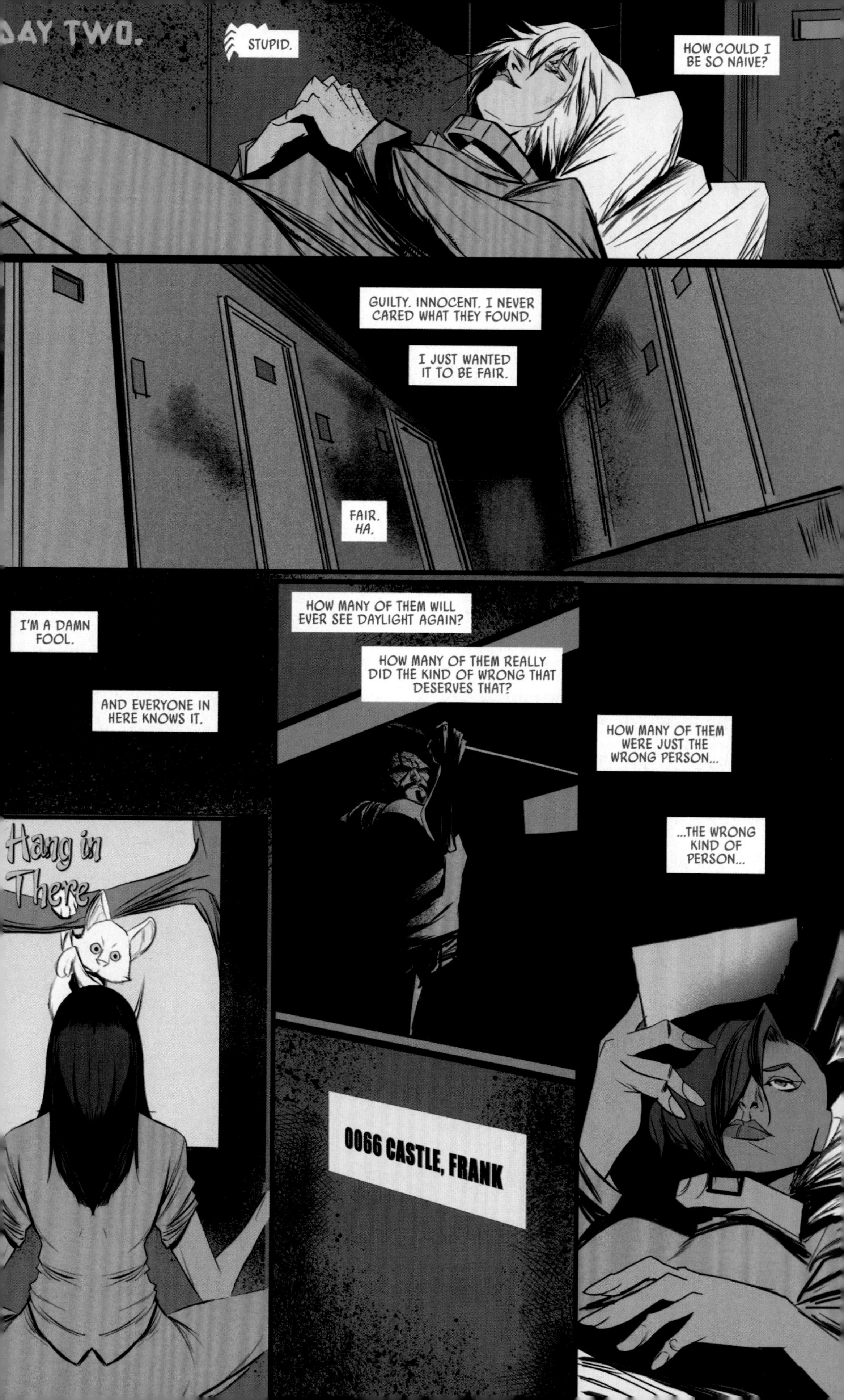
DAY TWO.
STUPID.
HOW COULD I BE SO NAIVE?
GUILTY. INNOCENT. I NEVER CARED WHAT THEY FOUND.
I JUST WANTED IT TO BE FAIR.
FAIR. HA.
I'M A DAMN FOOL.
AND EVERYONE IN HERE KNOWS IT.
Hang in There
HOW MANY OF THEM WILL EVER SEE DAYLIGHT AGAIN?
HOW MANY OF THEM REALLY DID THE KIND OF WRONG THAT DESERVES THAT?
0066 CASTLE, FRANK
HOW MANY OF THEM WERE JUST THE WRONG PERSON...
...THE WRONG KIND OF PERSON...

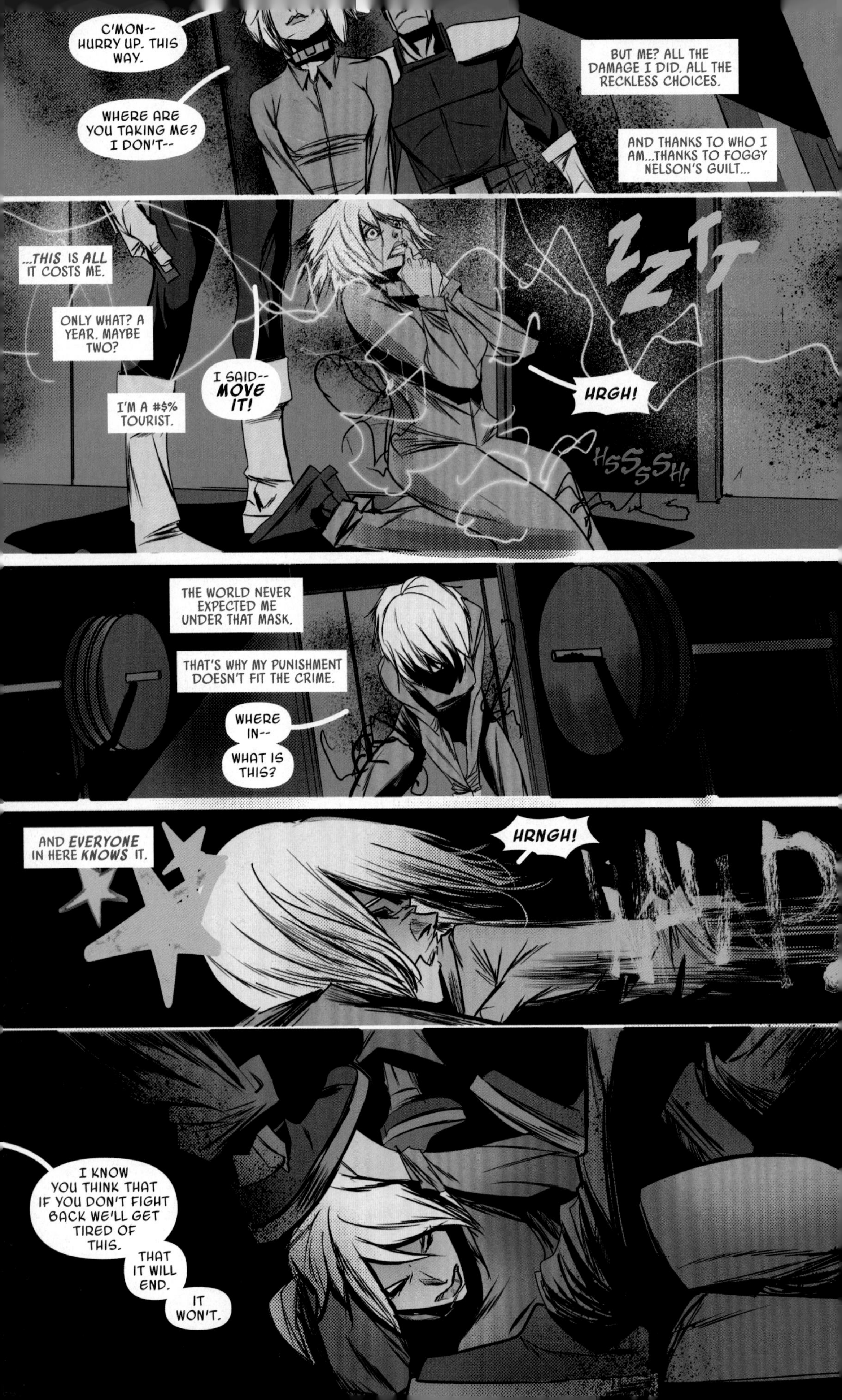
C'MON-- HURRY UP. THIS WAY.
WHERE ARE YOU TAKING ME? I DON'T--
BUT ME? ALL THE DAMAGE I DID. ALL THE RECKLESS CHOICES.
AND THANKS TO WHO I AM...THANKS TO FOGGY NELSON'S GUILT...
...THIS IS ALL IT COSTS ME.
ONLY WHAT? A YEAR. MAYBE TWO?
I'M A #$% TOURIST.
I SAID-- MOVE IT!
ZZTT
HRGH!
HSSSSH!
THE WORLD NEVER EXPECTED ME UNDER THAT MASK.
THAT'S WHY MY PUNISHMENT DOESN'T FIT THE CRIME.
WHERE IN--
WHAT IS THIS?
AND EVERYONE IN HERE KNOWS IT.
HRNGH!
I KNOW YOU THINK THAT IF YOU DON'T FIGHT BACK WE'LL GET TIRED OF THIS.
THAT IT WILL END.
IT WON'T.

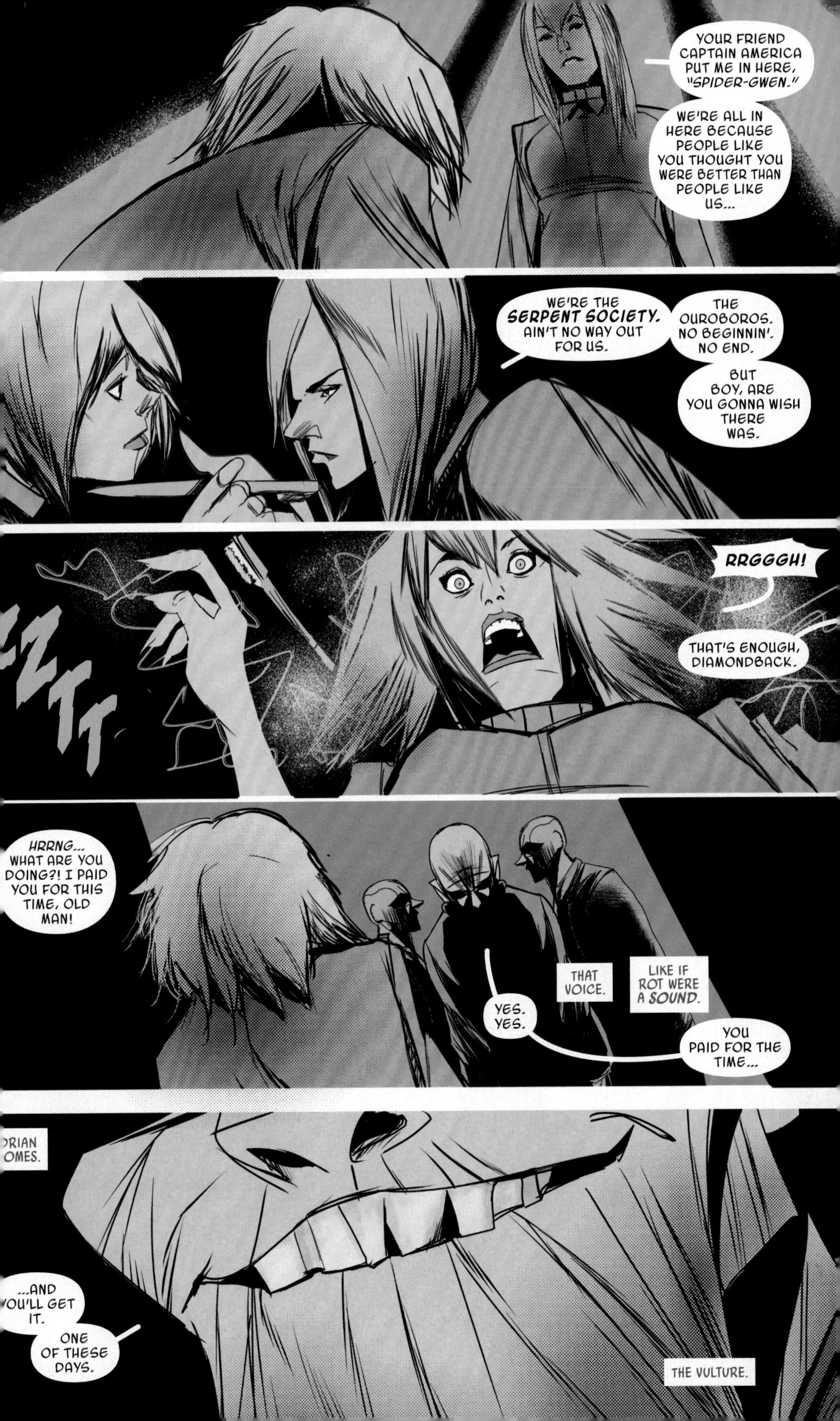
YOUR FRIEND CAPTAIN AMERICA PUT ME IN HERE, "SPIDER-GWEN."
WE'RE ALL IN HERE BECAUSE PEOPLE LIKE YOU THOUGHT YOU WERE BETTER THAN PEOPLE LIKE US...
WE'RE THE SERPENT SOCIETY. AIN'T NO WAY OUT FOR US.
THE OUROBOROS. NO BEGINNIN'. NO END.
BUT BOY, ARE YOU GONNA WISH THERE WAS.
ZZTT
RRGGGH!
THAT'S ENOUGH, DIAMONDBACK.
HRRNG... WHAT ARE YOU DOING?! I PAID YOU FOR THIS TIME, OLD MAN!
YES. YES.
THAT VOICE.
LIKE IF ROT WERE A SOUND.
YOU PAID FOR THE TIME...
RIAN OMES.
...AND OU'LL GET IT.
ONE OF THESE DAYS.
THE VULTURE.

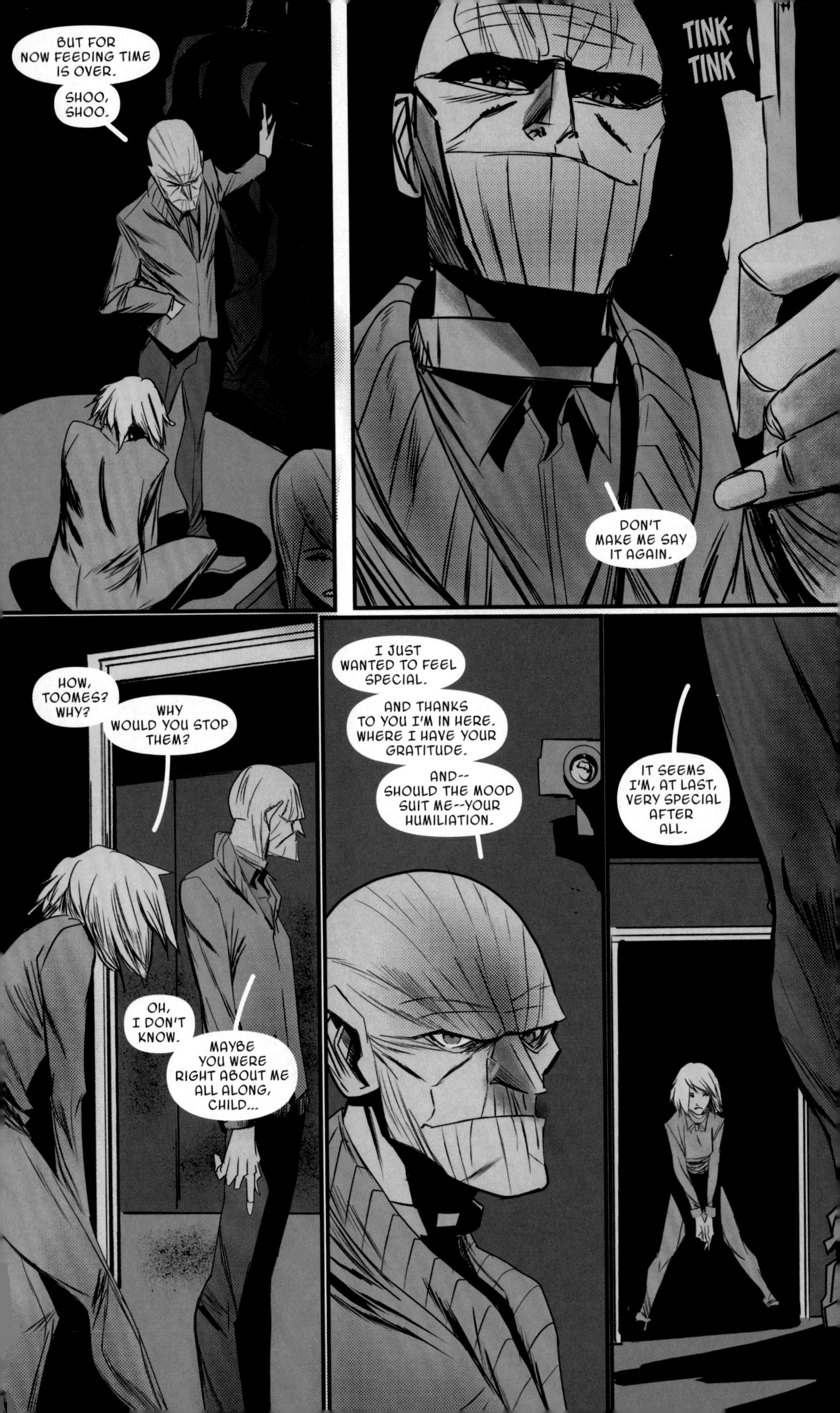
BUT FOR NOW FEEDING TIME IS OVER.
SHOO, SHOO.
TINK-TINK
DON'T MAKE ME SAY IT AGAIN.
HOW, TOOMES? WHY?
WHY WOULD YOU STOP THEM?
OH, I DON'T KNOW.
MAYBE YOU WERE RIGHT ABOUT ME ALL ALONG, CHILD...
I JUST WANTED TO FEEL SPECIAL.
AND THANKS TO YOU I'M IN HERE. WHERE I HAVE YOUR GRATITUDE.
AND--SHOULD THE MOOD SUIT ME--YOUR HUMILIATION.
IT SEEMS I'M, AT LAST, VERY SPECIAL AFTER ALL.

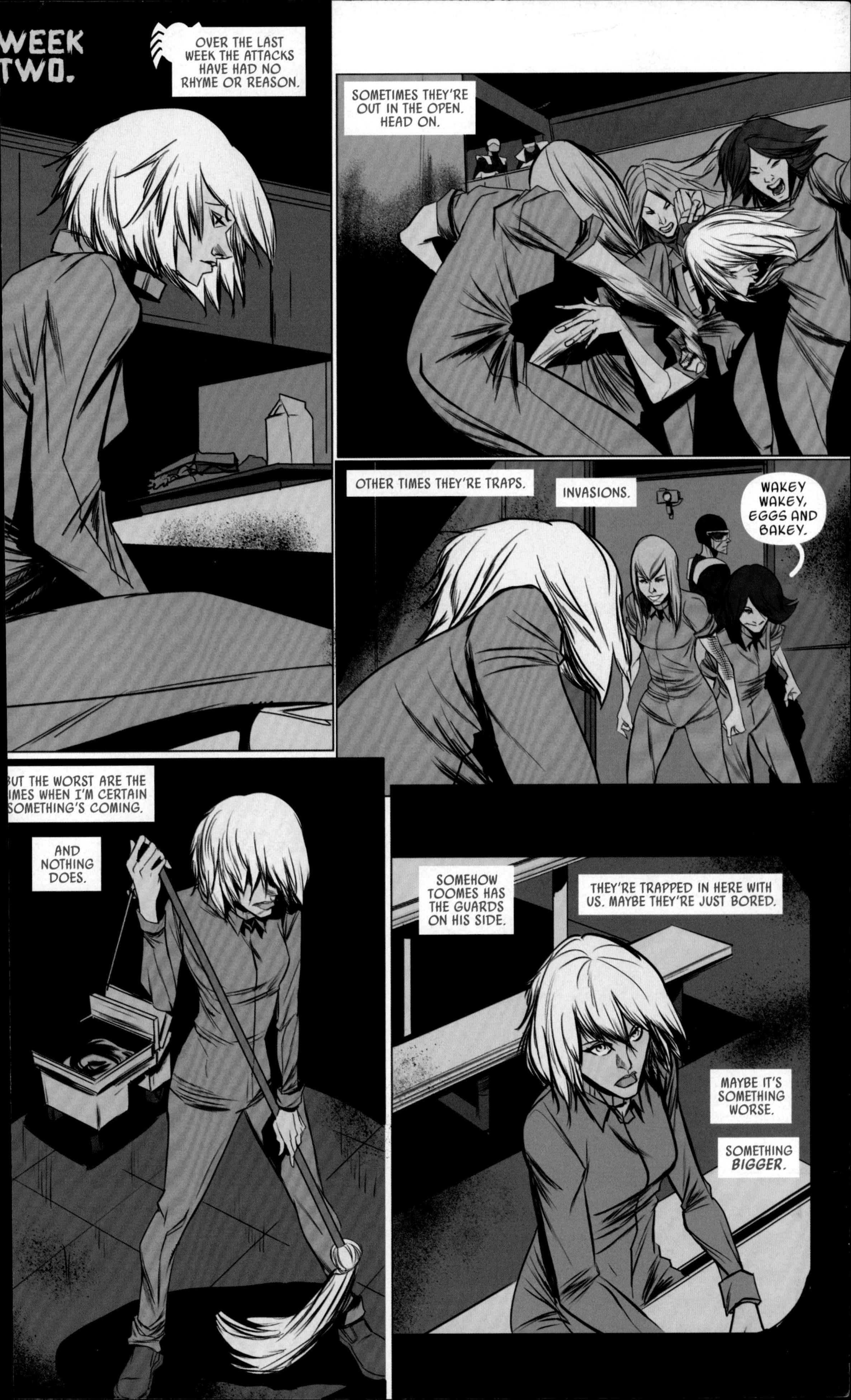
WEEK TWO.
OVER THE LAST WEEK THE ATTACKS HAVE HAD NO RHYME OR REASON.
SOMETIMES THEY'RE OUT IN THE OPEN. HEAD ON.
OTHER TIMES THEY'RE TRAPS.
INVASIONS.
WAKEY WAKEY, EGGS AND BAKEY.
BUT THE WORST ARE THE TIMES WHEN I'M CERTAIN SOMETHING'S COMING.
AND NOTHING DOES.
SOMEHOW TOOMES HAS THE GUARDS ON HIS SIDE.
THEY'RE TRAPPED IN HERE WITH US. MAYBE THEY'RE JUST BORED.
MAYBE IT'S SOMETHING WORSE.
SOMETHING BIGGER.

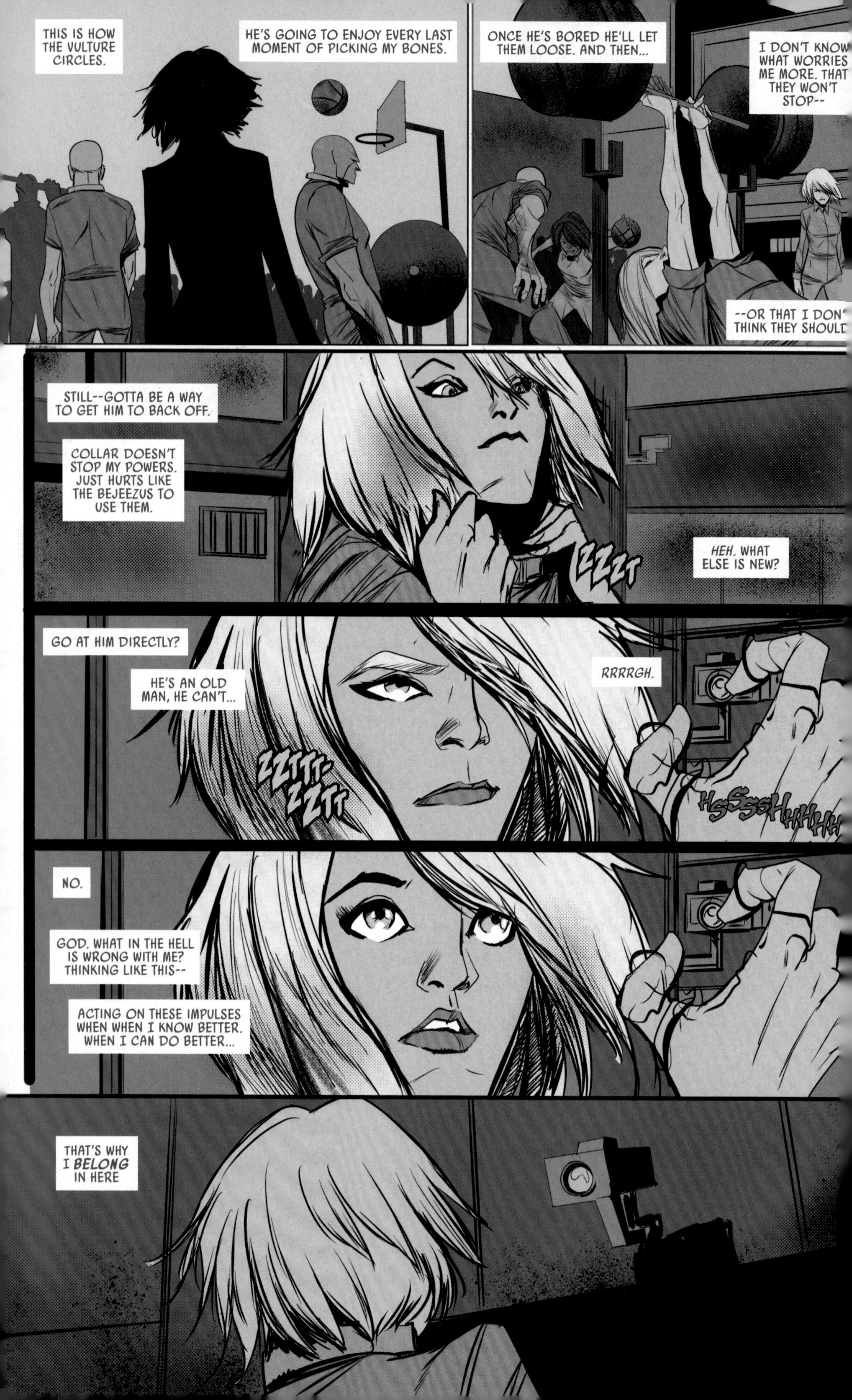
THIS IS HOW THE VULTURE CIRCLES.
HE'S GOING TO ENJOY EVERY LAST MOMENT OF PICKING MY BONES.
ONCE HE'S BORED HE'LL LET THEM LOOSE. AND THEN...
I DON'T KNOW WHAT WORRIES ME MORE. THAT THEY WON'T STOP--
--OR THAT I DON'T THINK THEY SHOULD
STILL--GOTTA BE A WAY TO GET HIM TO BACK OFF.
COLLAR DOESN'T STOP MY POWERS. JUST HURTS LIKE THE BEJEEZUS TO USE THEM.
ZZZT
HEH. WHAT ELSE IS NEW?
GO AT HIM DIRECTLY?
HE'S AN OLD MAN, HE CAN'T...
RRRRGH.
ZZTTT-ZZTT
HSSSSHHHHHH
NO.
GOD. WHAT IN THE HELL IS WRONG WITH ME? THINKING LIKE THIS--
ACTING ON THESE IMPULSES WHEN WHEN I KNOW BETTER. WHEN I CAN DO BETTER...
THAT'S WHY I *BELONG* IN HERE

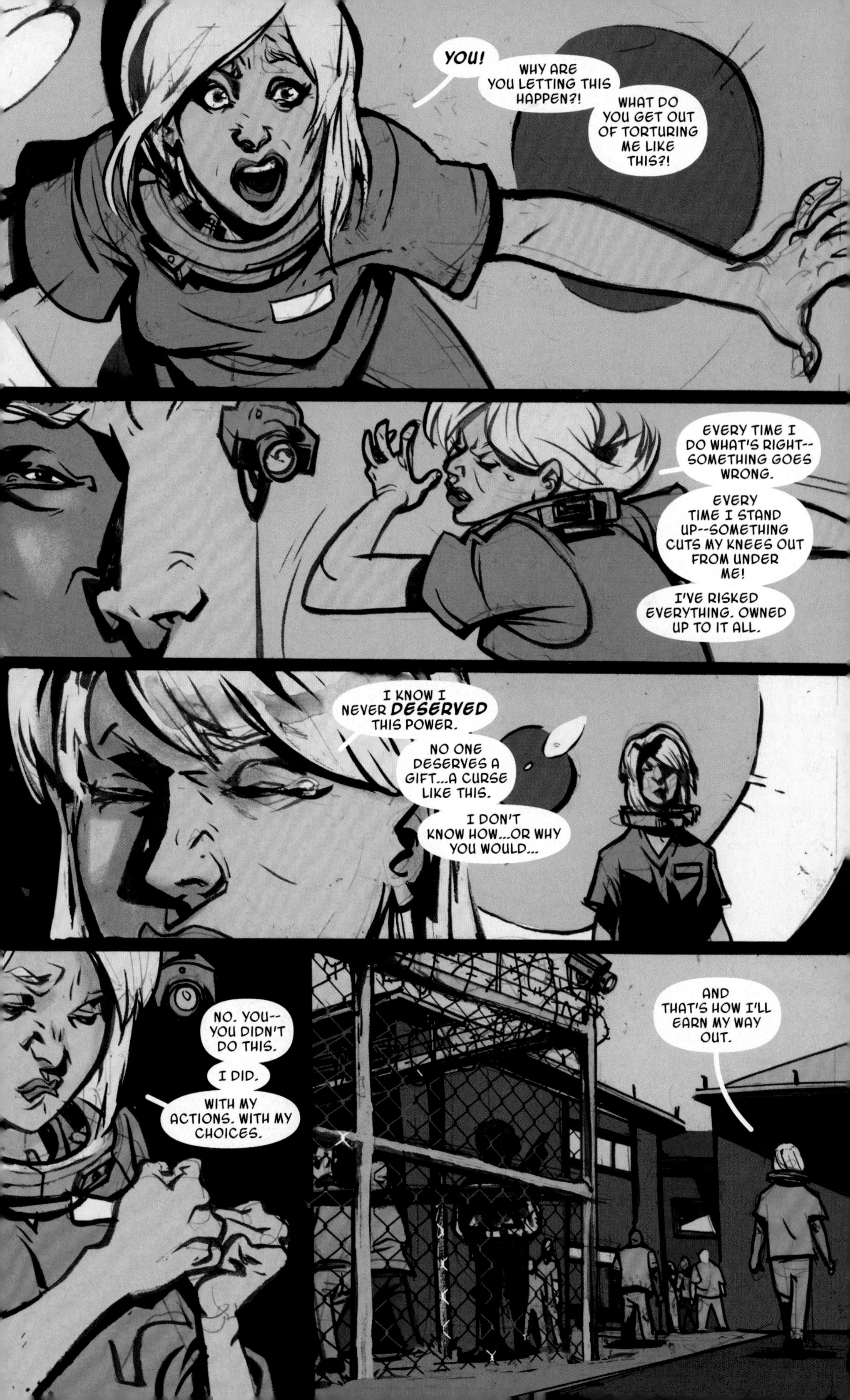
YOU!
WHY ARE YOU LETTING THIS HAPPEN?!
WHAT DO YOU GET OUT OF TORTURING ME LIKE THIS?!
EVERY TIME I DO WHAT'S RIGHT-- SOMETHING GOES WRONG.
EVERY TIME I STAND UP--SOMETHING CUTS MY KNEES OUT FROM UNDER ME!
I'VE RISKED EVERYTHING. OWNED UP TO IT ALL.
I KNOW I NEVER DESERVED THIS POWER.
NO ONE DESERVES A GIFT...A CURSE LIKE THIS.
I DON'T KNOW HOW...OR WHY YOU WOULD...
NO. YOU-- YOU DIDN'T DO THIS.
I DID.
WITH MY ACTIONS. WITH MY CHOICES.
AND THAT'S HOW I'LL EARN MY WAY OUT.

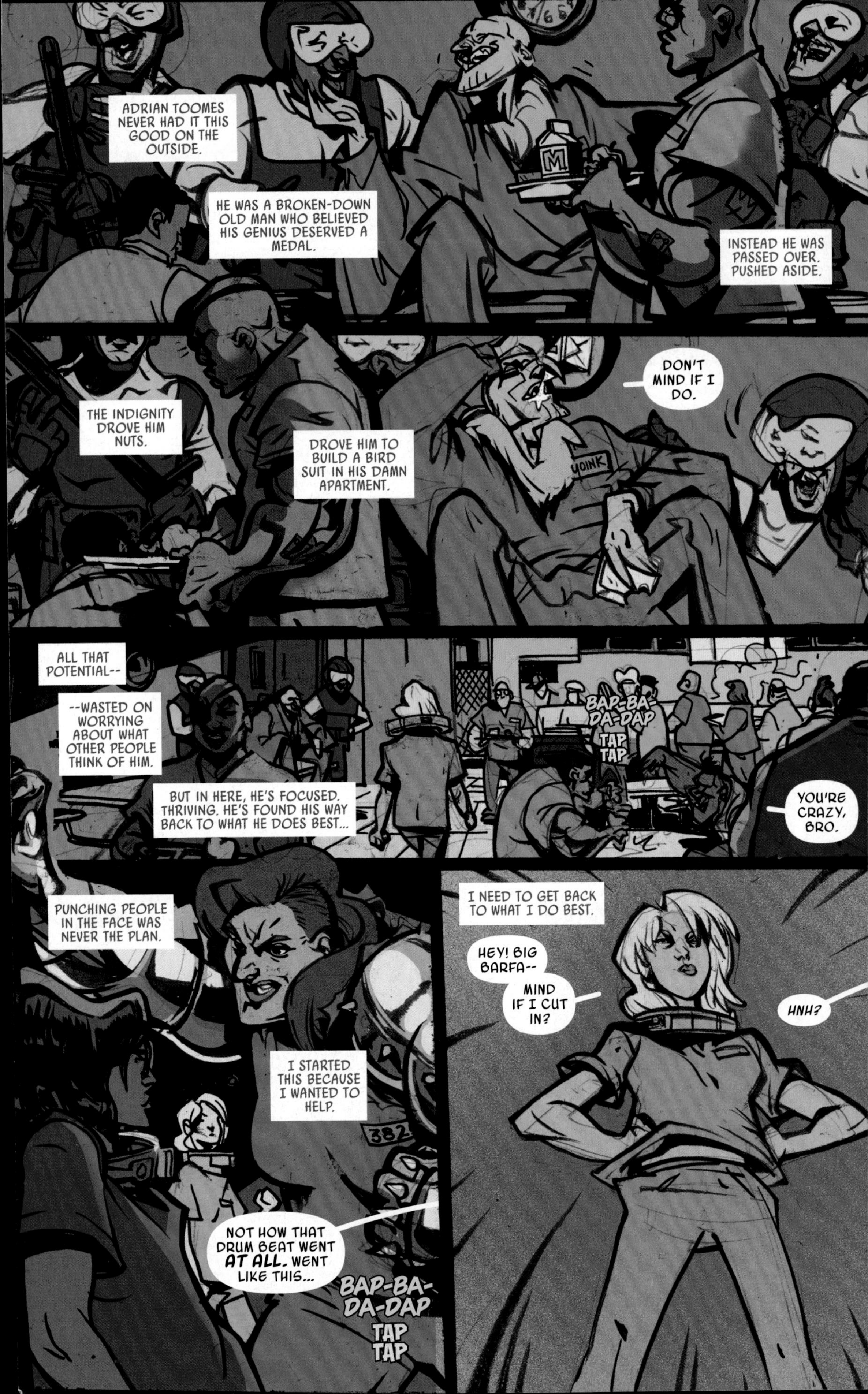
ADRIAN TOOMES NEVER HAD IT THIS GOOD ON THE OUTSIDE.
HE WAS A BROKEN-DOWN OLD MAN WHO BELIEVED HIS GENIUS DESERVED A MEDAL.
INSTEAD HE WAS PASSED OVER. PUSHED ASIDE.
THE INDIGNITY DROVE HIM NUTS.
DROVE HIM TO BUILD A BIRD SUIT IN HIS DAMN APARTMENT.
YOINK
DON'T MIND IF I DO.
ALL THAT POTENTIAL--
--WASTED ON WORRYING ABOUT WHAT OTHER PEOPLE THINK OF HIM.
BUT IN HERE, HE'S FOCUSED. THRIVING. HE'S FOUND HIS WAY BACK TO WHAT HE DOES BEST...
BAP-BA-DA-DAP
TAP TAP
YOU'RE CRAZY, BRO.
PUNCHING PEOPLE IN THE FACE WAS NEVER THE PLAN.
I STARTED THIS BECAUSE I WANTED TO HELP.
NOT HOW THAT DRUM BEAT WENT AT ALL. WENT LIKE THIS...
BAP-BA-DA-DAP
TAP TAP
I NEED TO GET BACK TO WHAT I DO BEST.
HEY! BIG BARFA--
MIND IF I CUT IN?
HNH?

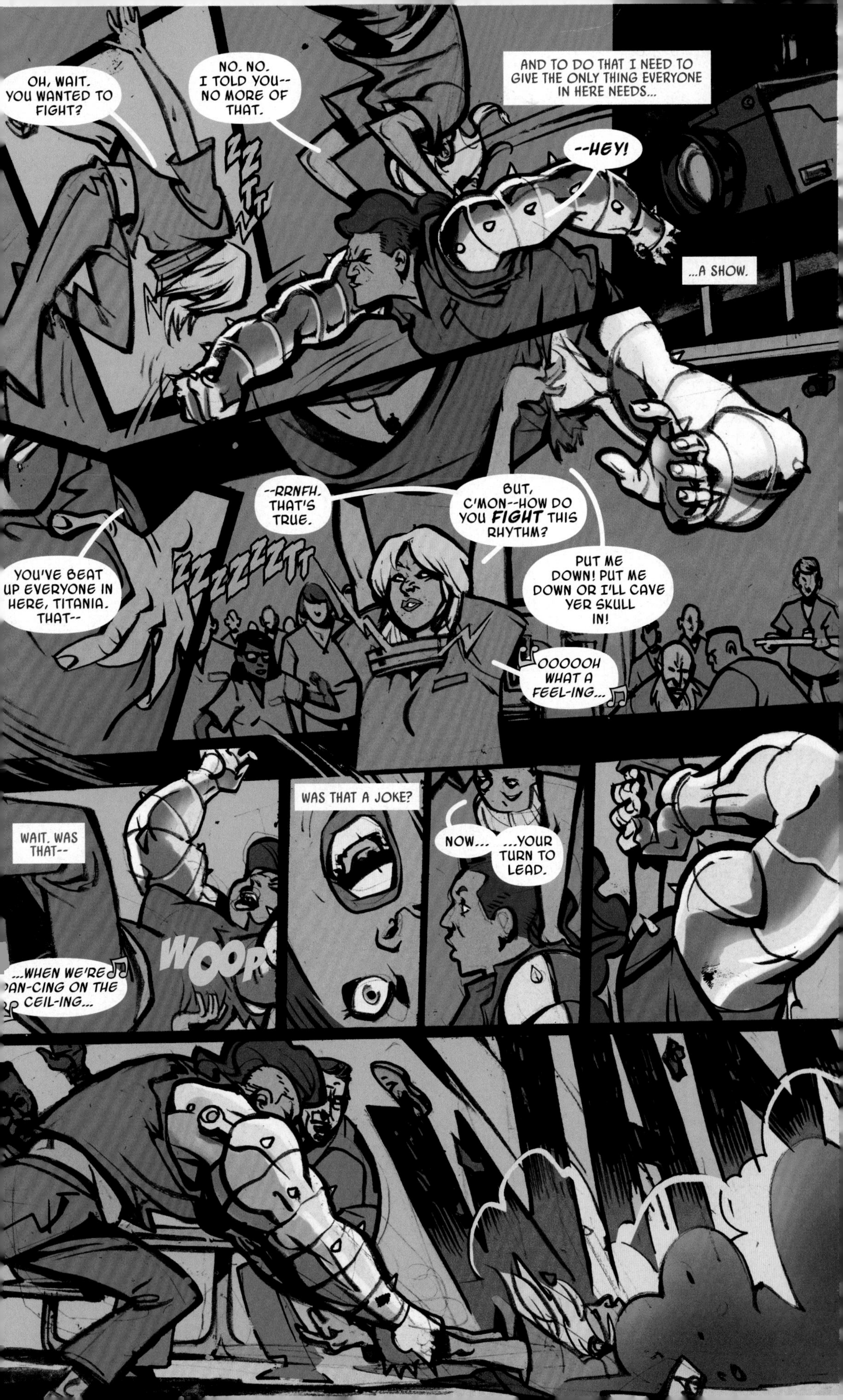
OH, WAIT. YOU WANTED TO FIGHT?
NO. NO. I TOLD YOU-- NO MORE OF THAT.
ZZZTT
AND TO DO THAT I NEED TO GIVE THE ONLY THING EVERYONE IN HERE NEEDS...
--HEY!
...A SHOW.
--RRNFH. THAT'S TRUE.
BUT, C'MON--HOW DO YOU FIGHT THIS RHYTHM?
YOU'VE BEAT UP EVERYONE IN HERE, TITANIA. THAT--
ZZZZZZTT
PUT ME DOWN! PUT ME DOWN OR I'LL CAVE YER SKULL IN!
OOOOOH WHAT A FEEL-ING...
WAIT. WAS THAT--
WOOP
...WHEN WE'RE DAN-CING ON THE CEIL-ING...
WAS THAT A JOKE?
NOW...
...YOUR TURN TO LEAD.

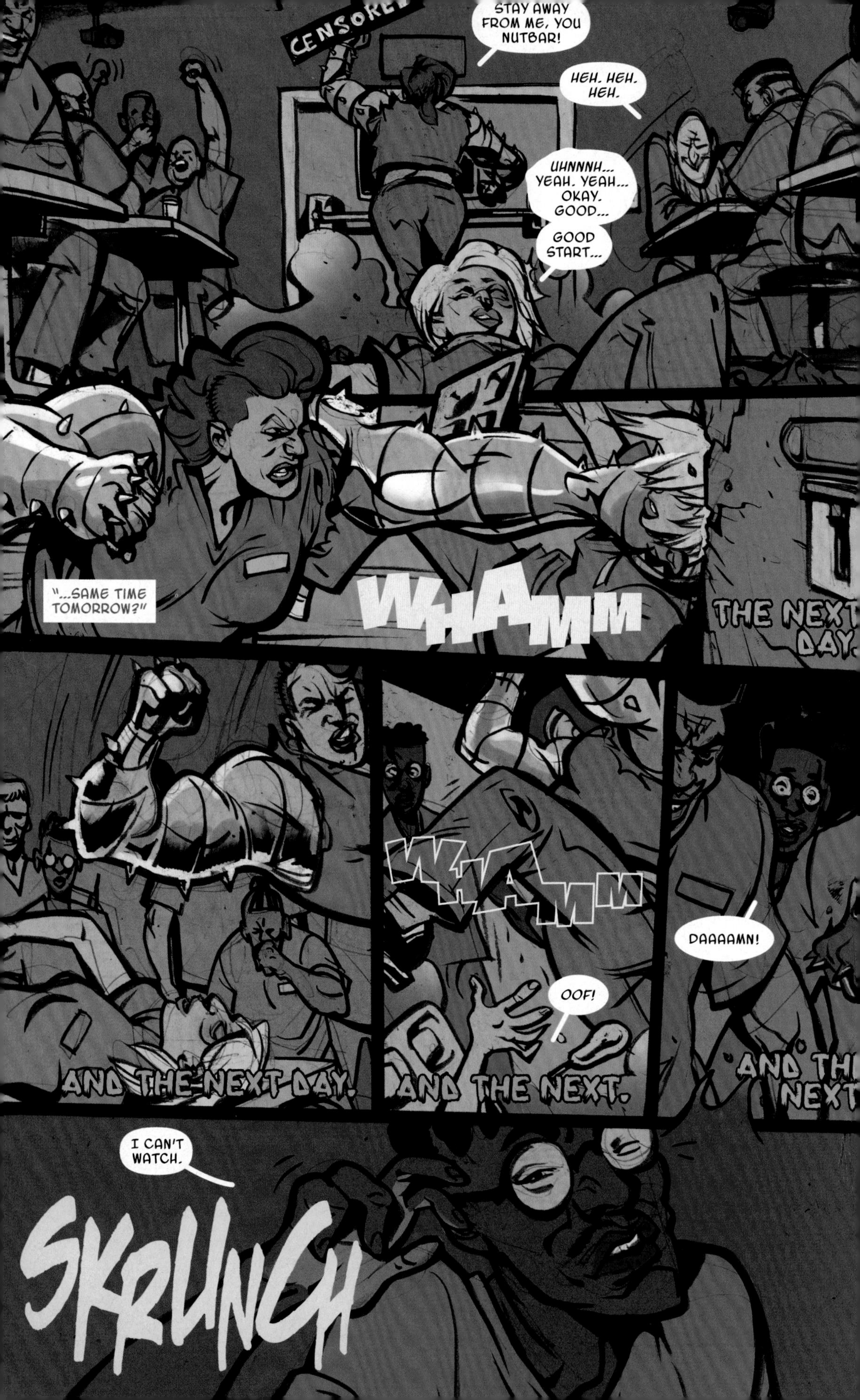
CENSORED
STAY AWAY FROM ME, YOU NUTBAR!
HEH. HEH. HEH.
UHNNNH... YEAH. YEAH... OKAY. GOOD...
GOOD START...
"...SAME TIME TOMORROW?"
WHAMM
THE NEXT DAY.
AND THE NEXT DAY.
WHAMM
OOF!
AND THE NEXT.
DAAAAMN!
AND THE NEXT
I CAN'T WATCH.
SKRUNCH

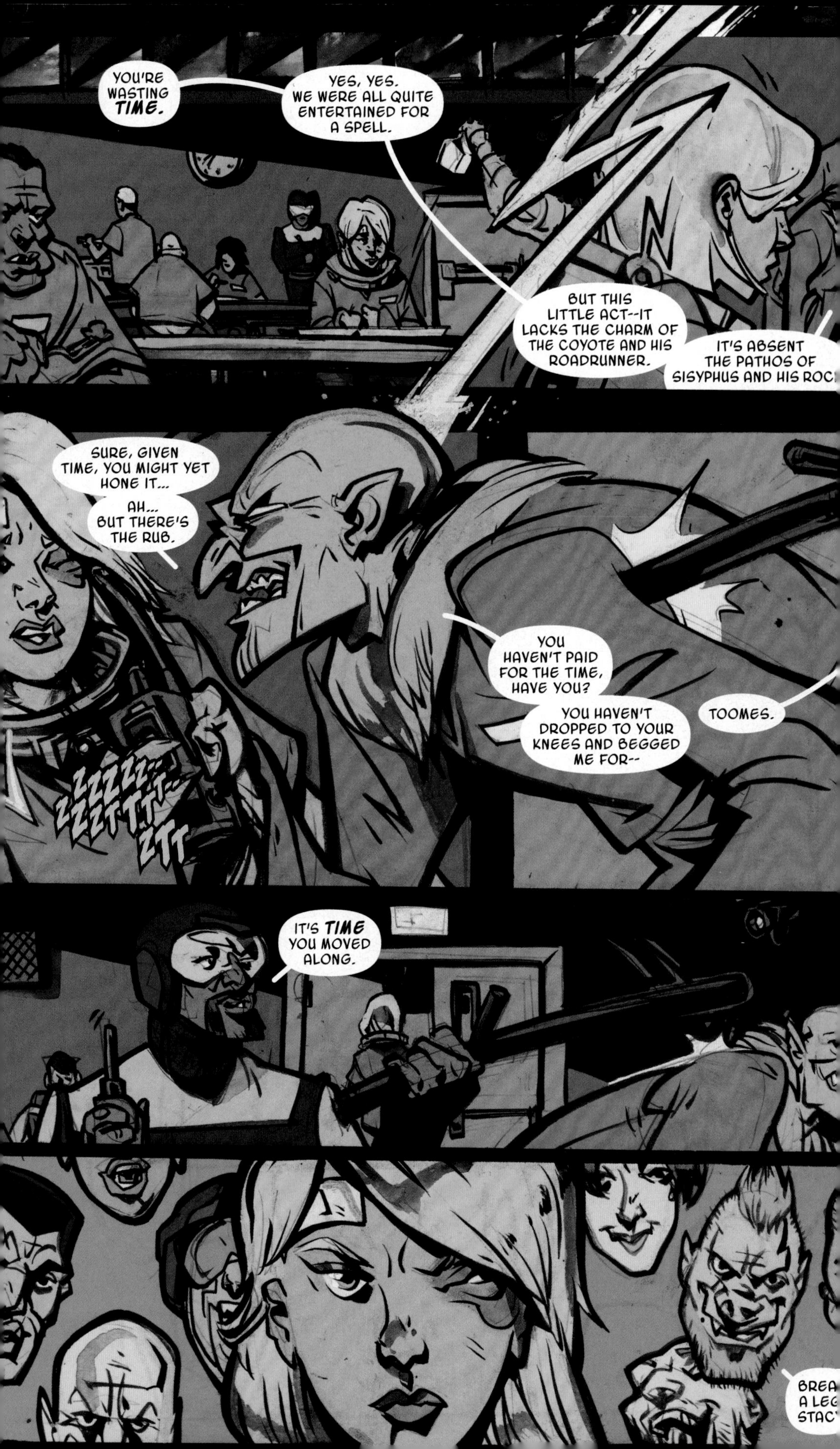
YOU'RE WASTING TIME.
YES, YES. WE WERE ALL QUITE ENTERTAINED FOR A SPELL.
BUT THIS LITTLE ACT--IT LACKS THE CHARM OF THE COYOTE AND HIS ROADRUNNER.
IT'S ABSENT THE PATHOS OF SISYPHUS AND HIS ROC
SURE, GIVEN TIME, YOU MIGHT YET HONE IT...
AH... BUT THERE'S THE RUB.
YOU HAVEN'T PAID FOR THE TIME, HAVE YOU?
YOU HAVEN'T DROPPED TO YOUR KNEES AND BEGGED ME FOR--
TOOMES.
ZZZZZZ-ZZZTTTT-ZTT
IT'S TIME YOU MOVED ALONG.
BREA A LEG STAC

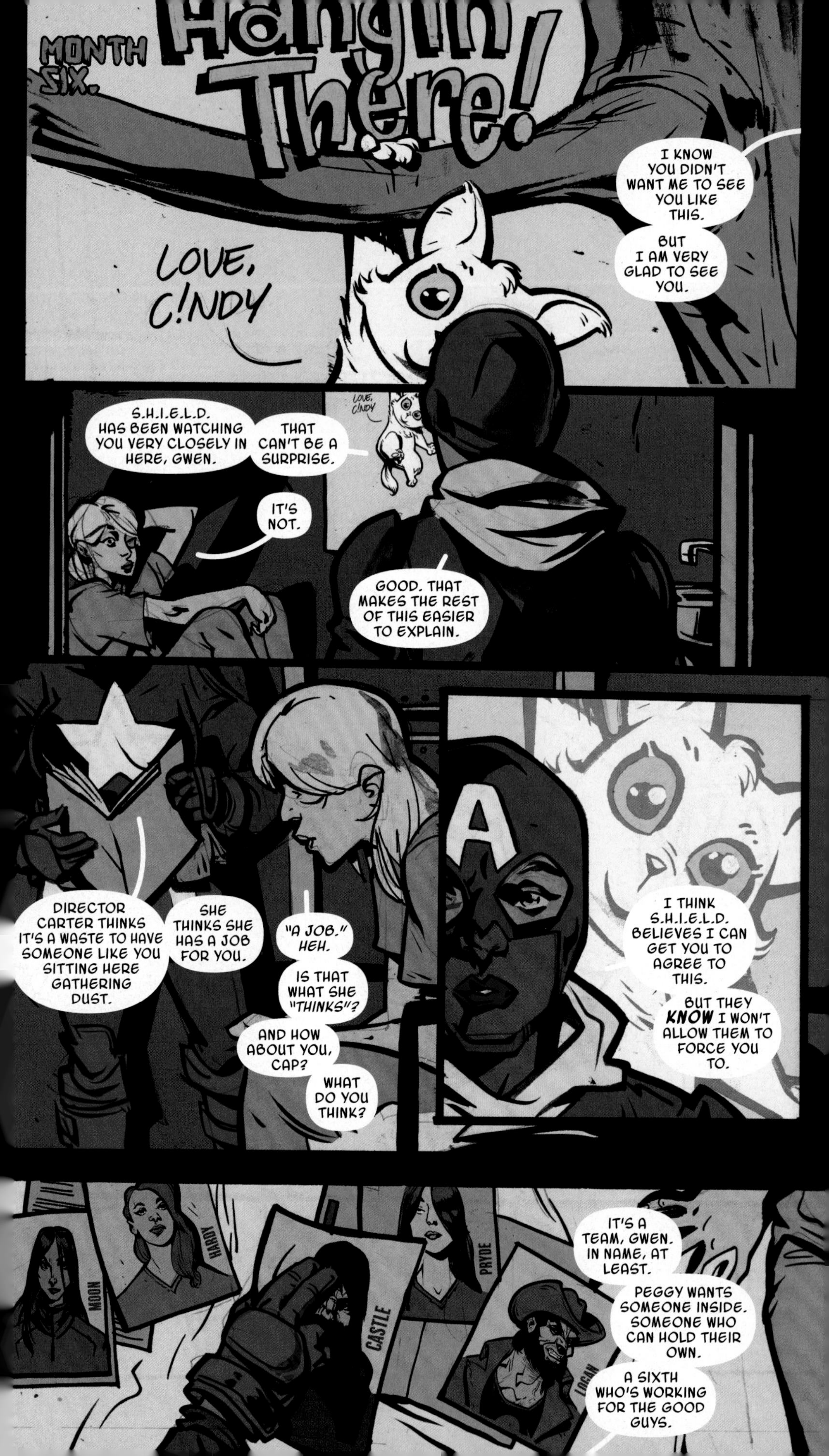
MONTH SIX.
Hangin' There!
LOVE, C!NDY
I KNOW YOU DIDN'T WANT ME TO SEE YOU LIKE THIS.
BUT I AM VERY GLAD TO SEE YOU.
S.H.I.E.L.D. HAS BEEN WATCHING YOU VERY CLOSELY IN HERE, GWEN.
THAT CAN'T BE A SURPRISE.
LOVE, C!NDY
IT'S NOT.
GOOD. THAT MAKES THE REST OF THIS EASIER TO EXPLAIN.
DIRECTOR CARTER THINKS IT'S A WASTE TO HAVE SOMEONE LIKE YOU SITTING HERE GATHERING DUST.
SHE THINKS SHE HAS A JOB FOR YOU.
"A JOB." HEH.
IS THAT WHAT SHE "THINKS"?
AND HOW ABOUT YOU, CAP?
WHAT DO YOU THINK?
I THINK S.H.I.E.L.D. BELIEVES I CAN GET YOU TO AGREE TO THIS.
BUT THEY KNOW I WON'T ALLOW THEM TO FORCE YOU TO.
MOON
HARDY
CASTLE
PRYDE
LOGAN
IT'S A TEAM, GWEN. IN NAME, AT LEAST.
PEGGY WANTS SOMEONE INSIDE. SOMEONE WHO CAN HOLD THEIR OWN.
A SIXTH WHO'S WORKING FOR THE GOOD GUYS.

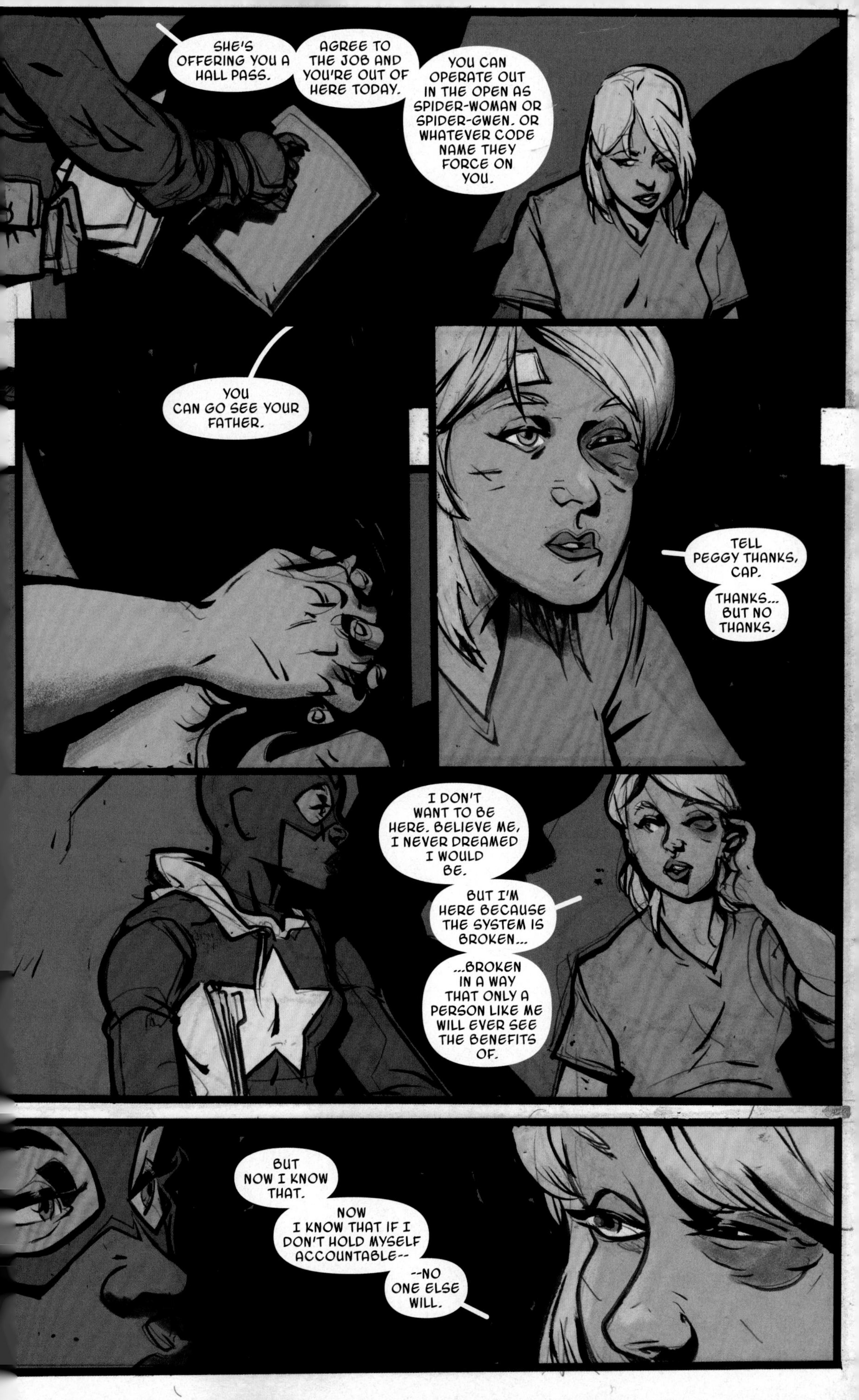

SHE'S OFFERING YOU A HALL PASS.
AGREE TO THE JOB AND YOU'RE OUT OF HERE TODAY.
YOU CAN OPERATE OUT IN THE OPEN AS SPIDER-WOMAN OR SPIDER-GWEN. OR WHATEVER CODE NAME THEY FORCE ON YOU.
YOU CAN GO SEE YOUR FATHER.
TELL PEGGY THANKS, CAP.
THANKS... BUT NO THANKS.
I DON'T WANT TO BE HERE. BELIEVE ME, I NEVER DREAMED I WOULD BE.
BUT I'M HERE BECAUSE THE SYSTEM IS BROKEN...
...BROKEN IN A WAY THAT ONLY A PERSON LIKE ME WILL EVER SEE THE BENEFITS OF.
BUT NOW I KNOW THAT.
NOW I KNOW THAT IF I DON'T HOLD MYSELF ACCOUNTABLE--
--NO ONE ELSE WILL.

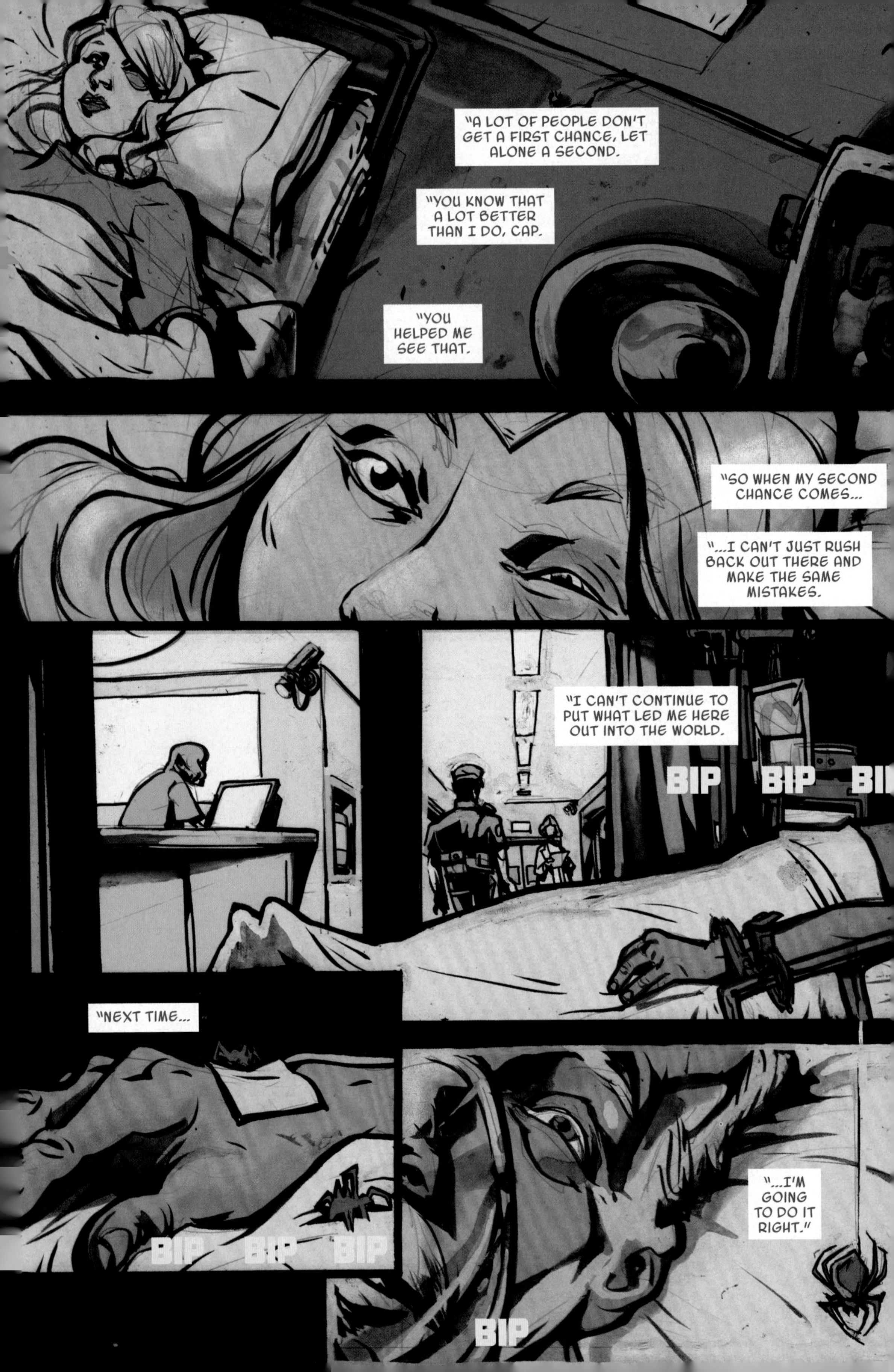
"A LOT OF PEOPLE DON'T GET A FIRST CHANCE, LET ALONE A SECOND.
"YOU KNOW THAT A LOT BETTER THAN I DO, CAP.
"YOU HELPED ME SEE THAT.
"SO WHEN MY SECOND CHANCE COMES...
"...I CAN'T JUST RUSH BACK OUT THERE AND MAKE THE SAME MISTAKES.
"I CAN'T CONTINUE TO PUT WHAT LED ME HERE OUT INTO THE WORLD.
BIP BIP BI
"NEXT TIME...
BIP BIP BIP
"...I'M GOING TO DO IT RIGHT."
BIP

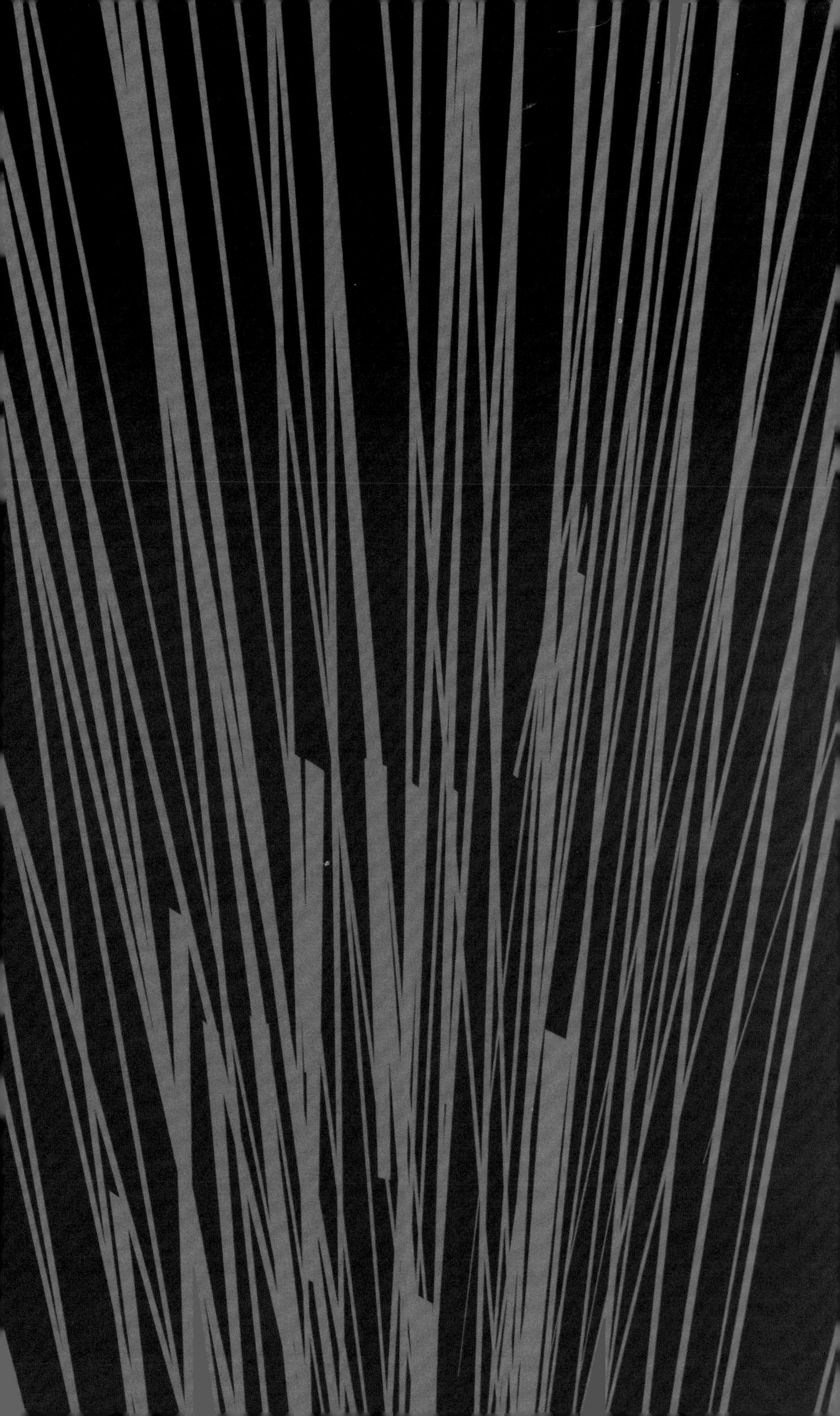

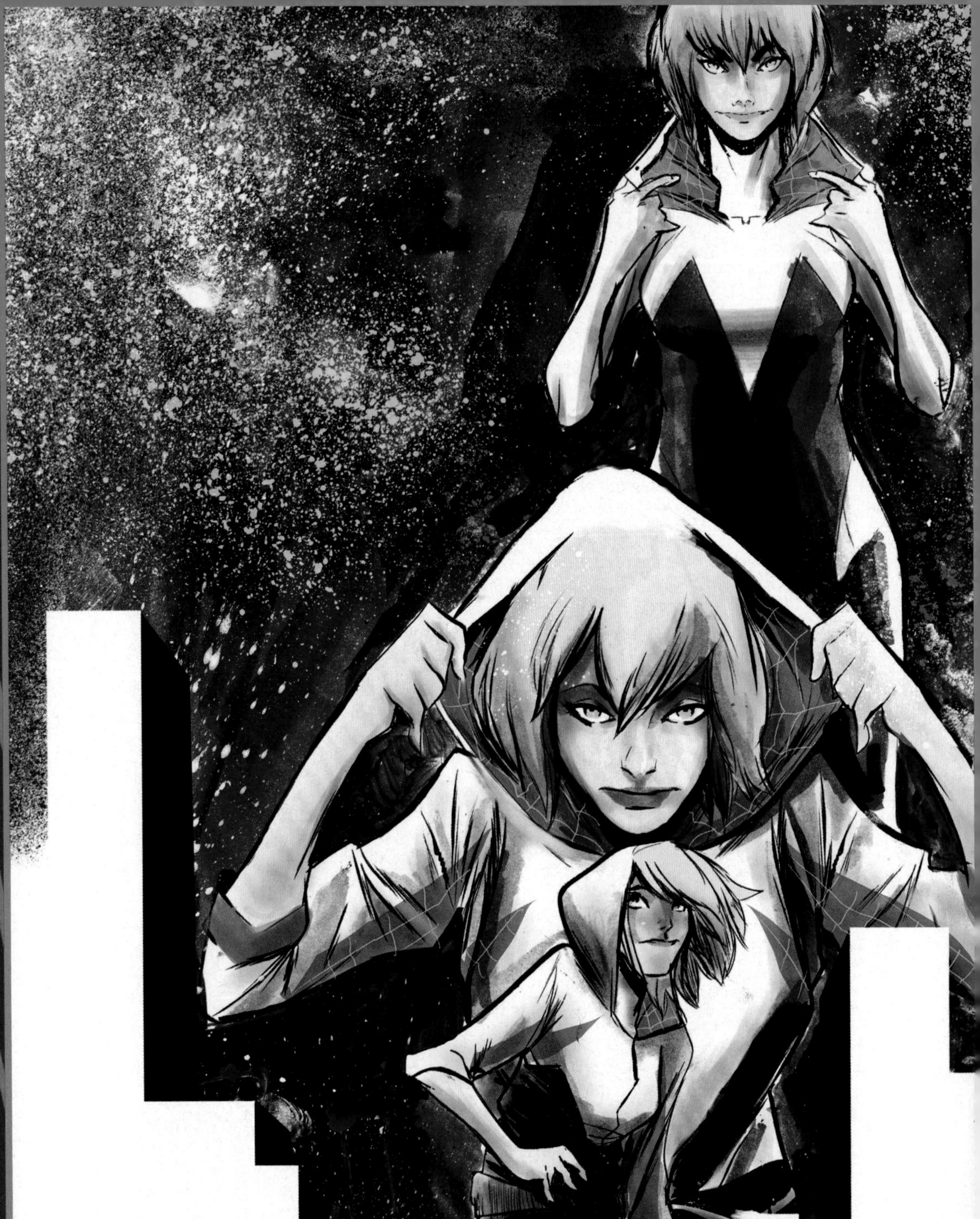

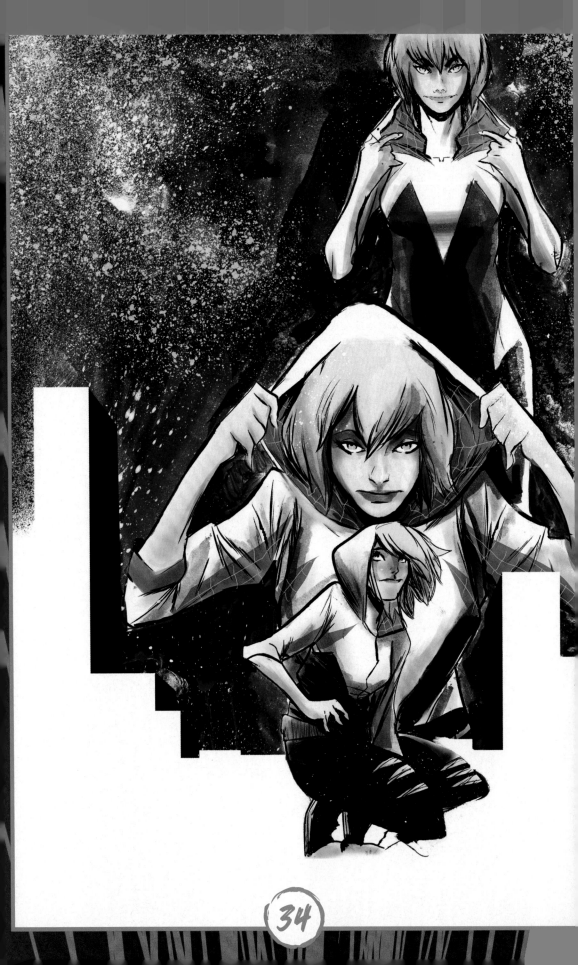

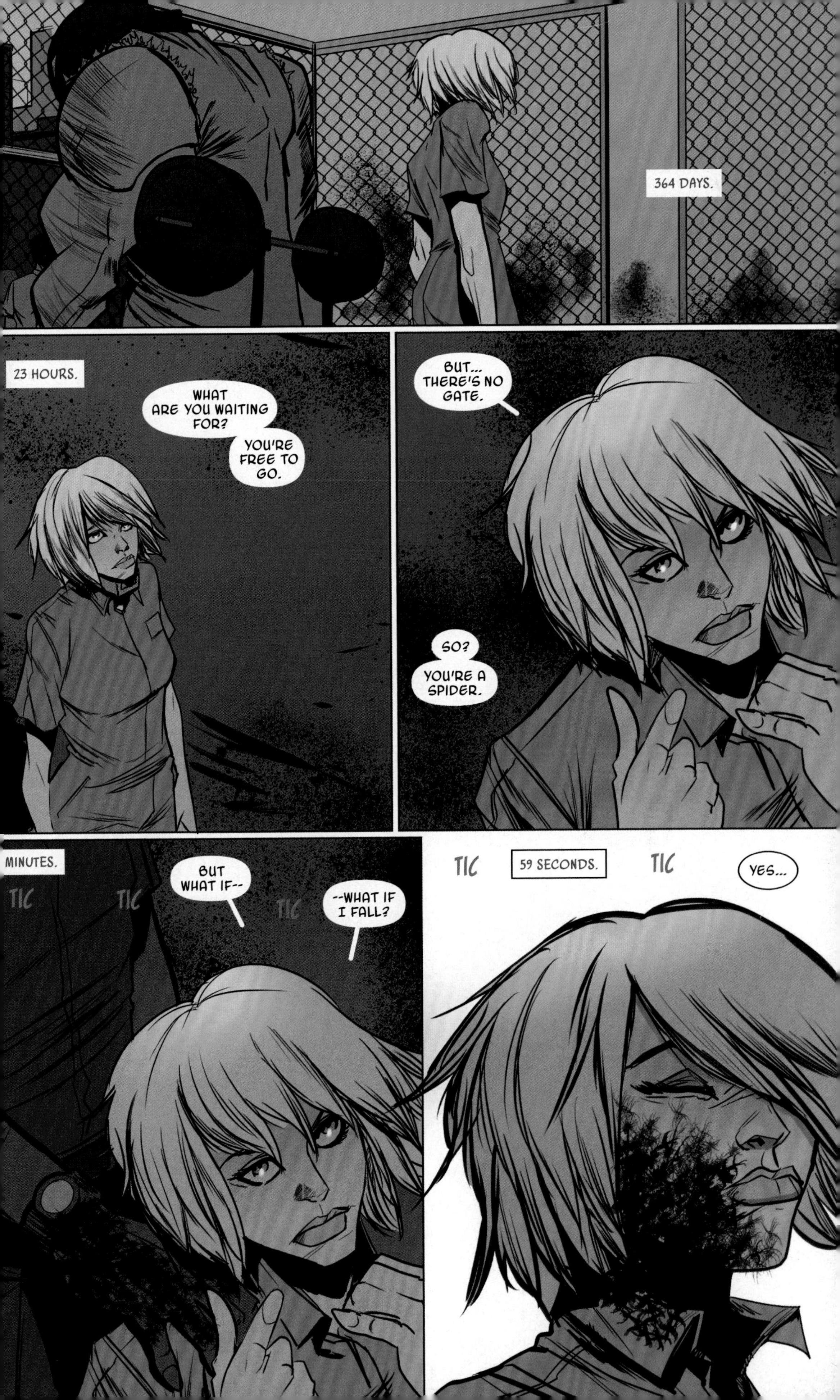
364 DAYS.
23 HOURS.
WHAT ARE YOU WAITING FOR?
YOU'RE FREE TO GO.
BUT... THERE'S NO GATE.
SO?
YOU'RE A SPIDER.
MINUTES.
TIC
TIC
BUT WHAT IF--
TIC
--WHAT IF I FALL?
TIC
59 SECONDS.
TIC
YES...

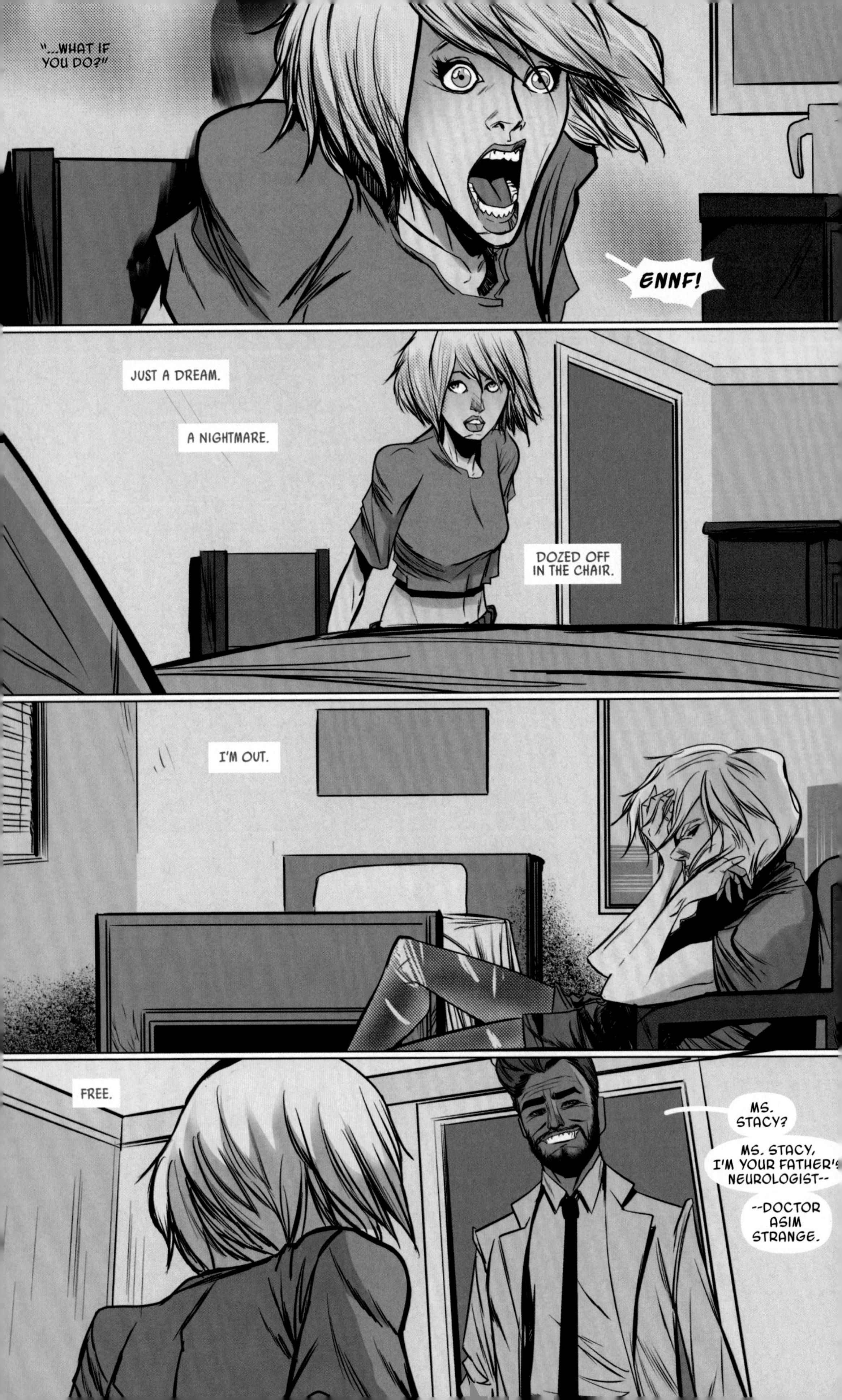
"...WHAT IF YOU DO?"
ENNF!
JUST A DREAM.
A NIGHTMARE.
DOZED OFF IN THE CHAIR.
I'M OUT.
FREE.
MS. STACY?
MS. STACY, I'M YOUR FATHER'S NEUROLOGIST--
--DOCTOR ASIM STRANGE.

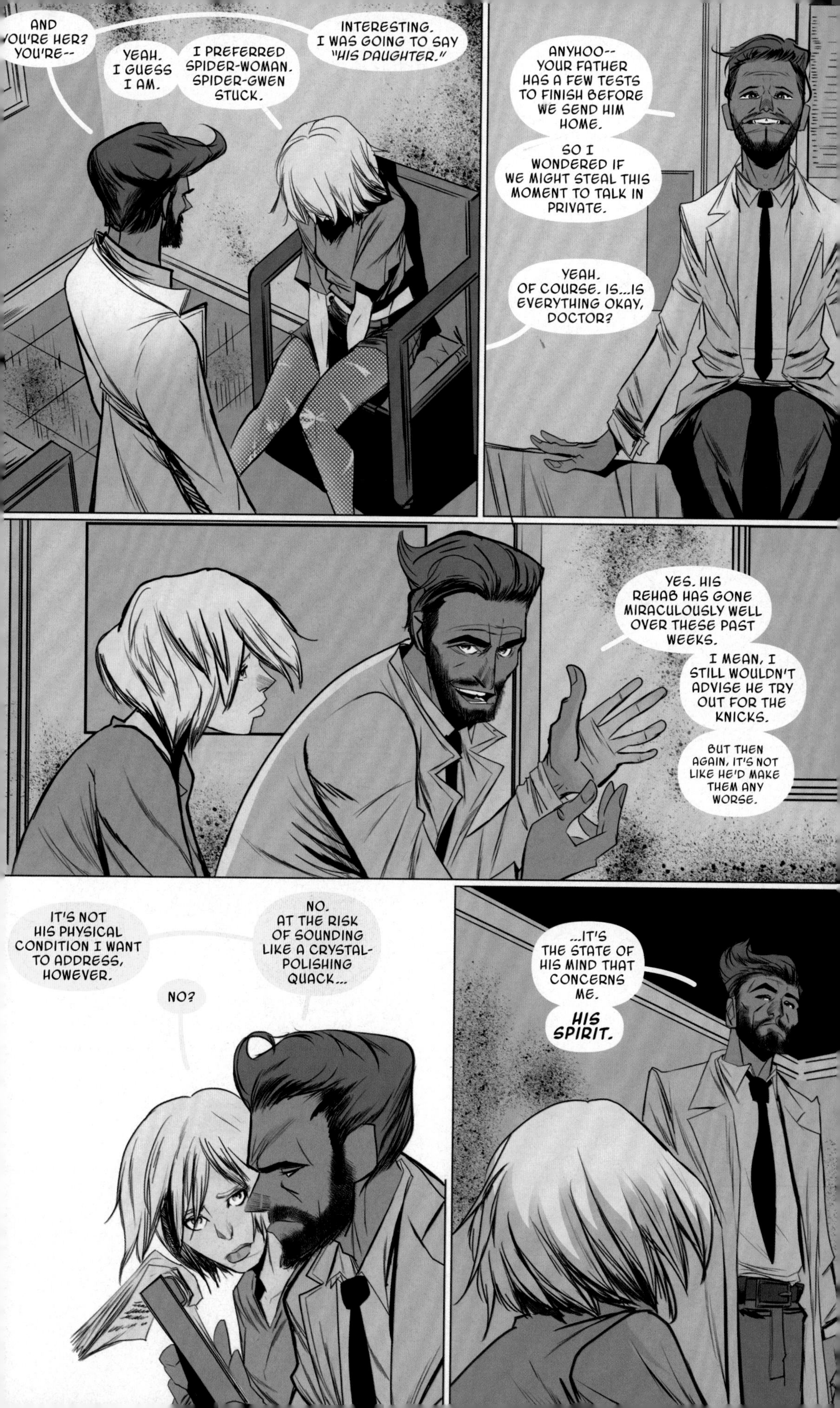
AND YOU'RE HER? YOU'RE--
YEAH. I GUESS I AM.
I PREFERRED SPIDER-WOMAN. SPIDER-GWEN STUCK.
INTERESTING. I WAS GOING TO SAY "HIS DAUGHTER."
ANYHOO-- YOUR FATHER HAS A FEW TESTS TO FINISH BEFORE WE SEND HIM HOME.
SO I WONDERED IF WE MIGHT STEAL THIS MOMENT TO TALK IN PRIVATE.
YEAH. OF COURSE. IS...IS EVERYTHING OKAY, DOCTOR?
YES. HIS REHAB HAS GONE MIRACULOUSLY WELL OVER THESE PAST WEEKS.
I MEAN, I STILL WOULDN'T ADVISE HE TRY OUT FOR THE KNICKS.
BUT THEN AGAIN, IT'S NOT LIKE HE'D MAKE THEM ANY WORSE.
IT'S NOT HIS PHYSICAL CONDITION I WANT TO ADDRESS, HOWEVER.
NO?
NO. AT THE RISK OF SOUNDING LIKE A CRYSTAL-POLISHING QUACK...
...IT'S THE STATE OF HIS MIND THAT CONCERNS ME.
HIS SPIRIT.

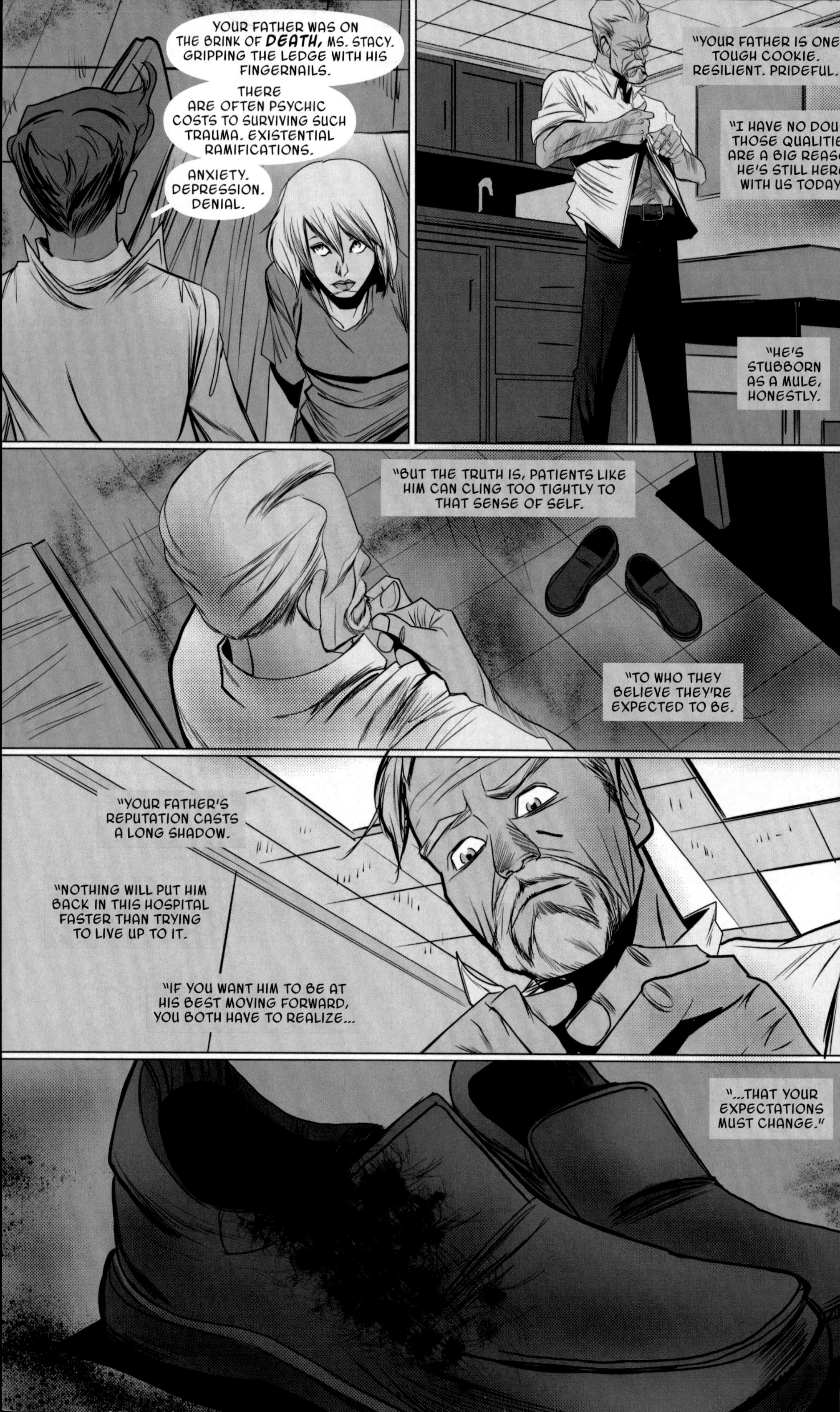
YOUR FATHER WAS ON THE BRINK OF **DEATH,** MS. STACY. GRIPPING THE LEDGE WITH HIS FINGERNAILS.
THERE ARE OFTEN PSYCHIC COSTS TO SURVIVING SUCH TRAUMA. EXISTENTIAL RAMIFICATIONS.
ANXIETY. DEPRESSION. DENIAL.
"YOUR FATHER IS ONE TOUGH COOKIE. RESILIENT. PRIDEFUL.
"I HAVE NO DOU THOSE QUALITIE ARE A BIG REAS HE'S STILL HER WITH US TODAY
"HE'S STUBBORN AS A MULE, HONESTLY.
"BUT THE TRUTH IS, PATIENTS LIKE HIM CAN CLING TOO TIGHTLY TO THAT SENSE OF SELF.
"TO WHO THEY BELIEVE THEY'RE EXPECTED TO BE.
"YOUR FATHER'S REPUTATION CASTS A LONG SHADOW.
"NOTHING WILL PUT HIM BACK IN THIS HOSPITAL FASTER THAN TRYING TO LIVE UP TO IT.
"IF YOU WANT HIM TO BE AT HIS BEST MOVING FORWARD, YOU BOTH HAVE TO REALIZE...
"...THAT YOUR EXPECTATIONS MUST CHANGE."

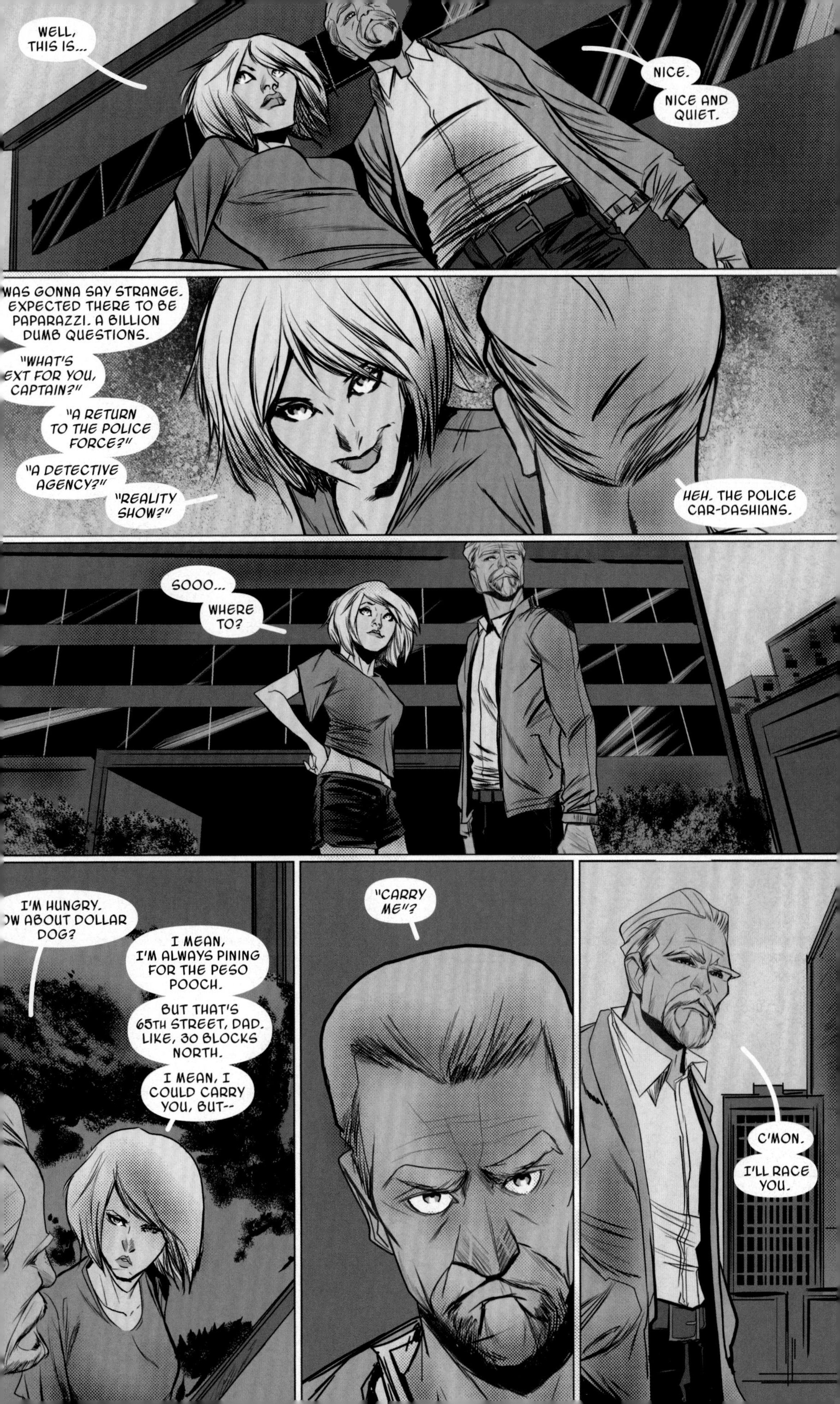
WELL, THIS IS...
NICE.
NICE AND QUIET.
WAS GONNA SAY STRANGE. EXPECTED THERE TO BE PAPARAZZI. A BILLION DUMB QUESTIONS.
"WHAT'S EXT FOR YOU, CAPTAIN?"
"A RETURN TO THE POLICE FORCE?"
"A DETECTIVE AGENCY?"
"REALITY SHOW?"
HEH. THE POLICE CAR-DASHIANS.
SOOO...
WHERE TO?
I'M HUNGRY. OW ABOUT DOLLAR DOG?
I MEAN, I'M ALWAYS PINING FOR THE PESO POOCH.
BUT THAT'S 65TH STREET, DAD. LIKE, 30 BLOCKS NORTH.
I MEAN, I COULD CARRY YOU, BUT--
"CARRY ME"?
C'MON.
I'LL RACE YOU.

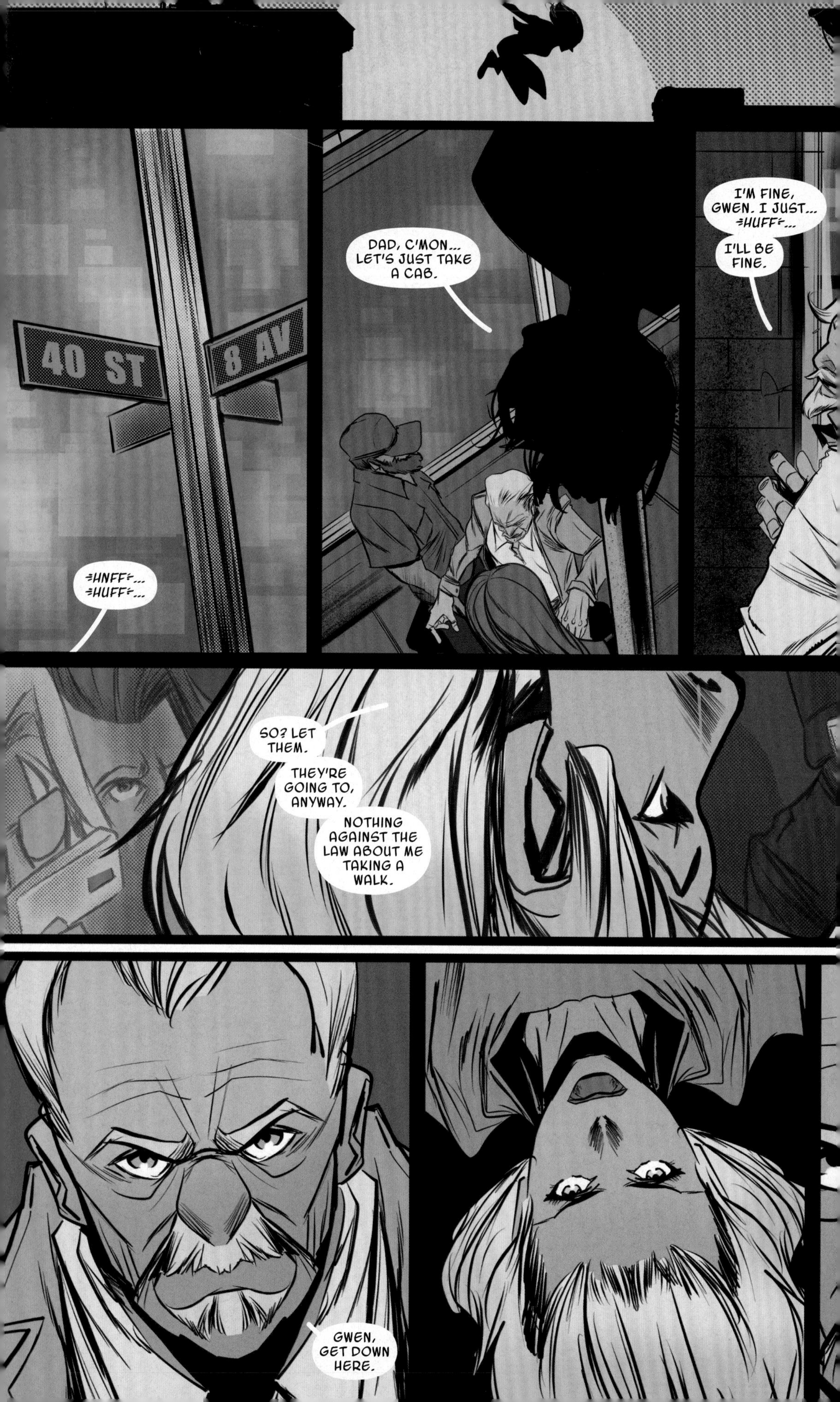
40 ST
8 AV
=HNFF=...
=HUFF=...
DAD, C'MON... LET'S JUST TAKE A CAB.
I'M FINE, GWEN. I JUST... =HUFF=...
I'LL BE FINE.
SO? LET THEM.
THEY'RE GOING TO, ANYWAY.
NOTHING AGAINST THE LAW ABOUT ME TAKING A WALK.
GWEN, GET DOWN HERE.

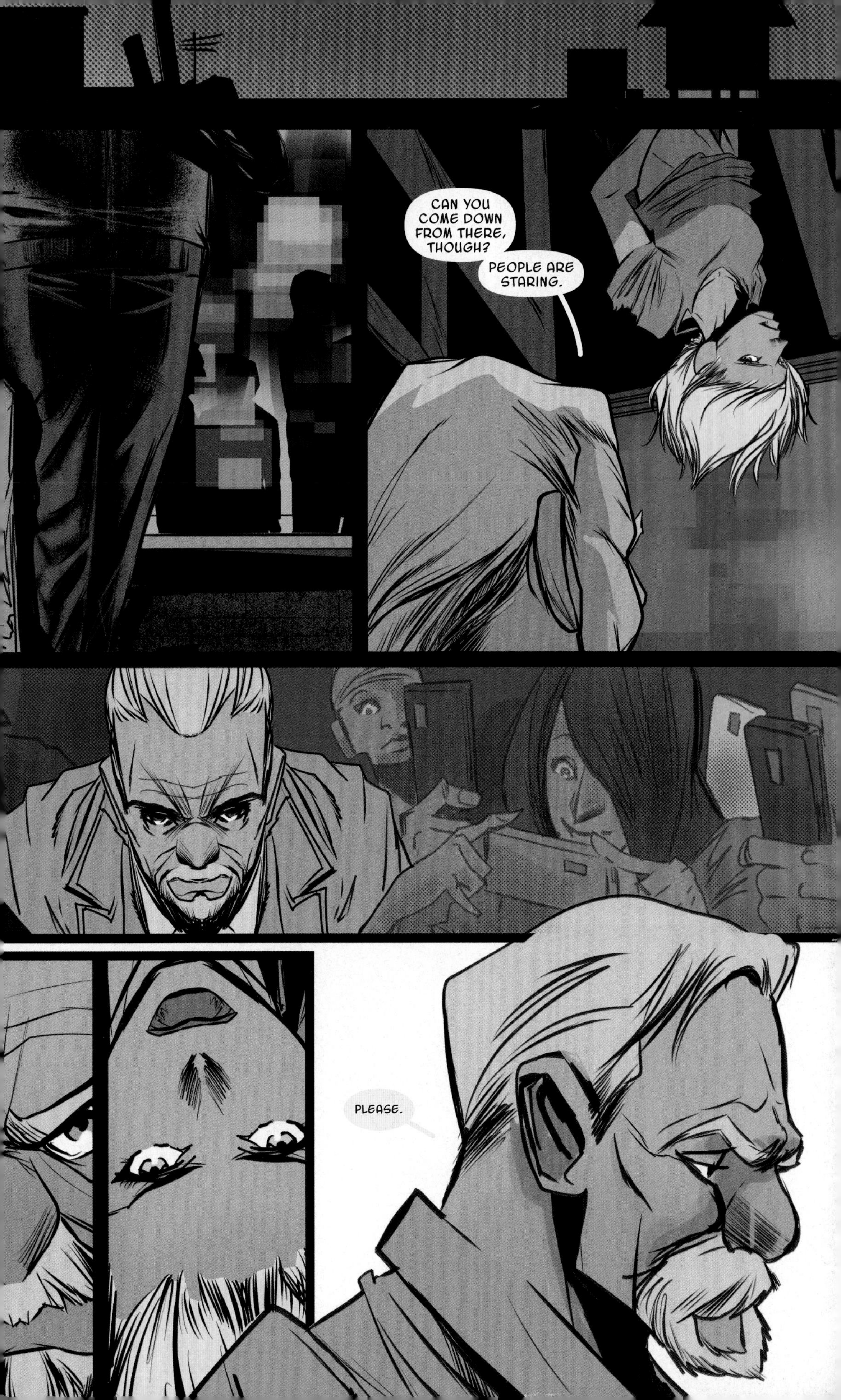
CAN YOU COME DOWN FROM THERE, THOUGH?
PEOPLE ARE STARING.
PLEASE.

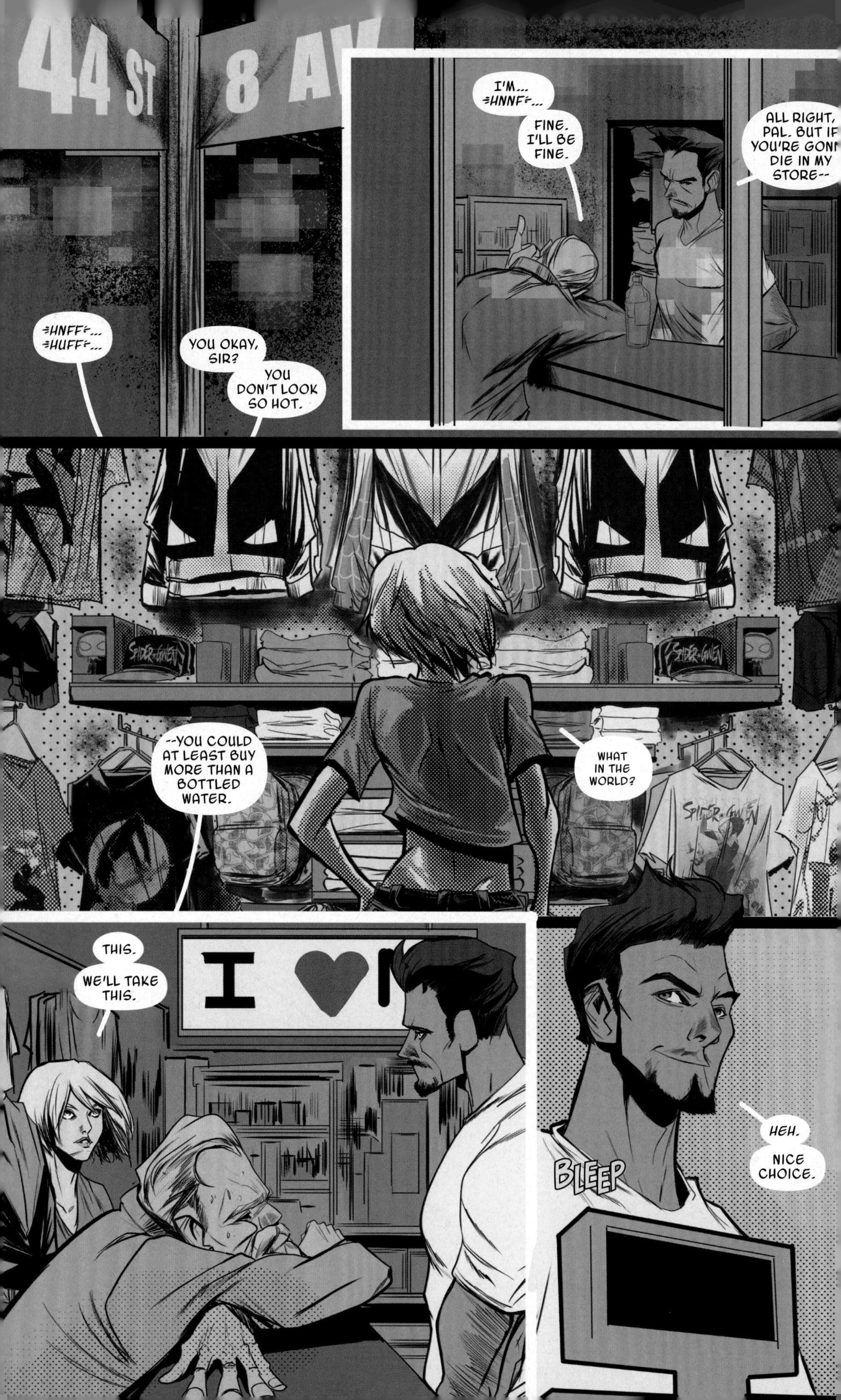

44 ST
8 AV
=HNFF=...
=HUFF=...
YOU OKAY, SIR?
YOU DON'T LOOK SO HOT.
I'M... =HNNF=...
FINE. I'LL BE FINE.
ALL RIGHT, PAL. BUT IF YOU'RE GONN DIE IN MY STORE--
--YOU COULD AT LEAST BUY MORE THAN A BOTTLED WATER.
WHAT IN THE WORLD?
SPIDER-GWEN
THIS.
WE'LL TAKE THIS.
I
HEH.
NICE CHOICE.
BLEEP

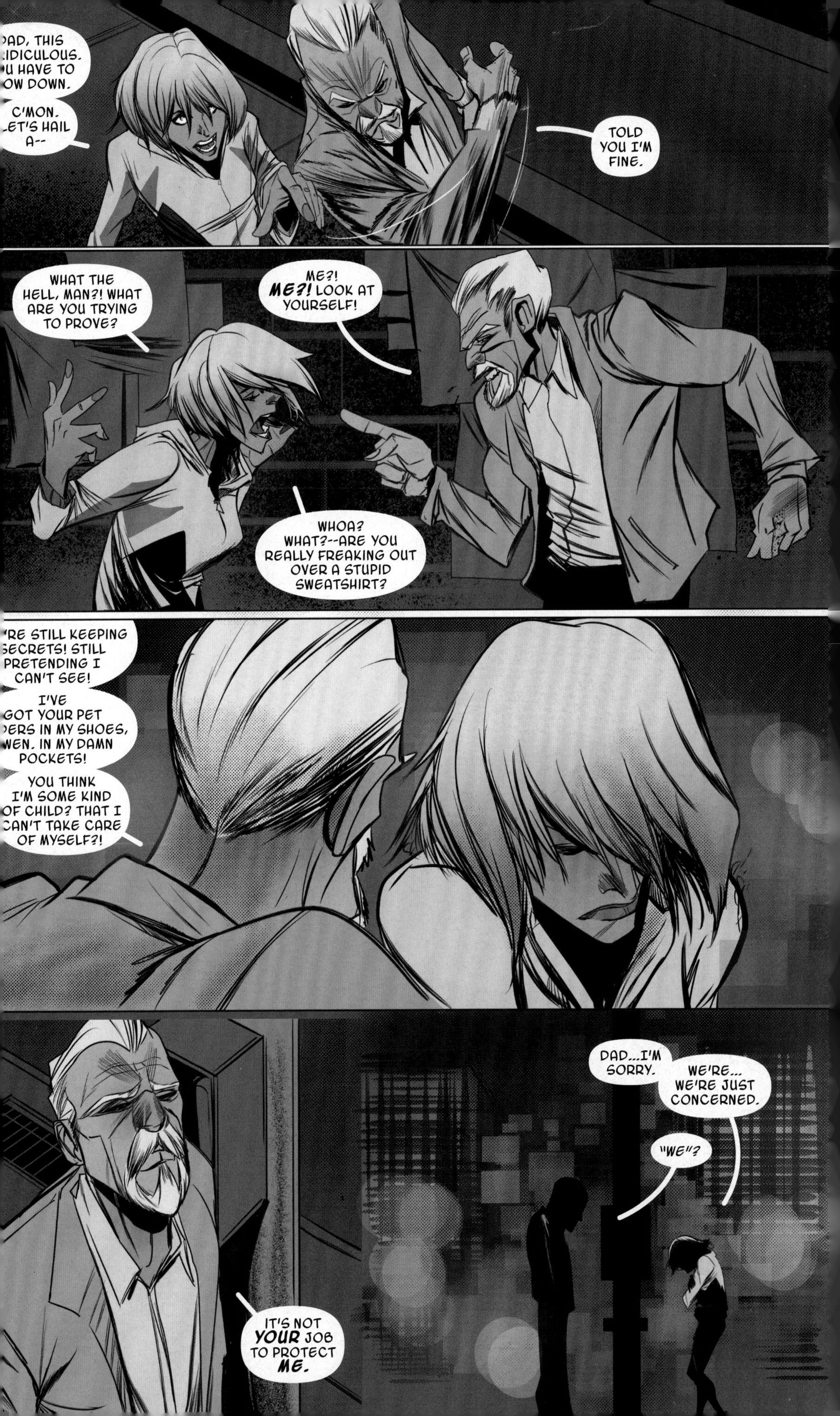
DAD, THIS IDICULOUS. U HAVE TO OW DOWN.
C'MON. ET'S HAIL A--
TOLD YOU I'M FINE.
WHAT THE HELL, MAN?! WHAT ARE YOU TRYING TO PROVE?
ME?! ME?! LOOK AT YOURSELF!
WHOA? WHAT?--ARE YOU REALLY FREAKING OUT OVER A STUPID SWEATSHIRT?
RE STILL KEEPING ECRETS! STILL PRETENDING I CAN'T SEE!
I'VE GOT YOUR PET DERS IN MY SHOES, WEN. IN MY DAMN POCKETS!
YOU THINK I'M SOME KIND OF CHILD? THAT I CAN'T TAKE CARE OF MYSELF?!
DAD...I'M SORRY.
WE'RE... WE'RE JUST CONCERNED.
"WE"?
IT'S NOT YOUR JOB TO PROTECT ME.

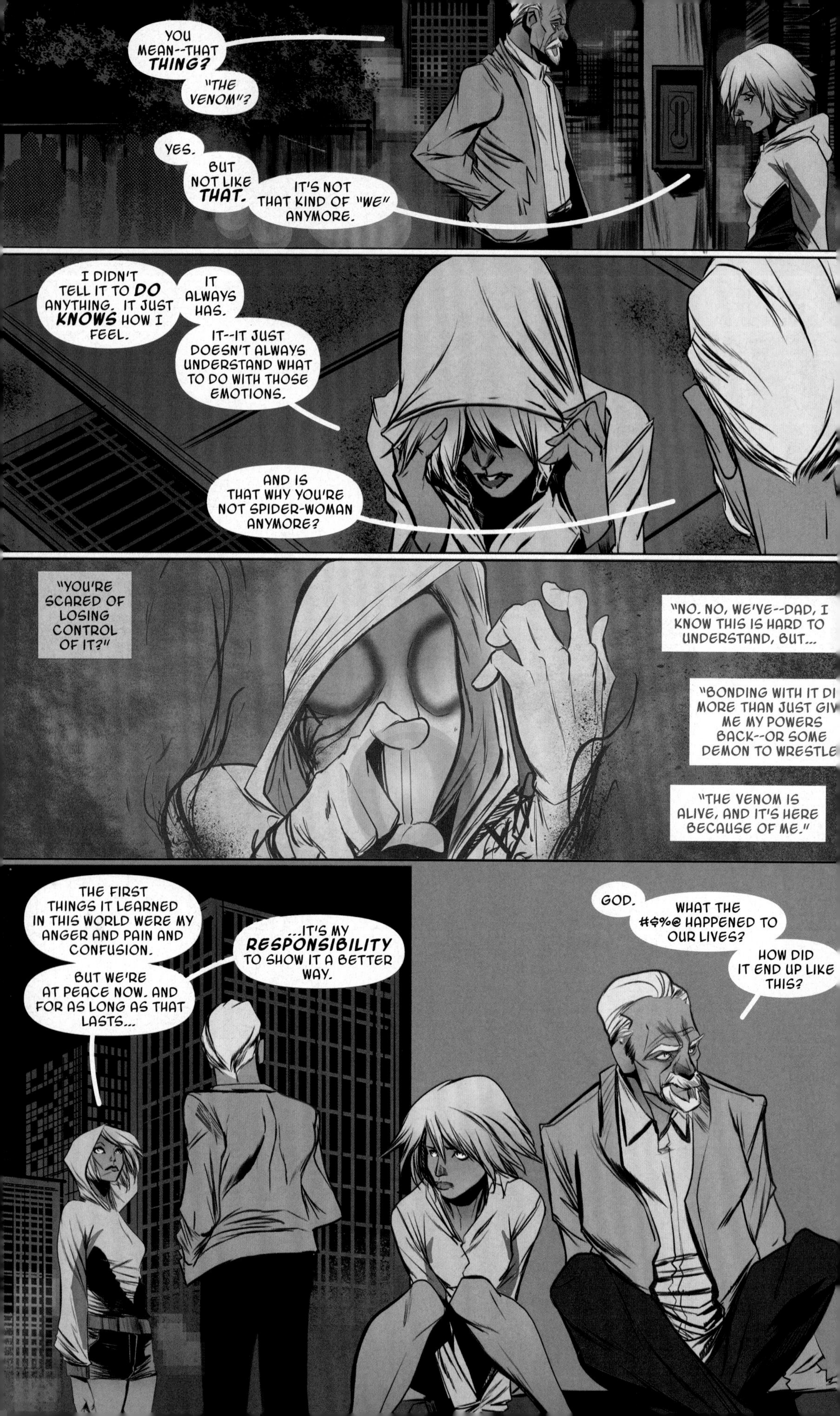
YOU MEAN--THAT THING?
"THE VENOM"?
YES.
BUT NOT LIKE THAT.
IT'S NOT THAT KIND OF "WE" ANYMORE.
I DIDN'T TELL IT TO DO ANYTHING. IT JUST KNOWS HOW I FEEL.
IT ALWAYS HAS.
IT--IT JUST DOESN'T ALWAYS UNDERSTAND WHAT TO DO WITH THOSE EMOTIONS.
AND IS THAT WHY YOU'RE NOT SPIDER-WOMAN ANYMORE?
"YOU'RE SCARED OF LOSING CONTROL OF IT?"
"NO. NO, WE'VE--DAD, I KNOW THIS IS HARD TO UNDERSTAND, BUT...
"BONDING WITH IT DI MORE THAN JUST GIV ME MY POWERS BACK--OR SOME DEMON TO WRESTLE
"THE VENOM IS ALIVE, AND IT'S HERE BECAUSE OF ME."
THE FIRST THINGS IT LEARNED IN THIS WORLD WERE MY ANGER AND PAIN AND CONFUSION.
BUT WE'RE AT PEACE NOW. AND FOR AS LONG AS THAT LASTS...
...IT'S MY RESPONSIBILITY TO SHOW IT A BETTER WAY.
GOD.
WHAT THE #$%@ HAPPENED TO OUR LIVES?
HOW DID IT END UP LIKE THIS?

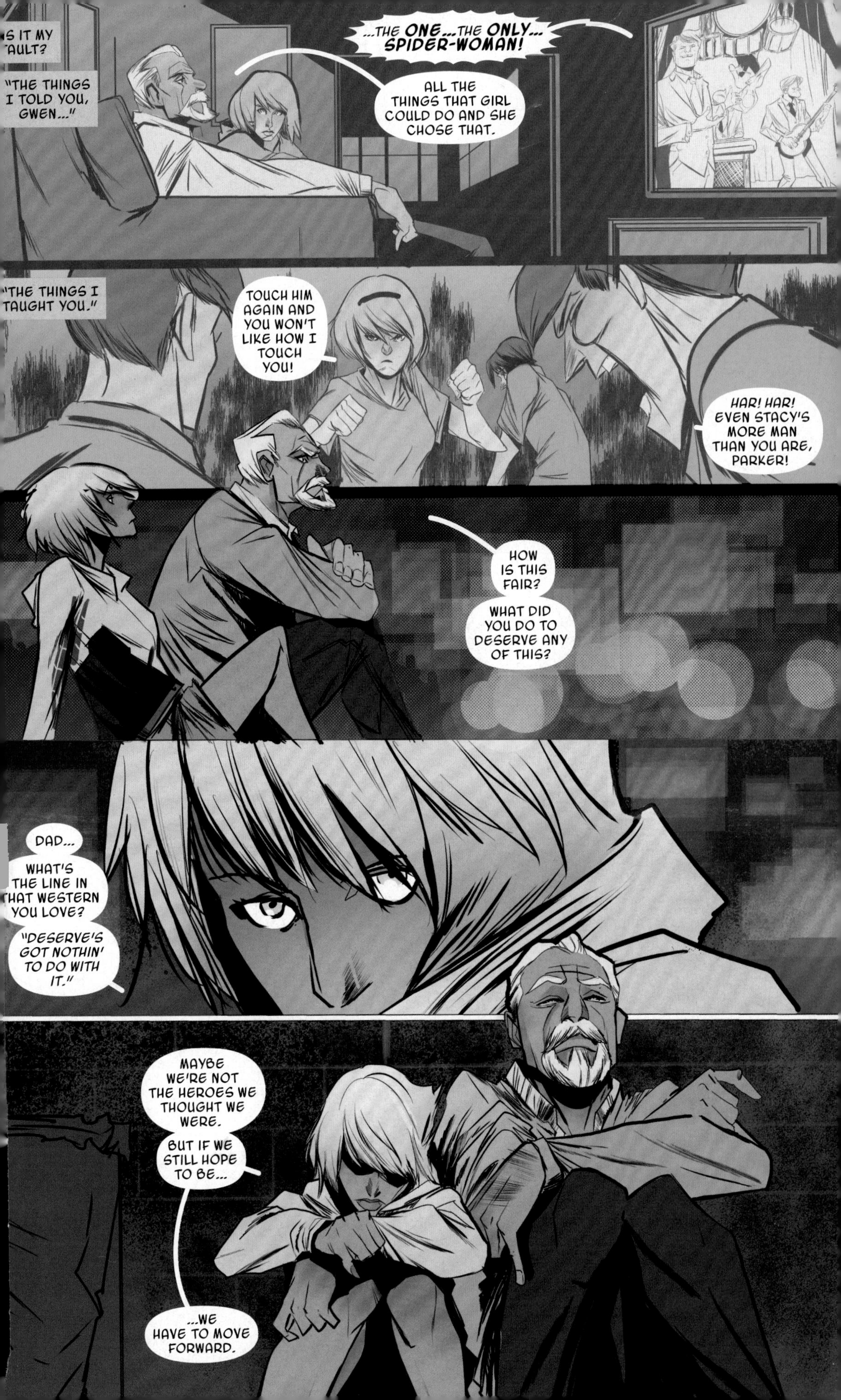

S IT MY
AULT?
"THE THINGS I TOLD YOU, GWEN..."
...THE ONE...THE ONLY... SPIDER-WOMAN!
ALL THE THINGS THAT GIRL COULD DO AND SHE CHOSE THAT.
"THE THINGS I TAUGHT YOU."
TOUCH HIM AGAIN AND YOU WON'T LIKE HOW I TOUCH YOU!
HAR! HAR! EVEN STACY'S MORE MAN THAN YOU ARE, PARKER!
HOW IS THIS FAIR?
WHAT DID YOU DO TO DESERVE ANY OF THIS?
DAD...
WHAT'S THE LINE IN HAT WESTERN YOU LOVE?
"DESERVE'S GOT NOTHIN' TO DO WITH IT."
MAYBE WE'RE NOT THE HEROES WE THOUGHT WE WERE.
BUT IF WE STILL HOPE TO BE...
...WE HAVE TO MOVE FORWARD.

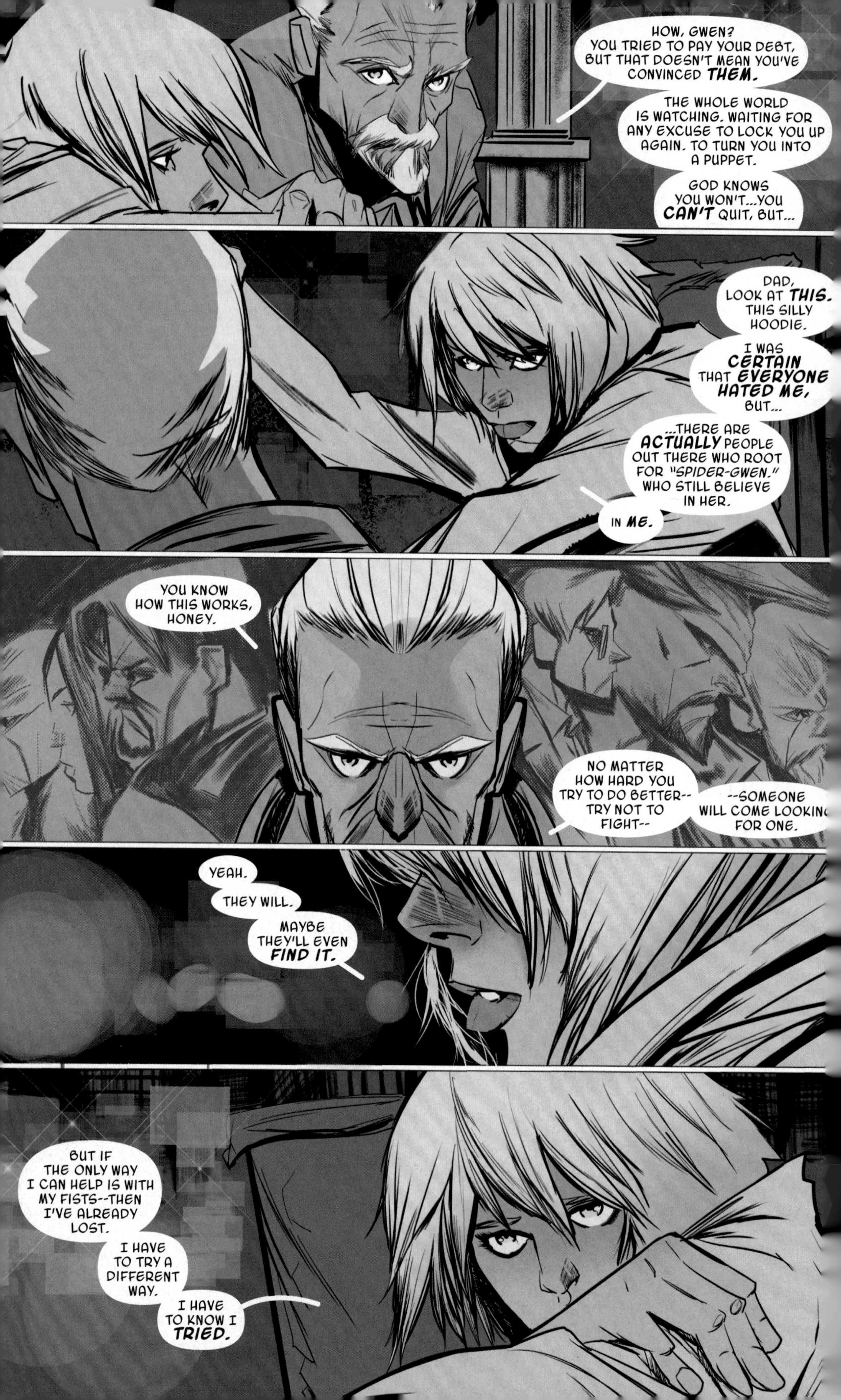
HOW, GWEN? YOU TRIED TO PAY YOUR DEBT, BUT THAT DOESN'T MEAN YOU'VE CONVINCED THEM.
THE WHOLE WORLD IS WATCHING. WAITING FOR ANY EXCUSE TO LOCK YOU UP AGAIN. TO TURN YOU INTO A PUPPET.
GOD KNOWS YOU WON'T...YOU CAN'T QUIT, BUT...
DAD, LOOK AT THIS. THIS SILLY HOODIE.
I WAS CERTAIN THAT EVERYONE HATED ME, BUT...
...THERE ARE ACTUALLY PEOPLE OUT THERE WHO ROOT FOR "SPIDER-GWEN." WHO STILL BELIEVE IN HER.
IN ME.
YOU KNOW HOW THIS WORKS, HONEY.
NO MATTER HOW HARD YOU TRY TO DO BETTER-- TRY NOT TO FIGHT--
--SOMEONE WILL COME LOOKING FOR ONE.
YEAH.
THEY WILL.
MAYBE THEY'LL EVEN FIND IT.
BUT IF THE ONLY WAY I CAN HELP IS WITH MY FISTS--THEN I'VE ALREADY LOST.
I HAVE TO TRY A DIFFERENT WAY.
I HAVE TO KNOW I TRIED.

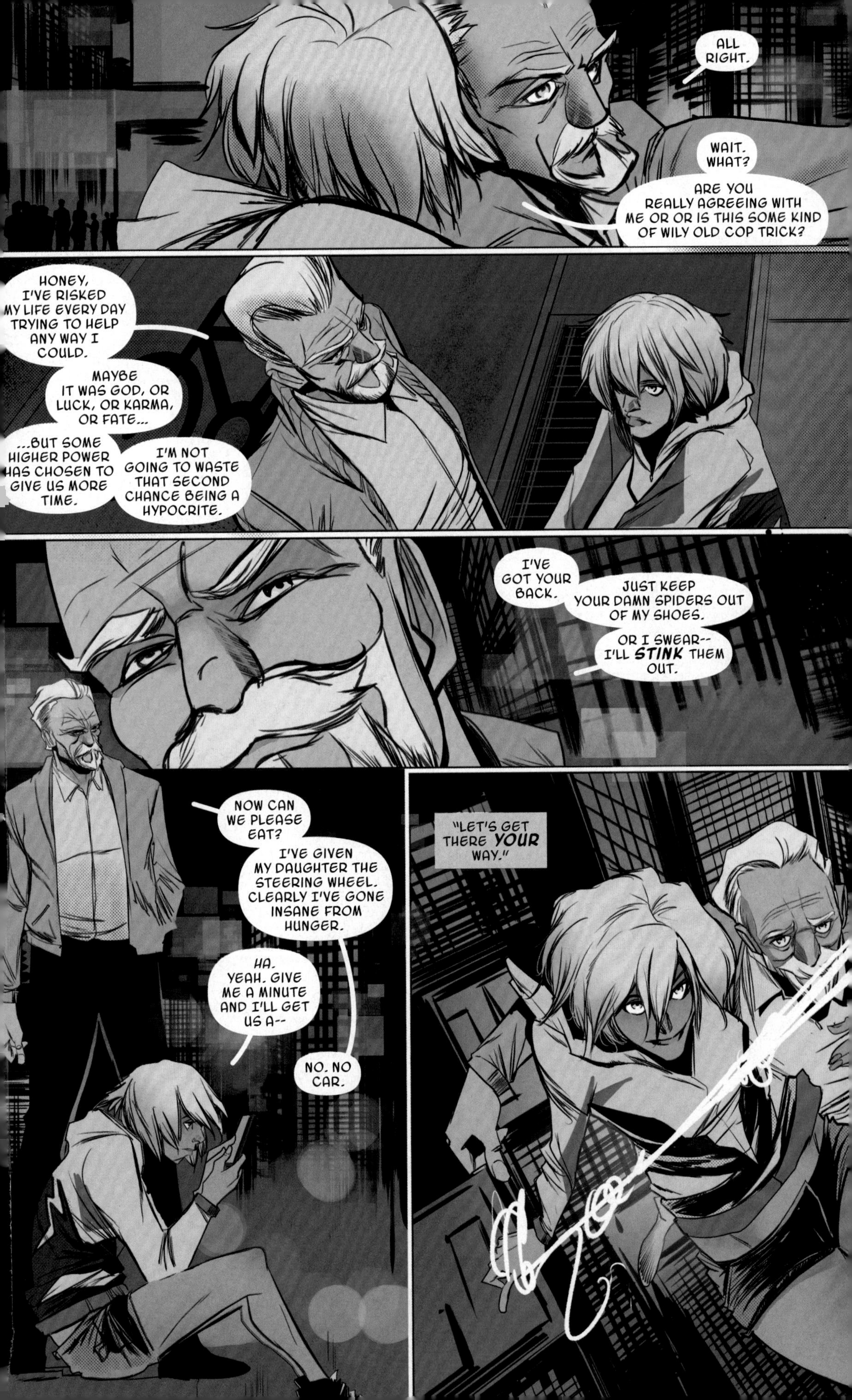
ALL RIGHT.
WAIT. WHAT?
ARE YOU REALLY AGREEING WITH ME OR OR IS THIS SOME KIND OF WILY OLD COP TRICK?
HONEY, I'VE RISKED MY LIFE EVERY DAY TRYING TO HELP ANY WAY I COULD.
MAYBE IT WAS GOD, OR LUCK, OR KARMA, OR FATE...
...BUT SOME HIGHER POWER HAS CHOSEN TO GIVE US MORE TIME.
I'M NOT GOING TO WASTE THAT SECOND CHANCE BEING A HYPOCRITE.
I'VE GOT YOUR BACK.
JUST KEEP YOUR DAMN SPIDERS OUT OF MY SHOES.
OR I SWEAR-- I'LL STINK THEM OUT.
NOW CAN WE PLEASE EAT?
I'VE GIVEN MY DAUGHTER THE STEERING WHEEL. CLEARLY I'VE GONE INSANE FROM HUNGER.
HA. YEAH. GIVE ME A MINUTE AND I'LL GET US A--
NO. NO CAR.
"LET'S GET THERE YOUR WAY."

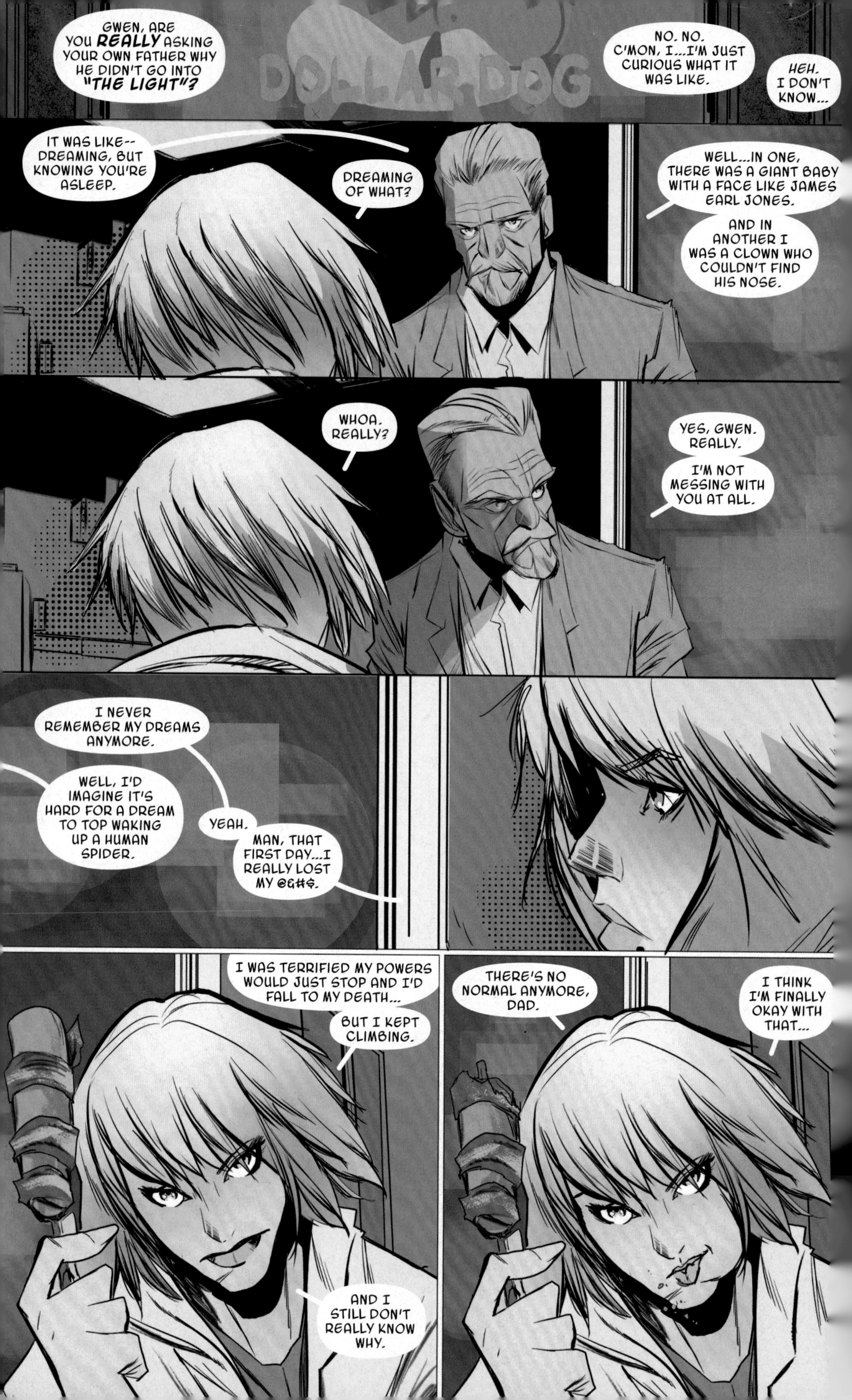
GWEN, ARE YOU **REALLY** ASKING YOUR OWN FATHER WHY HE DIDN'T GO INTO "THE LIGHT"?
DOLLAR DOG
NO. NO. C'MON, I...I'M JUST CURIOUS WHAT IT WAS LIKE.
HEH. I DON'T KNOW...
IT WAS LIKE--DREAMING, BUT KNOWING YOU'RE ASLEEP.
DREAMING OF WHAT?
WELL...IN ONE, THERE WAS A GIANT BABY WITH A FACE LIKE JAMES EARL JONES.
AND IN ANOTHER I WAS A CLOWN WHO COULDN'T FIND HIS NOSE.
WHOA. REALLY?
YES, GWEN. REALLY.
I'M NOT MESSING WITH YOU AT ALL.
I NEVER REMEMBER MY DREAMS ANYMORE.
WELL, I'D IMAGINE IT'S HARD FOR A DREAM TO TOP WAKING UP A HUMAN SPIDER.
YEAH.
MAN, THAT FIRST DAY...I REALLY LOST MY @G#$.
I WAS TERRIFIED MY POWERS WOULD JUST STOP AND I'D FALL TO MY DEATH...
BUT I KEPT CLIMBING.
AND I STILL DON'T REALLY KNOW WHY.
THERE'S NO NORMAL ANYMORE, DAD.
I THINK I'M FINALLY OKAY WITH THAT...

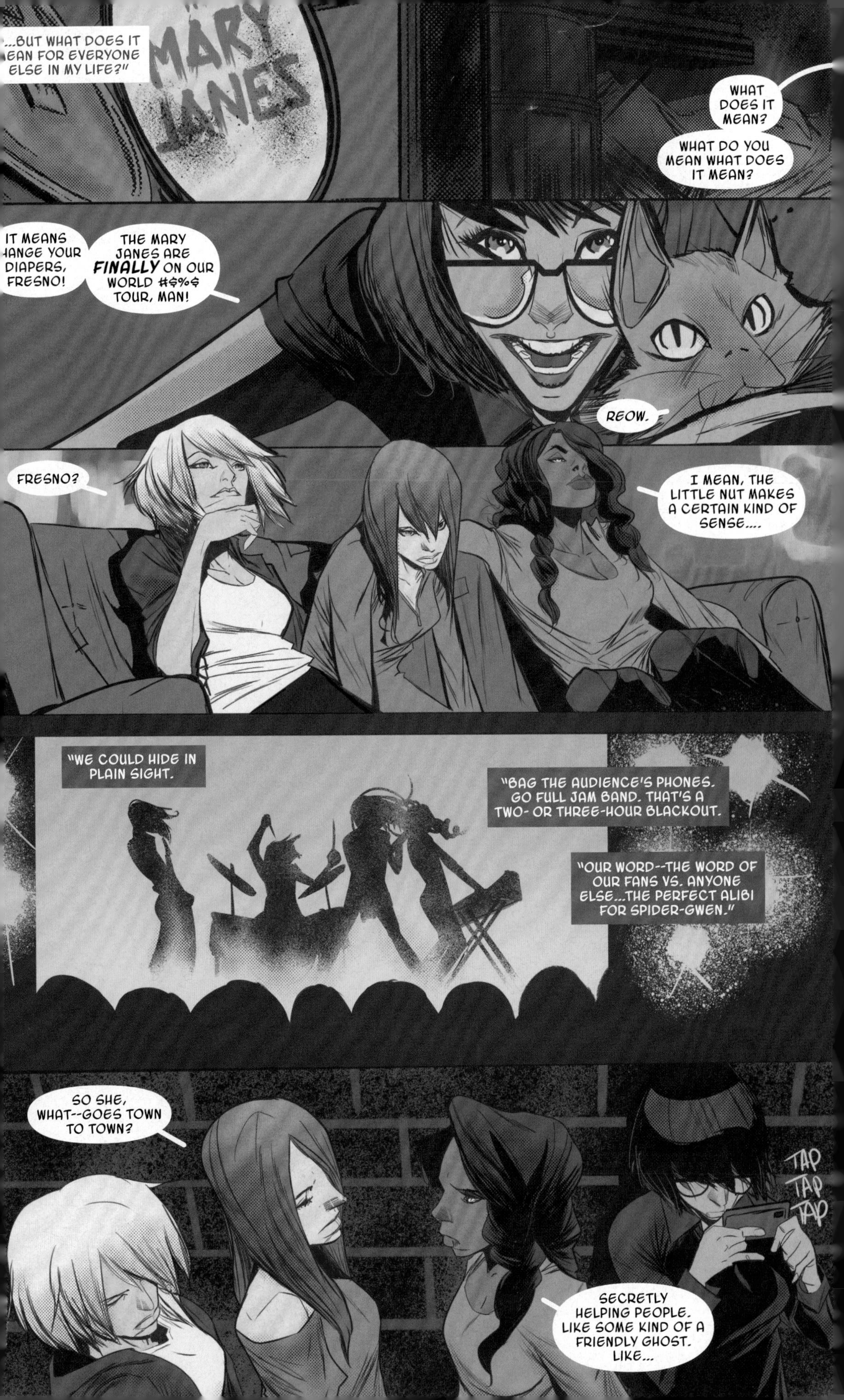
...BUT WHAT DOES IT
EAN FOR EVERYONE
ELSE IN MY LIFE?"
MARY JANES
WHAT DOES IT MEAN?
WHAT DO YOU MEAN WHAT DOES IT MEAN?
IT MEANS
HANGE YOUR
DIAPERS,
FRESNO!
THE MARY JANES ARE FINALLY ON OUR WORLD #$%$ TOUR, MAN!
REOW.
FRESNO?
I MEAN, THE LITTLE NUT MAKES A CERTAIN KIND OF SENSE....
"WE COULD HIDE IN PLAIN SIGHT.
"BAG THE AUDIENCE'S PHONES. GO FULL JAM BAND. THAT'S A TWO- OR THREE-HOUR BLACKOUT.
"OUR WORD--THE WORD OF OUR FANS VS. ANYONE ELSE...THE PERFECT ALIBI FOR SPIDER-GWEN."
SO SHE, WHAT--GOES TOWN TO TOWN?
TAP TAP TAP
SECRETLY HELPING PEOPLE. LIKE SOME KIND OF A FRIENDLY GHOST. LIKE...

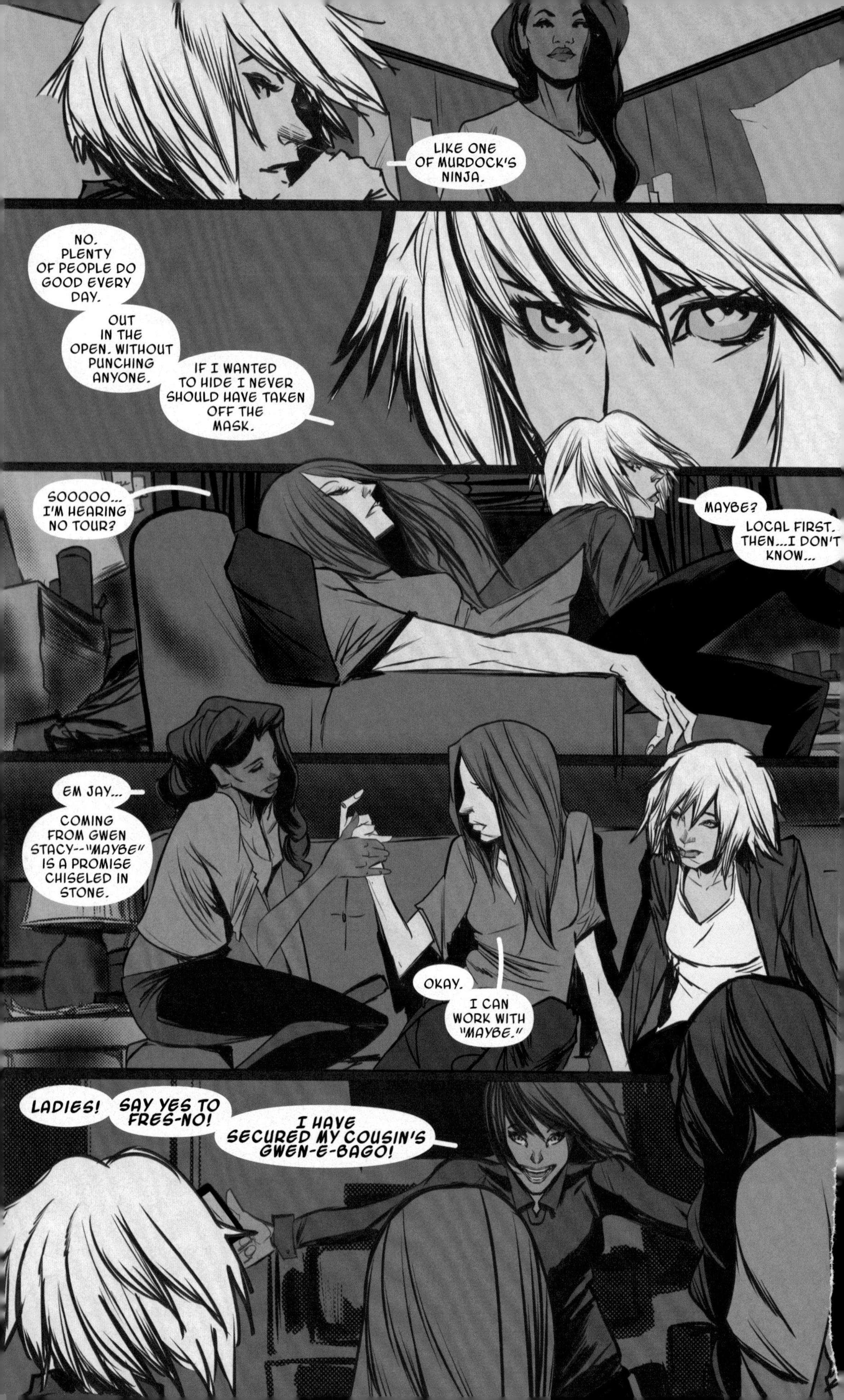
LIKE ONE OF MURDOCK'S NINJA.
NO. PLENTY OF PEOPLE DO GOOD EVERY DAY.
OUT IN THE OPEN. WITHOUT PUNCHING ANYONE.
IF I WANTED TO HIDE I NEVER SHOULD HAVE TAKEN OFF THE MASK.
SOOOOO... I'M HEARING NO TOUR?
MAYBE?
LOCAL FIRST. THEN...I DON'T KNOW...
EM JAY...
COMING FROM GWEN STACY--"MAYBE" IS A PROMISE CHISELED IN STONE.
OKAY.
I CAN WORK WITH "MAYBE."
LADIES!
SAY YES TO FRES-NO!
I HAVE SECURED MY COUSIN'S GWEN-E-BAGO!

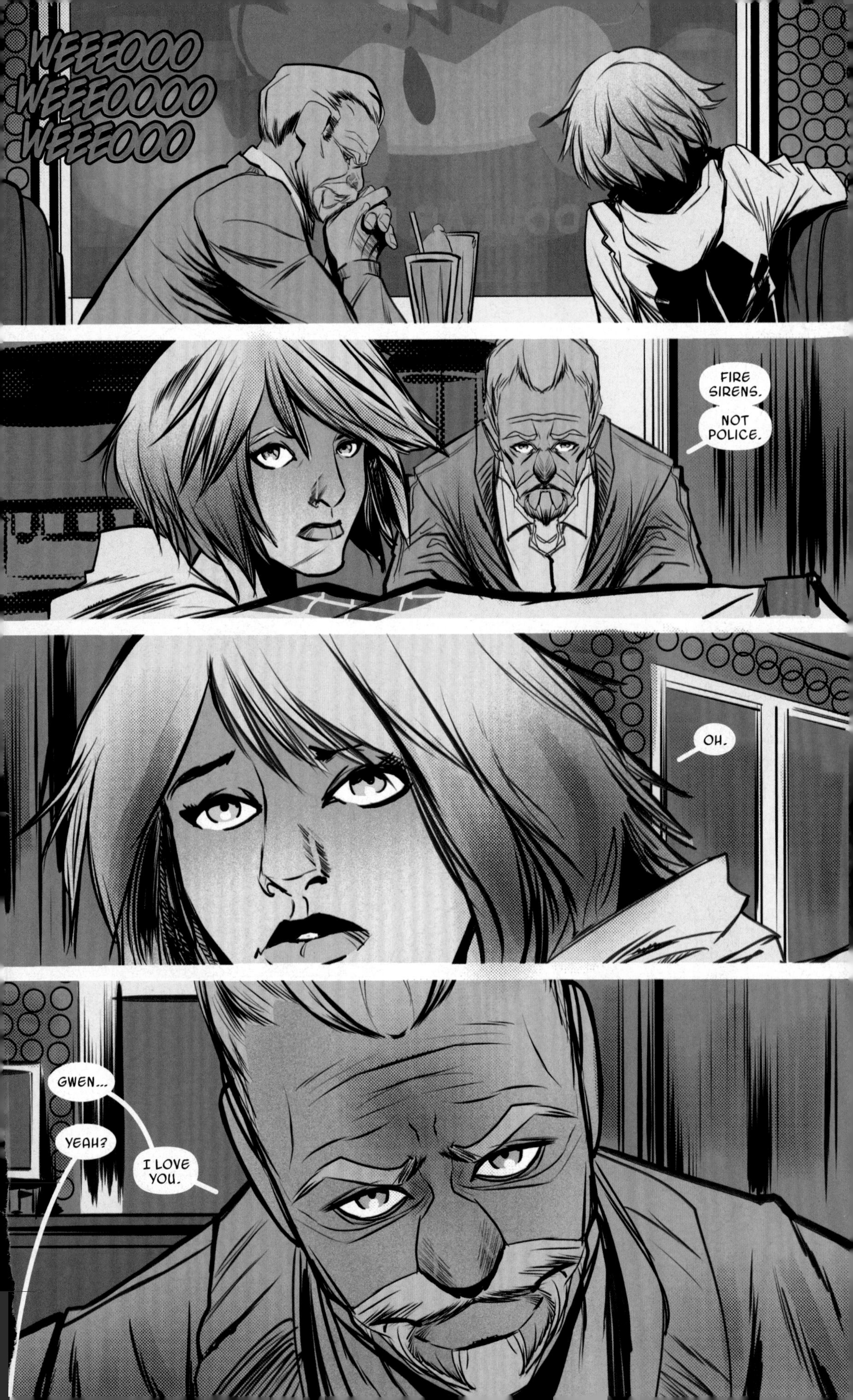
WEEEOOO
WEEEOOOO
WEEEOOO
FIRE SIRENS.
NOT POLICE.
OH.
GWEN...
YEAH?
I LOVE YOU.

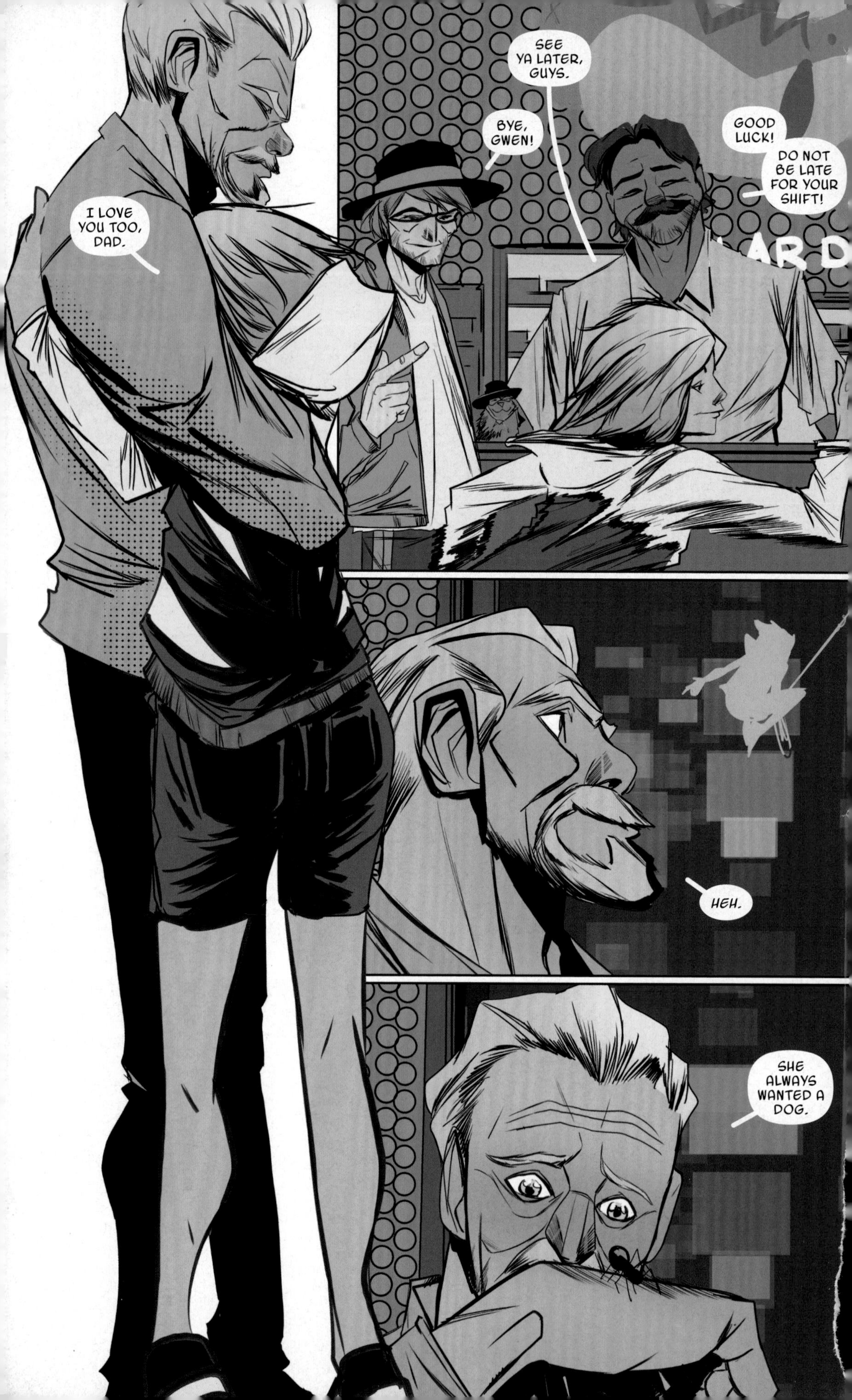
I LOVE YOU TOO, DAD.
SEE YA LATER, GUYS.
BYE, GWEN!
GOOD LUCK!
DO NOT BE LATE FOR YOUR SHIFT!
ARD
HEH.
SHE ALWAYS WANTED A DOG.

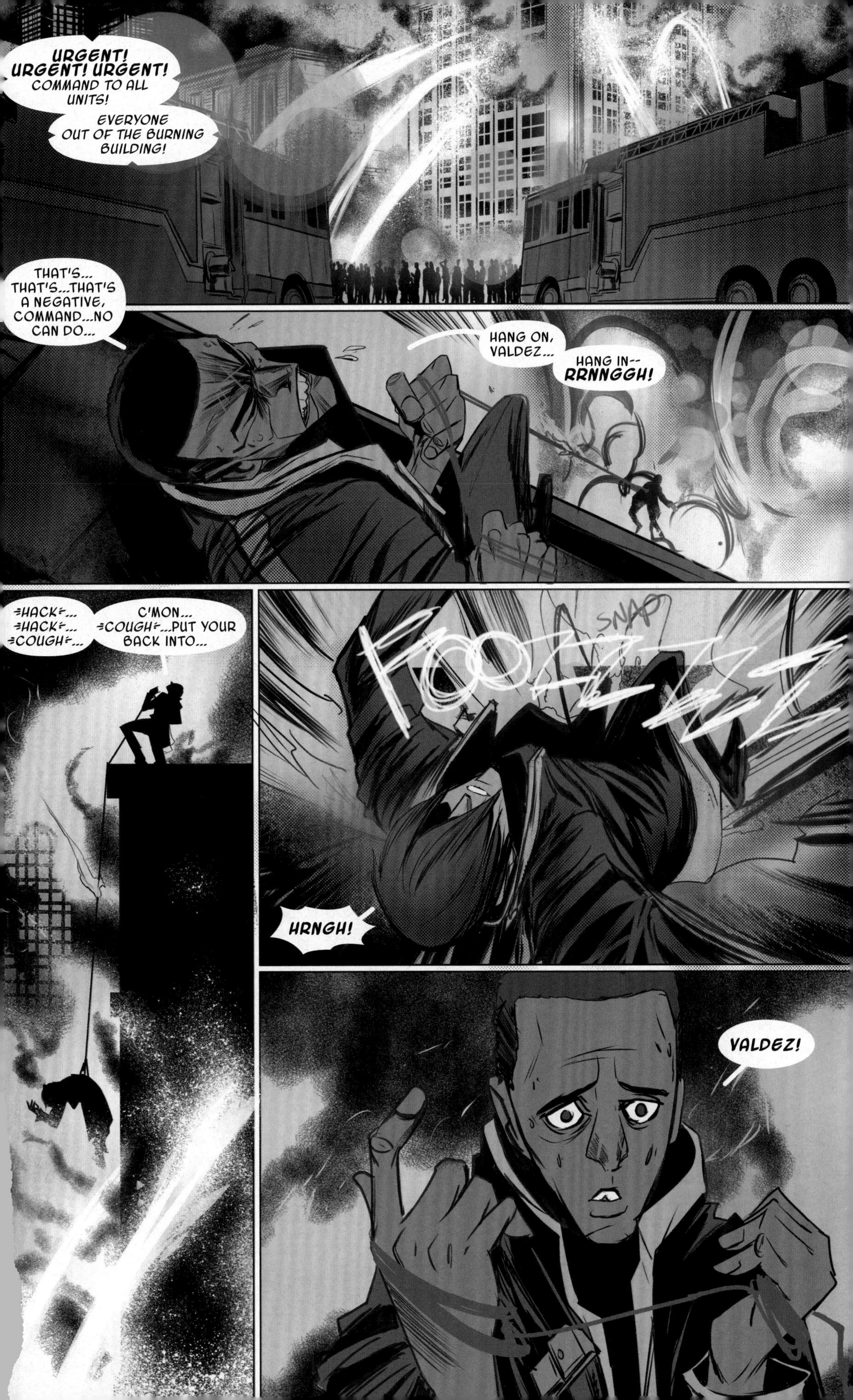
URGENT! URGENT! URGENT! COMMAND TO ALL UNITS!
EVERYONE OUT OF THE BURNING BUILDING!
THAT'S... THAT'S...THAT'S A NEGATIVE, COMMAND...NO CAN DO...
HANG ON, VALDEZ...
HANG IN-- RRNNGGH!
=HACK=... =HACK=... =COUGH=...
C'MON... =COUGH=...PUT YOUR BACK INTO...
SNAP
FOOZZZZZ
HRNGH!
VALDEZ!

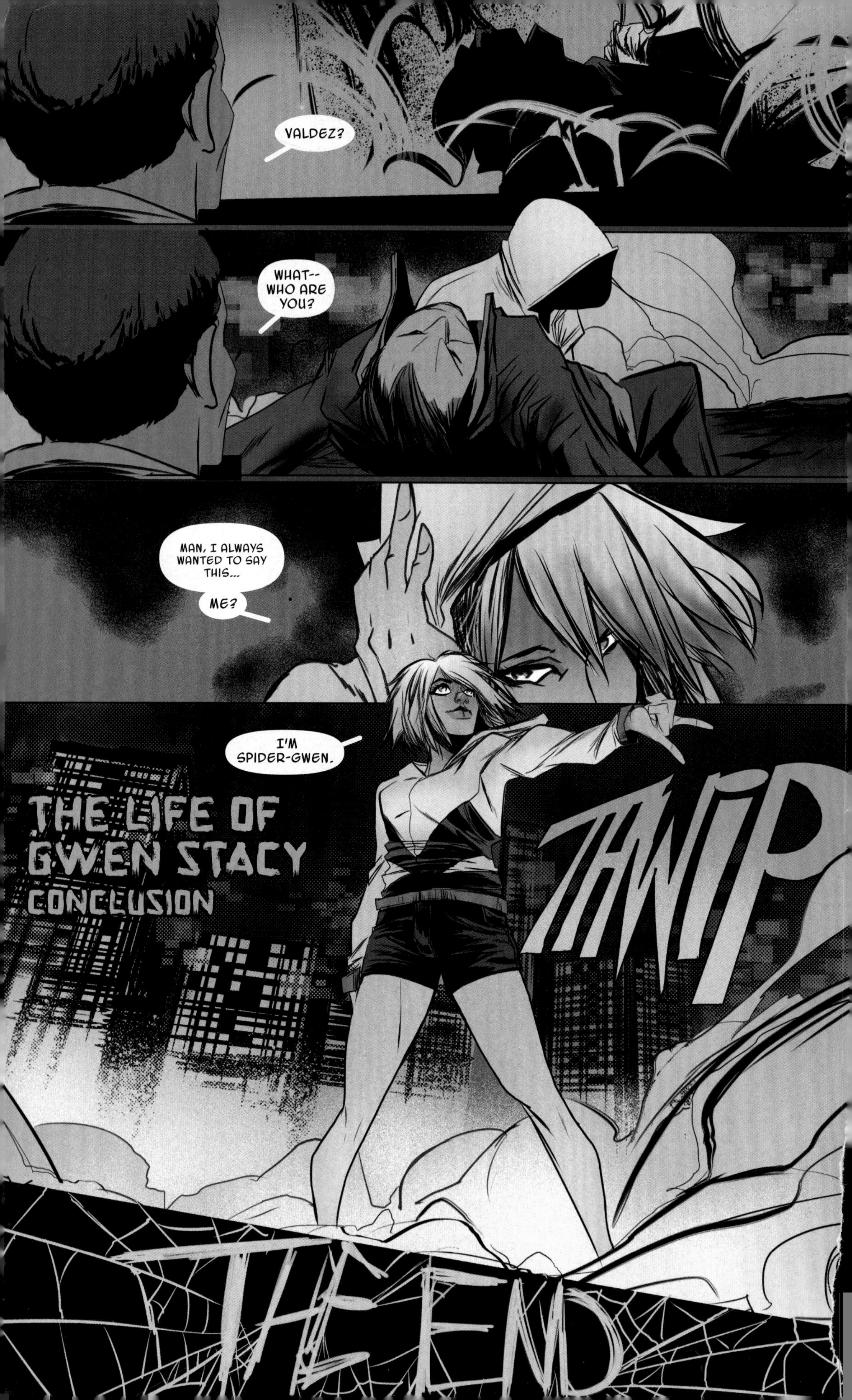
VALDEZ?
WHAT-- WHO ARE YOU?
MAN, I ALWAYS WANTED TO SAY THIS...
ME?
I'M SPIDER-GWEN.
THE LIFE OF GWEN STACY CONCLUSION
THWIP
THE END

Hello, in here, out there, around the world and aboard all the ships at sea! Earth-65 Editor Devin Lewis reporting to you live and in print from Marvel HQ in the heart of New York. As I type this, it's an absolute scorcher—SUMMER IS FINALLY HERE!

I dunno about you readers out there in Mighty Marveldom, but for me, especially when I was younger, summer was always bittersweet. I can't think of a time in my life more filled with wonder, excitement and fun. But those nights were also fraught with the ups and downs of being an adolescent. The two-a-day practices with the high school football team. That gnawing feeling at the back of my head that summer would almost be gone and that anxiety that came with trying to capitalize on every last second.

And so I can think of no season more fitting than this for us to say goodbye to Gwen Stacy and her cast of supporting characters—friend and foe alike—from Earth-65.

It was summer, too, when planning for Gwen-65's first appearance started to swirl amidst the earliest stages of SPIDER-VERSE. I was the editorial assistant in the Spider-Man office at the time, and I'll never forget how slack-jawed I felt (and must have looked!) when Ellie Pyle and Nick Lowe brought me up to speed on how the event was shaping up—and all of the new Spiders that were about to be introduced to the Marvel Multiverse, including one Gwendolyn Stacy of Earth-65.

At the time, I thought it was sacrilege. It had been my long-held belief, as a child of the '90s, that Mary Jane Watson was Peter Parker's true love. As a rookie here in the offices I had only just begun to get wise to the fact that it is in fact Gwen who should be the bearer of that particular title.

The idea of Gwen Stacy alive struck me as crazy! And crazier still, reimagining her as a Spider-Woman?! And a multiversal one at that?!

Surely, Gwen Stacy should be treated with more reverence.

Fortunately, I was just an editorial assistant at the time and mine was not the deciding vote, because what a wonderful story and world we would have missed if it had been.

It was Nick and Ellie who shepherded Gwen, and the rest of SPIDER-VERSE, into the world, but it was Jason Latour, Robbi Rodriguez and Rico Renzi who were, almost magically, able to craft an incredibly exciting introduction to Gwen's world, her family and even her origin story in EDGE OF SPIDER-VERSE #2.

It's a tough thing in super hero comics to make these characters who, to us mortals, seem larger than life and are paragons of virtue.

And yet, this Gwen was wonderfully human. Venerable. Through the alchemy of comic books, Jason, Robbi and Rico were able to put their own unique, modern spin on a character who has appeared in Spider-Man stories, quite literally, since before mankind landed on the moon.

That's a testament not only to the creativity, collaborative spirit and hard work of everyone involved, but to Gwen herself, as well. Because in an event story that hinged on the deaths of dozens of Spider-Men and -Women alike, Gwen was among the special things that came OUT of that story (Along with SP//DR! And WEB-WARRIORS! Oh, my sweet, sweet Web-Warriors…) and bounded into our hearts, the Marvel Universe and, soon, your television sets as part of MARVEL RISING.

Maybe it's the headband. Maybe it's because she's a drummer in a band. Or maybe it's that vaporwave costume. Whatever it is that brought you to Earth-65, I'm sure glad so many of you stayed for the long haul.

But I'm not the only one! Some of the creative team wanted Gwen to get a proper send-off, too, and to thank all you Gwen-Heads who were with us from the jump.

Over and out!
Devin
6.20.2018

The impossible has happened. I don't know what to say. I thought when I sat down to write this that one of those big, dumb, sappy Gwen Stacy speeches would just pour out. That all the things I have left to say would crystalize into the perfect goodbye.

But maybe it's fitting that I can't quite get it there. That it doesn't end with a perfect bow. SPIDER-GWEN was always about taking chances. Risk was the whole point. And even now with her story told, she's reaching out to tell me there are challenges ahead. That maybe it'll never be over.

So instead of goodbye, I'll just say THANK YOU.

Thank you to Robbi and Rico. I know there were times when it was impossibly hard. How much you put into it and how much you bled for it. I will never forget that all this happened because you said "yes" when I asked you to help me. I'm eternally grateful to you both. And I hope you find the kind of success ahead that makes this just a blip on the radar. Just know I'm always your fan. That I love y'all.

Thank you, Nick Lowe, Devin Lewis, Kathleen Wisneski and Allison Stock for all your tireless support and never-ending patience. To Clayton Cowles for the letters and words that bridge the gap between what we imagine and what you take in. To every creator who contributed to Gwen's story both within and without these pages. Thanks for picking us up when we were down, or inspiring us to do better when we needed a lift.

Thank you to the readers and fans—we may have written and drawn and colored what Gwen thinks and says and does, but she BREATHES because of you. It's been one of the great thrills of my life to connect with you all—the countless folks who tell me it was their first comic or the first one to bring them back. It's very strange to make some of you sad. But I'm truly grateful you are.

I know this comic wasn't perfect. But I do believe it was honest. We didn't have the answers. But we were always in pursuit of better questions.

It's my truest hope that Gwen lives on. That she can grow and change and permute. That the folks who get to tell her stories after us can find a way to challenge us and her further.

At a convention a couple of weeks back, a little girl stood in a line of gruff old *Southern Bastards* fans to tell me Gwen was her hero because she gave Bodega Bandit her guinea pig when he was sad.

Never in my wildest dreams did I ever think I'd hear something like that. I'm not sure what I did to deserve it, that I have or that I ever will. But thank you for letting me try. Till next time…

Love,
Jason Latour

The name Gwen Stacy was just that—a name—when it crossed my path. I'm not sure what that name means to you or who comes to mind when you hear it, but I hope over the course of our series it meant rebellion, change, taking chances, heartbreak and triumph. Within the words, lines, colors of this series is 100% a portrait of our thoughts, pain, joy and our hearts. Gwen means more to us than you could ever imagine. She is our daughter. One raised by three dads who shared our views on the world and ourselves so that one day she could change the game. I think she is on her way. I would like to thank the Spider-Man editorial office for trusting us and protecting us so we could make something special. I would like to thank my comic book husbands, Jason Latour and Rico Renzi; Rico and Jason's families for the support over the course of the series; David Latour and Ron Carlson for providing the model of what a great father figure is for Captain Stacy. To Chris Visions, Clayton Cowles and Lauren Affe; To Dai Kou, Matt Bracy, Spencer, Noal, Donny and of course Club 21. But most of all, to the ones that I shed all that blood, sweat and tears for over this series, my kids: Shaun, Mr. Kitty, Watson and Mei.

"I have a lot of regrets, but I'm not going to think of them as regrets." —Debbie Harry
Robbi Rodriguez

Thanks for sticking with us! It's been a pleasure putting our twist on the Spider-Mythos. The rare privilege of working on a Marvel book with the same creative team for this long is not lost on me. The fact that the team happened to be some of my oldest and dearest friends made it that much sweeter. The support of our readers has been amazing, and I look forward to seeing new spins on our Earth-65 creations.

Rico

SPIDER-GWEN got me an Eisner nomination, so thanks to the team for having me on, and thanks to you for reading!

Clayton

Be sure to follow Robbi, Jason, Rico and Clayton on social media for thoughts on Gwen and to learn what's next for them. You know it's going to be amazing. As a fan, I'm grateful to this team for SPIDER-GWEN. As someone who worked on the book in a small capacity, allow me to once again thank you, readers, for joining us.

Kathleen

#32 DEADPOOL VARIANT BY BENGAL

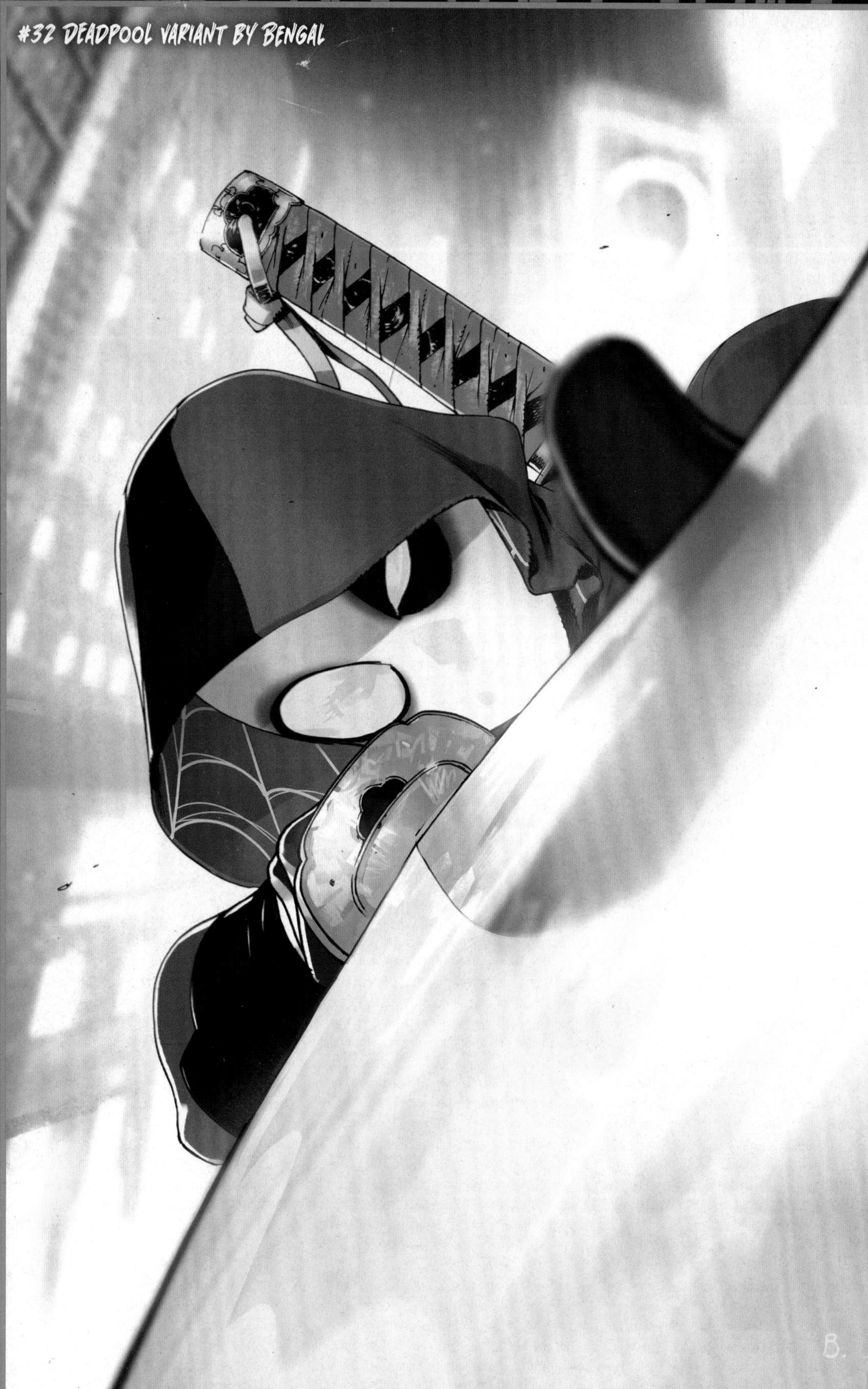

B.